Square John

SquareJohn

MARLENE WEBBER

TONY McGILVARY

UNIVERSITY OF TORONTO PRESS
Toronto Buffalo London

© University of Toronto Press 1988
Toronto Buffalo London
Printed in Canada

ISBN 0-8020-5776-4

To cons inside struggling to get their lives together,
to ex-offenders on the street struggling for a chance,
and to young potential offenders struggling to stay out of
the 'corrections' system

Canadian Cataloguing in Publication Data

Webber, Marlene
    Square John

ISBN 0-8020-5776-4

1. Webber, Marlene. 2. Recidivists – Canada – Biography.
3. Ex-convicts – Canada – Biography.
4. HELP (Program). 5. Rehabilitation of criminals – Canada.
I. McGilvary, Tony. II. Title.

HV6248.M236W42 1988   364.1'092'4   C88-093447-6

Contents

ACKNOWLEDGMENTS vii
PREFACE ix

Prologue 3
1 Beginnings: Rejection, Guilt, and Gangs 6
2 Alfred: Training School for Crime 23
3 Detention Barracks: You're in the Army Now 37
4 Life on the Carnival Circuit 47
5 Beachcombing in Vancouver 57
6 Doing Crime, Doing Time 68
7 Incorrigible Crook: Bordeaux and St Vincent de Paul 80
8 From Burwash Prison to Bootlegging, Brothels, and Boosting 97
9 Seven-Year Sentence on a Fifteen-Year Instalment Plan 110
10 A Fugitive Hiding with Gypsies 125
11 Freedom Is a Score: Deciding To Go Straight 142
12 HELP: Finding Jobs for Ex-offenders 153
13 A Critical Partnership: HELP Meets Frontier College 168
14 A Strong Legacy: Tony Leaves HELP 184
    Epilogue 194

Acknowledgments

Collaborating with Tony was such a daunting challenge that I feel I owe first thanks to friends and associates who weathered my woes. Tessa Stein bore more of the brunt than most. Others heard more than their fair share of groaning – Miria Ioannou, Jamie Brown, Valerie MacIntosh, Don Fitz-Ritson, Ed Wadley, and Fiona Griffiths. Jack Bond made me laugh when I felt like screaming. Thanks, guys.

Many people helped me figure out how to approach the writing. Janet Turnbull's suggestions got me started. Cape Breton farmer and author David Newton's critique of the early chapters helped shape the style. Vancouver writers Alison Griffiths' and David Cruise's ideas contributed much to a more readable manuscript.

Roger Caron helped me figure out how to market the idea for the book. Our agent, Sara Parker, enthusiastic from the first paragraph, was an important support and a fast worker. University of Toronto Press Managing Editor Virgil Duff was eager and accessible. Editor Susan Kent was kind with her sharp pencil and reassuring words. Dennis Curtis at Correctional Service Canada helped with contacts and encouragement, plus a manuscript review. John Wilson offered valued technical assistance.

Tony and I thank the people mentioned – and many more unmentioned, especially all the people who generously gave interview time and rummaged through their memories of Tony.

But thanks from me are due most of all to six people: Jack Pearpoint for pushing me beyond my reluctance to work with Tony and for having the patience to mediate when Tony and I were at loggerheads;

Marsha Forest, my dear friend, and cheerleader throughout; Ethel and Harvey Webber, my parents and helpful literary critics; David Carter, my mate and patient project consultant; and Tony, who, in spite of being the most frustrating and infuriating collaborator (our relationship was more collision than collaboration), did something so worthy with his life that my effort was minuscule by comparison.

MARLENE WEBBER

Preface

'Could you rob a bank? I mean, seriously, could you really do it – brandish a weapon, threaten a teller – rob the sucker?' an ex-con challenged me.

'No, not a chance,' I answered reflexively.

'Well, if you can imagine how impossible it would be for you to commit a felony, then you have some idea how impossible it is for habitual cons to stop committing crimes. We think about square life the same way you think about criminal life – an impossibility. Once you're in the game, once it's in your blood, and especially once you're in the prison system, it's almost impossible to turn yourself around.'

He went on to explain that a minority of habitual cons do succeed at square life. 'You squares don't hear about these turnarounds, though, because they become "sleepers" – guys who avoid crime cronies and even hide their past from new wives.'

However, he concluded, the majority of cons, once securely in the underworld's clutch, never surface.

When I had that conversation some years ago, it didn't have much impact. How could anyone regard crime as a normal daily grind, like going to a regular job, I wondered casually to myself, without giving the question much thought.

Years later the conversation came back to me. That ex-con's words played over and over in my mind, a slow background chant as I listened to Tony McGilvary tell tales of his crimes and his eventual turnaround. Finally, it struck me. It is truly remarkable for any habitual con to turn his life around, to become a square john – remarkable, given an underworld and a 'corrections' world that conspire to make every petty pilferer into a professional prisoner.

Practically every con, at some point in his criminal career – usually while doing time – decides to go straight. To make that decision is conventional. To make it stick is unconventional. For those who do somehow manage to make it on the street, becoming law-abiding citizens will likely be the highest accomplishment of their lives.

For ex-con Tony McGilvary, however, becoming just an ordinary civilian wouldn't have been good enough. He was too compulsive to be an ordinary crook – stealing, living off the booty, then stealing again – and too compulsive to become an ordinary square john. For thirty-three years, age seven to forty, Tony was a relentless rounder, a non-violent, habitual flimflam man. He stole as if every day were his last chance to rob, and then he turned his compulsion for theft into a compulsion for doing good. He converted a twenty-four-hour-a-day crime habit into a full-time crusade against crime. He has never understood that there is a slow track on either side of the law.

Tony paid for his fast life; in fact, he spent more time doing time than doing crime – twenty-two years behind bars, twenty-two years of revolving doors. He did his first bit in foster homes and his last in the Big House – penitentiary.

I first met Tony by chance at Frontier College in 1982. Almost before we said hello he started a monologue about his HELP program, which I gathered had something to do with helping ex-cons to find jobs, get straight, and stay on the street. I was intrigued more by the man than by the program. He was big and round with bulging eyes, a bully's manner, and a gruff voice. 'I wouldn't want to meet you in a dark alley,' I thought inwardly while listening politely to his harangue about HELP. He threw me off-balance when he abruptly changed the subject.

'What's wrong, little girl, what are you sad about?'

I blundered an evasive answer, made a fast get-away, unnerved by this burly stranger who was getting so personal. That was enough of Tony McGilvary for me; I wasn't eager to meet again.

Inevitably, since we both had business at Frontier, we did meet again. He tried to befriend me; I kept my distance. Over the next year I learned more about HELP and more about him. A very bad boy turned very good boy – that's how I started to view him. My experience with Tony, plus the college gossip, confirmed my developing view. Yes, he had worked a minor miracle with his unorthodox cons-helping-cons scheme, and he had to be a man of heroic qualities to have pulled off this improbable thing called HELP. But the man who did it was probably the most mysterious and difficult individual I'd ever met.

Even brief encounters revealed his extremes and his contradictions. Like the socially dense guy who met me first time with a blather about HELP. No hello, no how do you do. Minutes later, he abandoned the blather, resonating to pain that he perceived in me, an unforthcoming stranger. One minute his judgment was absurdly bad, the next dead on. Even the way he used language spoke of the contradictions in his life: the weak education that produced ain'ts in every sentence, and the bold, often funny attempts to use high-flown words. 'It ain't like her ta have that much prospect' (read perspective) issues comfortably from his lips. He asked me recently, 'Ain't it just like me ta not leave the meeting graciously?' (read gracefully).

It surprised me that he almost never swore. This tough barrel of an ex-con whose presence suggested rude and crude was mostly polite.

His chauvinism didn't surprise me. Proud of his womanizing, he often referred to women as 'pretty little things.' He often called me 'little girl.'

From occasional chance meetings I began to get a picture of his personality. There wasn't much eye-contact because he wandered around in a halo of exhaust fumes from chain-smoking. Despite his awkward bulk – about three hundred pounds on a squat five-foot ten-inch frame – he was always running – even, I felt, when he was sitting still. His commanding voice reverberated off the college walls. He took up more psychological space than any three Type A people. Tony was always in the throes of a crisis. Or rather, he perceived almost everything as a crisis and he was always at its centre, Tony the rescuer, who would intercede and patch things up. He was needed everywhere – at HELP offices, in the prisons, at the homes of just-released cons.

He changed subjects faster than he replaced a dying butt with a fresh fag. Ideas flowed into each other without logical conclusions or clear beginnings. It was always as if his mouth were trying to keep up with his brain. I could rarely follow his diatribes, though I recognized the common theme: saving would-be criminals, current culprits, and ex-cons from life on the lam. Tony was obsessed with saving a particular piece of the world.

In his fervour to act he couldn't sit still. He leapt from person to person, conversation to conversation, idea to idea, crisis to crisis. When there was no one around the college to talk to, he'd grab a phone and find someone to rap. He had everyone around him – HELP staff in satellite offices and Frontier staff who played support roles in the program – running. Wherever Tony was, a storm was bound to be.

From a distance I watched him, amused and amazed by his ability to control people and wowed by his capacity to get things done. He was an unknown from nowhere – just a trouble-maker from prison holes all over the country – setting the corrections world on its heel. He was building a program that was doing what no one had effectively done before, helping a large number of people from a particular population of losers – habitual cons – to reshape themselves into winners, turn long-lost and given-up-on lives around.

By 1984 Tony had created such a stir in the corrections world that it made sense to record his story and the burgeoning success of HELP in a book. He and Jack Pearpoint, Frontier's president, asked me to write it. Almost without hesitating, I said, 'Thanks, but no thanks.' I turned it down because I understood how impossible it would be to work with Tony, how erratic, unreliable, and flighty he would be. I never doubted the merit of his story or the significance of his accomplishments, but I doubted his ability to sit still, reconstruct his past, focus on the task at hand.

No matter how much good he was doing, no matter how hard he was trying to make amends for his life of crime, no matter how hard he was trying to help others after a lifetime of hurting victims, what I mostly saw was a man who could not stop hurting himself. The hundred cigarettes a day was a clue. The excessive overweight meant something. The nicotine, the caffeine, the addiction to crises, the compulsiveness in face of severe health problems – arthritic legs, emphysema, high blood pressure, borderline diabetes, advanced circulation problems – made me feel he'd need to wreck, not write, this proposed book. As well, I was a little frightened. Working with Tony was a challenge I wasn't sure I could manage.

None the less, Tony had obviously had an intriguing life. He'd had five sons – by five different women – and had named all of them Michael Anthony after himself! He had a sometimes-on, often-off relationship with Audrey, his then-current wife. I knew there was a story there, and it wasn't a happily-ever-after fable. For all the people Tony was helping, there was lots of evidence that he was hurting others too.

xiii Preface

A year later the story of Tony McGilvary and HELP was still unfinished business on the Frontier HELP agenda. Tony was still breathing his raspy breath and walking his laboured walk. He was the same, but more so. His program was the same – in essence – but much greater. He, and others whom he had recruited and trained, had built perhaps the most significant force in Canada, certainly in Ontario, helping ex-cons to lead productive lives.

By 1984 HELP had five offices, four across Ontario and one in Winnipeg. Thirty-three ex-offenders worked in the program finding jobs for thousands of other invisible rejects pouring out of prisons into predictable lives of more crime. HELP already had a record in beating down the high recidivism rate; most of its clients were still on the street a year after release. HELP had fanned out from its job-finding core into scores of crime-prevention and -diversion activities. Its workers persuaded young school audiences that crime wouldn't pay, and they lured young delinquents into trading B&Es for baseball.

Tony and his ex-chain gang were turning an old truth on its head. The truth was as a John Howard Society ad read: 'Release. Now the Punishment Begins.' They were rewriting this bit of wisdom. 'Release. Now the Chances Begin.'

However, by 1985, I too felt more convinced that the story, whatever obstacles to its re-creation Tony would throw in its path, should be told. This time, when Tony and Jack Pearpoint asked me to write it, I said yes. However, my original fears about working with Tony quickly proved all too accurate. From one day to the next in the on-again-off-again eighteen months of this book's creation, I could not predict what Tony would do.

Sometimes, though rarely, it was his pet project and he was compliant as a lamb. He'd meet me at the appointed time and place. He'd rummage through his memory to re-create painful scenes from his childhood. He'd stick with it through laughing and weeping and wishing to run away, to forget. He'd work hard at the knotty business of untangling the past, of finding chronology and meaning in the amorphous mass of fifty years lived. It's a daunting enough task for most of us to recall last week's events with any freshness or reliability, let alone the story of a lifetime. Tony's memory proved almost as lively as his imagination, which found full play in embellishing his bandit tales.

On good days Tony struggled to make this book happen. More often, however, he'd miss appointments, misuse our time together with whatever distractions he could manufacture. He'd stall endlessly in delivering documents and bits of information that only he had access to and to which I needed access. Many of those documents I never saw, though he'd reassure me that they were in the mail. He'd imagine me his enemy rather than his collaborator, betraying the con's reflexive distrust of everyone. He'd advance and retreat, one day all enthusiasm and co-operation, the next all resistance and sabotage.

On one subject – his personal life – Tony's resistance never diminished. He ached visibly at questions about his relationships with women, beginning with his mother. Probes about his feelings were toughest. Sometimes it was as if he was protecting the women; more often I felt he was protecting himself.

He was perpetually angry with me for not writing his story the way he wanted it told. I was perpetually angry with him for not giving me enough material to write his story his way. Time after time I implored, 'I want to write it the way you want it told, but I need anecdotes and information. Talk to me, Tony – I'm not a mind reader.' He'd answer – when I'd finally reach him a dozen phone calls later – 'I'm too busy,' or 'I got to go out on a call,' or 'I ain't feelin' good,' or any other of his myriad excuses, usually punctuated with claims that 'I ain't tryin' ta dodge ya.'

'Deadline' has no meaning to Tony. The irony is that Tony wanted the book's successful completion rather badly, though his behaviour would never reveal that desire. Intense contradictions, always.

Forgive the armchair psychology, but Tony's destructive impulses go straight back to his childhood. He is a classic, textbook example of an unloved, unwanted kid who, desperate for the love he never got, struck back by hurting others and hurting himself. He is still doing it today. I am sure he does not know why he needs to upset things when they are running smoothly – but that is the story of his life. Misread cues, missed clues. A man whose ability to destroy things for himself is equalled by his opposite ability to have created HELP, which is about saving lives.

In the end I no longer saw in Tony's accomplishment the story of a bad guy turned good guy. He didn't change; he just changed what he did. For a time in his life Tony McGilvary did something worthy that will have lasting importance for losers languishing in prison cells. By creating HELP, he created hope – hope of becoming a winner.

Square John

Prologue

The twenty-second of June 1984. The St Lawrence Golf Club in Kingston. Perfectly manicured greens. A perfect late spring evening, balmy and bright. Rows of long tables covered in starchy white linens. Rows of guests in Sunday best, the men squirming under the starchy feel of new dress shirts and ties. Convicts, after all, aren't accustomed to form-fitting uniforms.

Few of the 215 people gathered here to celebrate are accustomed to the scene they are part of tonight. A party of jailbirds and jailers, hand shaking, back slapping, chatting, embracing – socializing. The mood is jubilant, like a victory party.

End-to-end at the head table there are dignitaries – the likes of MP *Flora MacDonald, Kingston Mayor John Gerretsen, the federal deputy commissioner of prisons for Ontario, Art Trono, and Ontario's regional director of corrections, Sidney Schoom. Mixed in the crowd is the who's who of agencies that work with inmates and ex-cons –* Frontier College, AA, *John Howard, Elizabeth Fry, Seven Steps, Salvation Army, and many more.*

There are a few ex-cons at the head table. It is easy to tell the cons from the square johns. The squares look comfortable in their bureaucratic blues. They don't have tattoos peeking out from open-necked shirts or decorating the backs of their hands. The squares grace the head table with the élan of men and women who eat there regularly. The ex-cons, even Go-Boy, Roger Caron, *a success in the straight world, exude lack of confidence. They carry themselves with the I-don't-belong here bearing of people who've lived their lives in institutions.*

It's going to be an interesting evening. Tony McGilvray, focus of the festivities, the man being roasted, has a hard time getting to his head-table seat. Many well-wishers stop him en route. 'Just look at him,' a journalist in the next seat says to me; 'he looks like such a menacing type ... who would imagine that he could achieve what all these people are here to hail?'

The look of him certainly bespeaks a hard life. Only forty-nine, but with a face deeply lined from many years not lived softly. Three hundred pounds and no taller than five-foot ten. He looks awkward in his dress clothes. The pants hang below his belt line; he keeps hooking his thumbs under the belt to haul his pants up. Tony is wearing a blue newsboy cap. His face, like his midriff, is a perfect moon. A cigarette hangs from his mouth, the smoke curling around his salt and pepper beard. Images of Burl Ives and William Conrad come irresistibly to mind.

Eating over, the speeches begin. Bob Young, a smaller and younger carbon copy of Tony, is master of ceremonies. He shares his role with a succession of others, like Millhaven lifer Tom French, another Tony clone at 350 pounds, and with ex-con and writer Roger Caron. As you'd expect at a testimonial dinner, they have come here to praise.

It is quickly obvious that the praise is deserved, not manufactured. Tony McGilvary, habitual crook and flimflam man, has worked miracles. He has not only turned his own life around – more than a minor miracle for anyone who's grown up in the 'corrections' system – but he has also helped thousands of others to do the same. He has helped hardened – and not so hardened – ex-cons and potential offenders get straight and stay on the street. How? Through his ingenious program called HELP, a job-placement program run by ex-offenders for ex-offenders. HELP helps ex-cons get jobs instead of pulling them.

Tony's vision and tenacity have stunned all the doomsayers. Deputy Commissioner of Prisons Art Trono later tells me that he didn't think Tony could make it on the street himself, let alone help anyone else. Now Trono, who was once Tony's warden at Joyceville Pen, is congratulating him publicly and handing over a twenty-five-thousand-dollar down payment on a seventy-thousand federal corrections grant to the HELP program.

Flora can't be effusive enough. She is clearly in awe of the most crusading anti-crime ex-con she's ever met. Mayor John Gerretsen speaks for Kingston city council. 'Because of programs like this, the members of city council have over recent years changed their attitudes about prisons and prisoners.'

One after another, head-table guests recount anecdotes to illustrate Tony's single-mindedness, his blind determination to build a program that would give habitual losers a new chance to become winners.

Finally, Tony speaks. The empathy between him and the cons in the crowd is palpable. He speaks their language, their pain, their experience, and their hunger for hope and chances.

You could hear a pin drop on the velvety grass when Tony, in his deep rasp, says 'This night means I don't owe nothin' more ta society; all my debts is cancelled. Many of the keepers that kept me in jail close ta twenty-two years is here tonight honourin' me. If that can happen ta me, then anybody can achieve whatever they want. If they want, they can come out and make a good life. An' tonight shows me that people really cares, 'cause when I look over this crowd, I see people here that's been helped by HELP *and people that's helped the program.'*

He goes on to name a long list of helpers — from funding foundations to friends — to whom he attributes HELP*'s success. I hear in his turns of phrase a man struggling to play a team game but who hungers to hog the limelight.*

When the applause hushes, Bob Young, HELP*'s second-in-command, who organized the roast, rises. With obvious pride he unveils a model of Freedom Farm,* HELP*'s next venture. He is using the roast to test the waters. Will funders in the audience come forward to bankroll a bold new project? Will* HELP *supporters support a farm where ex-felons can learn work skills and social skills that every square john needs to make it on the street? In this unveiling the* HELP *method reveals itself: push forward; use every occasion to educate and enlist your allies in creating more chances for ex-offenders.*

I listen to the ambitious scheme unfold. Bob is not talking about any ordinary farm with a couple of barns and a couple of cows; he is talking about a temporary home for ex-cons, a modified trades school, a commercially viable business. He presents it with the same fervour that all the speakers attribute to Tony — total conviction, obsessive drive. As he elaborates the dream, I have no doubt that the Freedom Farm will become a reality. Others in the audience look equally convinced.

It dawns on me — Tony, Bob, these men are still cons. They are still conning, only now they are doing it on the right side of the law.

Beginnings: Rejection, Guilt, and Gangs

I was born in Cornwall, Ontario, on a cold Depression-era morning – 15 January 1935. Six months later my mother tried to kill herself. That event was going to have more impact on my life than anything else that would ever happen. To this day I don't know exactly what was wrong with her. I do know that everyone thought she was crazy, that they locked her in an insane asylum where she died of mysterious causes some thirty-five years later, after spending her whole adult life in an institution. Like mother, like son, I guess. I was sure destined to do more than my share of time locked up.

I wonder why she wanted to die so bad that she made a bunch of suicide attempts? I dunno. Maybe you can figure it out if I tell you what I know about her. First of all, she was only twenty-five when my father married her; he was fifty-five. Besides the age difference, he was English and she was French. Each of them could only speak a few words in the other's language. The old man's first wife had died, and he already had a grown family. The youngest was more than a quarter-century older than me. All his kids, four daughters and one son, was already living on their own. In fact, my father had several grandkids when I come into the world. I remember the old man as a loner type of guy, just like I was going to be.

My father was a real bugger. Although he was far from perfect, he was a real square john, an honest and hard-working labourer

7 Rejection, Guilt, and Gangs

that worked for the city of Cornwall. Poor but not hungry poor. For thirty years he drank his case of wine on weekends, and he loved his women. He didn't how to be a father, but he sure knew how to chase skirt. A real rogue, always running around. Even a pretty young bride couldn't keep him home nights. Just ask my half-sister – she'll tell you what a Romeo he was.

Tony's half-sister, Rachel, was mother of a two-year-old when Tony was born. Now seventy-five and a widow, Rachel sits at her arborite kitchen table in a Cornwall basement bachelor busily decorated with bric-a-brac, plastic floral arrangements, and religious knick-knacks. The round face and brown eyes, the quick changes in mood from ebullient to tearful as she recalls her family's past, make me think of Tony. Although she is a half-sister, the family tie is unmistakable. Rachel talks about her father and his young bride around the time of Tony's birth.

'Yes, he liked the girlfriends. He never brought them home when my mother was alive, but he did when he lived with Tony's mother. He'd get drunk on the weekend and bring them home, right in front of her.' *Rachel is nervous, embarrassed by the memory. She absently crumples a scrap of paper.* 'He'd be sitting in their living-room under her nose with some girl on his knee. Can you imagine? It's no wonder the woman went crazy.

'Tony's mother was a real good-looking woman in spite of being tall and stout, at least two hundred pounds. With those big blue eyes and rosy cheeks, she had a real innocent look about her. It's not surprising because she lived with her mother till the day she married my father. Her mother kept her like a spoiled child, almost like a baby, did everything for her. When she and Dad were first married, I'd go to visit and I'd have to do all the housework because she didn't know how to do anything. She had no interest in cooking or cleaning. She just liked to sit around, talk, and eat. I liked her, but I felt sorry for her because she was so childish.

'I remember my father telling me she was a virgin when he married her. But she was soon pregnant and she treated her pregnancy like it wasn't really happening. You never got the feeling she didn't want the baby, but she certainly never did anything to prepare for the arrival of an infant. Then, soon after Anthony was born, she had a nervous breakdown. Who knows why? I don't know why, and my father couldn't explain it. Maybe it was the childbirth; some women do go out of their mind after childbirth, you know. She was out of control, trying to kill herself. My father couldn't take care of *her and she certainly couldn't take care of a baby, so my father sent her to the Hotel Dieu, a hospital in Cornwall. Later, she was moved to the Brockville Psychiatric Hospital, where she eventually died. My father didn't know how to raise a child alone, so he sent Anthony to the Brodeur family — that was his wife's people, her brother.'*

Like my mother, I got sent away too, sent to live with Aunt Alma and Uncle Alphonse. Till I was six, I thought they were my natural parents – even called them Maman and Papa because my mother's side of the family is French. I thought their four kids was my natural brothers and sisters. Except it was kind of confusing because I never really felt like I fit into the family. Their place didn't seem like my home. Even as a little kid I felt like a roomer.

I had good reason to feel like an outsider. In all kinds of small ways I was treated different from the others. Like haircuts: the other kids went to a barber, but my uncle cut mine. I used to feel real bad and all alone, but I didn't know why. My aunt was a good, loving woman that tried to make me feel like one of her own. But my uncle was very strict. He beat me every time I didn't behave exactly the way he wanted. He never beat his own kids, just me. I still don't know why he didn't like me. Maybe he blamed my father for my mother's sickness and he was taking it out on me. Or maybe he thought I put my mother in that mental hospital. I dunno. All I know is that he was always mad at me.

The other Brodeur children, still family and friends to Tony, have a hard time admitting their father treated Tony harshly. But they do agree that there was tension between Tony and Alphonse. Hector Brodeur, with the moon-round face and easy smile characteristic of the family, remembers that tension.

'My mother really loved Tony and she always took his part in any arguments. You know Tony likes to eat a lot. One time my father was complaining about all the food Tony was devouring. Immediately, my mother started to stand up for Tony. My father, who had quite a temper, got mad and turned the table upside-down. I think he was jealous because my mother paid so much attention to this kid who wasn't his son. Besides, he resented Tony's father for the way he treated our aunt. He took it out on Tony.'

9 Rejection, Guilt, and Gangs

He took it out on me, all right. As a result I spent the first five or six years of my life in emotional chaos, till one day when the confusion started to clear. As usual, my uncle was ordering me around. I protested.

'No, Papa. I won't do that.'

Uncle Alphonse, in a rage, hollered 'I'm not your Papa, Anthony. You're not our son.'

'I'm not?' I felt mixed up, scared. 'Am I adopted?' I asked, all bewildered.

'No, not adopted, just boarding with us. Your father – the man who visits and plays with you sometimes – he's your real father. Grace, Rachel, Emily, and Joe too – they're your real sisters and brother. Your father can't take care of you because he lives alone. Your mother is away someplace to get looked after. She can't look after herself.'

I was too scared to ask questions. I wanted to know more and I didn't want to know. I felt my mother must be someplace very bad. I thought about my so-called sisters. Someone in our family had had a baby out of wedlock and one of my so-called sisters had adopted it. But none of my three sisters (I don't include Anne because she died before I was born) or my brother's family wanted me – that's why I was boarding with the Brodeurs. I brooded on that. My little head – don't forget, I was only six – was full of big questions, but I never asked no one for the answers. I remember feeling very confused, very upset, and very angry but not knowing what was making me feel so mad.

It was about another year before I found out more about my mother. My Uncle, quick to temper, quick to strap me with his leather belt or sting me his with words, really blew one day.

'You're the reason my sister is in that place,' he thundered. 'You drove your mother crazy – that's why she tried to kill herself.'

There was more but I couldn't listen. I was feeling too much pain from the few words he had already spoken. I ran to my bed and threw myself down, bursting with hurt. Very clearly, I remember what I thought about through all the pain – getting back at my uncle. I plotted ways to get even.

Steal. It was the only revenge my seven-year-old mind could come up with. A couple of days later I saw my chance. His pants were draped over a chair in his bedroom. I shoved my hand into a pocket, my heart pounding in my throat, grabbed some bills and change, then fled the house. It felt good. Stealing definitely felt good. Exhilarating! Now I was going to spend the stolen money on having fun and feeling even better. Wandering downtown on my way to the movies, I bumped into a schoolfriend.

'C'mon,' I said, 'let's go to the show.'

'Can't. Haven't got any money.'

'I do,' I bragged. 'I'll pay your way in.' I paid his way and bought us popcorn and pop. We had a great time watching Roy Rogers get the bad guys.

I was scared to go home, but I had no place else to go; so I went back. It was a bit late and that got me in a bit of trouble, but to my relief and surprise no one mentioned the money. I got off so easy that I decided then and there to make stealing a regular habit. It went real smooth for a while till one day Uncle Alphonse must have got suspicious.

'Anthony, you taking my money?'

'No.' Surely he didn't expect me to confess. But I fled as the denial was lying off my lips. As I ran out, I heard my aunt come to my defence, tell Alphonse that he was always misplacing things. That was one of the many kind things she done for me. Because she loved me, I never stole from her. After that my uncle got more careful with his money, but by now I was used to having it, to using it to buy friends and have fun and push away the guilt and loneliness. If I couldn't get cash from my uncle's pocket, I was going to find another source.

It wasn't hard. I spotted a parked car with keys in the ignition. I couldn't steal the car, of course – though it occurred to me – but I could steal spare tires. It was 1942. The was a war on, so tires was scarce, easy to sell. I snuck the keys to open the trunk, wrestled the spare out of there, and rolled it down the street to the nearest junkyard.

'Whatcha got, kid? A tire, eh?' The junkyard man squatted down to examine it. 'Almost new. Tube holds air. Complete with wheel.' He peered at me over his glasses. 'Not yours, is it, kid?'

I turned to take off but he grabbed hold of my arm. 'Hold on, sonny. Here, take this.' He shoved two dollars in my hand. That was big money. I was thrilled.

11 Rejection, Guilt, and Gangs

'Listen, kid. My customers don't ask where I get my merchandise and I won't ask you. I'll give you that much for every tire you bring. Now beat it.'

It was so easy! I was reeling with joy. I'd heard my uncle talk about 'honest businessmen.' 'So that's what an honest businessman is,' I thought to myself. That lesson was going to come in handy the next thirty-three years. I never had a problem finding a straight citizen looking for a crooked bargain. Never.

I quickly expanded my line – rubber lawn hoses with brass fittings, and hood ornaments, which the junkyard man showed me how to remove from cars. I was stealing lawn-mowers from one family man and selling it to another. No one asked where a seven-year-old got the stuff. Before long I was making and spending more money than I imagined existed.

To make up for days when stealing wasn't going too good, I figured out how to have an emergency fund. I'd go house to house on a regular route, stealing money from milk bottles. I thought of the change sitting around on other people's verandas in milk bottles as my bank balance. Once I found stores that would buy the empties, I stole the bottles as well.

By the time I was eight, my business had outgrown a one-kid operation. So I organized gangs. Incidentally, it was in working with my gangs and with our fences that I learned to speak English. Cornwall – at least my family and people I knew – was mostly French. We even spoke French in school, not that I was there enough to know what they was speaking. But in stealing I realized I had to learn the language of commerce, you might say, so I picked it up on the street while I was picking up hot merchandise. Anyway, with a bunch of us working a car, it was quicker and easier to get all four tires, the spare, the hood ornament, plus anything else we could pry off.

We got caught, of course. But only sometimes, not every time. Some suspicious citizen would sic the cops on us. They'd chase us and usually catch one or two kids. They'd take us home or down to the station, then call our parents. When some of the gang quit after they got caught once or twice, I'd just replace them with new recruits. Every time the cops took me home, it was the same routine.

'Stealing again, Anthony. Why?'

I couldn't explain. I couldn't explain about the loneliness and hurt. The questioning would go on for a while; then the strapping would begin. But it didn't do no good. Maybe I was already incorrigible. Looking back, I realize that I just had to hurt my uncle and I guess I had to hurt myself too, punish myself for all the guilt I felt.

Anyone that drove his mother crazy, anyone that wasn't good enough to live with no one in his immediate family, must be a pretty bad person deserving lots of punishment.

There was more hurt and punishment coming. Total rejection – a foster home. My aunt and uncle couldn't manage me; I was wrecking the peace at home. I think they was scared I'd corrupt their kids too. So I got shipped off once again, got put away just like my mother did. They told me it was for my own good; that's what adults always tell kids when they're plotting something you're not going to like.

Was Tony such an unmanageable kid? The Brodeur children who grew up with him reluctantly confess that he was out of control. Yet, they remind me repeatedly, he seemed to love people and was always generous and kind-hearted to a fault. In spite of his eagerness to do for and give to other kids, he was more of a loner. They describe that contradiction in his nature – a love of people, yet a tendency to withdraw from others – in precisely the terms everyone uses to describe him today.

Soft-spoken and slow-spoken Anita Brodeur, a year older than Tony, was the closest to him of the Brodeur clan. She remembers the rebellious exploits he organized as a kid – like convincing her to run away with him when they were five and six years old respectively. They ran, but they got cold and hungry sitting on train tracks, not knowing where to go.

'When we came home, Anthony got a licking. I didn't. He always got heck for everything, even the good things he did. One time when I was supposed to do the dishes, he said he'd do them for me so I could go skating. I did go and I broke my leg, had to drag myself home on it. My mom told me that God had punished me for not doing the dishes. Tony got a beating for letting me go.'

That beating didn't hurt nearly as much as the sting of being sent to a foster home. Tony's cousin, Cecile (Brodeur) Jodoin, today a chambermaid at the Flamingo Motel in Cornwall, recalls that foster home with horror.

'How could I forget?' she asks as tears fill her eyes. 'We – the four

13 Rejection, Guilt, and Gangs

Brodeur kids, that is — we loved Anthony like a brother. It broke our hearts, and our mother's heart, to see him in that place. The foster home wasn't far from our house, so we'd see him a lot. When I'd go by their yard I'd see him tied on a rope like a dog. And the woman talked real mean to him.

'Sometimes he'd come by our place on his way to school. My mother would see the kind of sandwiches he had for lunch — usually molasses and bread. She'd throw them away and make him good sandwiches. It was no wonder he was always running away from that place. But my father would always take him back to the foster family.'

I'll never forget where they put me after that foster family; I'll never forget that hell-hole of an orphanage. Next to Alfred, a training school where I'd end up wasting my early teens, that orphanage is the worst place I ever done time. The nuns that run the place was so cruel they turned me off the church and anything to do with religion for a long, long time. It's kind of funny that a nun would be so much help to me in turning my life around thirty years later.

There were ninety reject kids in that 'home,' living in two dorms: one had thirty kids; the other had sixty. The six nuns, their few helpers, and the priest that overseered the place – a soft-hearted but turn-a-blind-eye kind of guy – treated us the way a rancher treats a herd of animals. We were just a mass a flesh to be moved, moulded, and manipulated with no thought to our comfort or our needs. We weren't individuals. They gave us enough food to keep us alive – that was all.

Every night after supper the nuns went to church. They prayed maybe two, three hours. Meanwhile, they'd lock us in the dorms with no toilets, not even chamber-pots. I'd get so desperate, I'd have to piss out a window. The routine was always the same. After breakfast we were herded to church for Mass, then to school. After school it was move the flock back to the orphanage for dinner and lock-up.

Brother Valentine was my teacher. He wasn't such a bad guy but he was absent-minded. One time, a community kid gave him the ten-dollar fee that outside kids had to pay for books. Brother Valentine tucked it in a book and forgot about it. Then, by mistake, he gave me the book. The kid's parents got billed again, so they come to complain. Brother realized that one of the kids must have the money.

'Children,' he says to the class, 'who found ten dollars in his textbook?'

A few of the kids answered together 'Anthony.' 'It must be him because he has lots of money,' one kid added. These were my 'friends' I was treating to popsicles and gum!

Brother Valentine decided to save me from myself. He got me involved in a boy's club where I could exercise my chubby body and open my delinquent mind. It was a nice gesture, but I was already too far gone. For me the club was just another opportunity to scam. I'd show up at the right time, make my presence known to the adults in charge. When the sports got going and there was lots of action and noise, I'd leave through the washroom window. After a couple of hours at liberty, mostly stealing and selling hot tires, I'd head back to the club just in time for refreshments. I was always eager to be on time for food, but I always tried hard to be late for sports. The only sports that interested me was eating and stealing.

I ran away a lot, too. Once I discovered the trapdoor to a storage area that extended under the veranda, I used that route to run. Sometimes I came back on my own and got beaten, sometimes I got caught and got beaten. I think those nuns invented the idea of 'spare the rod and spoil the child.' They weren't into spoiling kids. I was beaten bad many's the time, but I seen kids abused worse, so bad they couldn't walk afterwards. They was always trying to make us into miniature adults; they never let us act like normal kids. I kept running, and I kept stealing – anything that wasn't tied down. They kept running after me and strapping me, harder and harder all the time. They didn't care where that strap landed – they just swung.

One day Sister Mona come looking for me in the dorm. She had blood in her eyes. I knew that my ass was going to be bloody if I let her get hands on me. Funny, I don't even remember what misdemeanor she was on me for. Since I wasn't in the mood for a beating, I dashed – out through the window on to the roof. It was midwinter, freezing cold. I only got cotton pyjamas on. If I come in off that roof, I was in for a worse whaling than she originally planned. So I couldn't back down. I squatted just out of their –

15 Rejection, Guilt, and Gangs

Mona had help by now – reach and wondered how to get out of this jackpot.

'Anthony, come in before you catch your death of cold.'

'Better a cold outside than a rear warmed inside,' I thought to myself.

'Anthony, if you don't come in immediately, you'll get the licking of your life.' There was no news in that.

My mind kept working. I was getting very cold and the roof was slippery. How was I going to get out of this alive?

'Come in, Anthony. Think how nice hot chocolate would be right now.' That was tempting, very tempting. But I knew better than to trust them. After a few more minutes – it seemed like hours, I was so cold – of their threats and promises, I got an idea.

'I'm not coming in. I want my uncle. I'm staying out here till he comes to take me to his place.' I still couldn't call it home but anything was better than this hell-hole.

This was serious stuff. I was serious cold, afraid my shivering would make me lose my grip and fall off the roof. I hunkered down as best I could to get out of the wind and waited it out till my uncle come. He wasn't pleased about taking me back, but before I came back in, stiff and chilled to the bone, I made him promise to take me to his place. One good thing about my uncle, he never broke his word.

My little stunt on the roof made me very sick with a flu which I recovered from with my aunt's loving care. Soon as I was feeling okay, my uncle shipped me back to the orphanage. Back again, I went back to my old tricks. Stealing, running, and beatings, that was my life. When I was nine, the sisters gave up hope of reforming me and sent me away.

For a while I stayed with my father. He lived alone in a small apartment, trudged off to his outside job with the city of Cornwall, drank his ration of booze, and fed his appetite for women. He had no experience or talent for dealing with an unmanageable kid like me. He just gave me a little money, a long leash, and let me do my thing. The only way he had of being responsible for me and showing me he cared was buying me things and paying my board at my uncle's. More than that, we really never had nothing much between us.

16 Square John

'Like father, like son' believes Tony's half-sister, Rachel. In the 1980s she has watched Tony try to establish a relationship with his own son from his first marriage.

'He does just what our father used to do with him. He gives his Michael Anthony money and he lets him run. He tries to express his caring and his love by buying things for Michael ... and it isn't working any more than it worked when my father tried to buy Tony's affection.'

Audrey McGilvary, Tony's wife, has seen the same thing. 'I think Tony wants to have a relationship with his son but he doesn't know how. When Michael comes to our house to visit, Tony just sits in front of TV and he doesn't even know how to answer questions when Michael tries to start a conversation. He can be so understanding and supportive of kids getting out of prison, but he doesn't know how to relate to his own son. I think it's how Tony's father treated him — either ignored him or bought him gifts.'

My father tried to make a go of us living together, but we didn't have enough family feeling to play happy household. I just more or less used his place to sleep. When I wasn't sleeping, I was on the streets stealing, hustling, hawking the goods, and going to shows. I loved the westerns and the war movies, especially anything with Gene Autry — he was my hero.

One night I went to the Palace on Pitt. I fell asleep during the show. I woke up to pitch darkness. Locked inside! I groped to the door and pounded and yelled till a passer-by heard me. He called the cops. When the cops brought me home, my father was mad. He got madder — though he never hit me — when he caught me stealing some money from his pocket.

One time after that I lifted a two-dollar bill from his pocket, the only cash he had. Since he'd got in the habit of feeling inside his pockets to check I hadn't stolen his money, I got the idea to replace the stolen two dollars with a piece of paper. It worked! He went out happy as a lark, and I went to the movies. I guess that was my first real flimflam.

Next shunt — back to my uncle's. The old battles raged. I'd steal, he'd abuse me, so I'd steal more and he'd abuse me more. Stealing was habitual for me, a way of life. I was incorrigible. I went out to steal the way other kids went out to school. I was real good at it and I didn't even mind getting caught sometimes. To me, it seemed like I was doing what I wanted to do.

17 Rejection, Guilt, and Gangs

Speaking of school, that wasn't a place you'd often find me, although when I did go, I paid attention in class and actually learned something, enough to pass every year except grade two. You might expect me to be misbehaving in the classroom, but I didn't. I wasn't one of the kids considered a classroom troublemaker. Maybe I wasn't in the classroom often enough to make trouble. I was known to be bad outside of class. Every school's got its bad kids that plays hookey and steals. At my school that was me and a few others. We'd meet at recess and take off, or at lunch, or maybe not make it to class at all if we met on the way to school in the morning.

The city was too full of temptations for me to be wasting my days in school. The truant officer, however, didn't agree with my priorities, so he was often my shadow. When he managed to catch me, we'd trundle off to the police station, where they'd threaten me, then throw me in what they called the 'women's cell' because it had a mattress. Women gets it softer even in jail! They'd leave me in there to stew a while. I guess they thought that would scare me off crime. I just lay in there plotting my next heist. It was better than being in school.

My uncle wasn't any happier having me this time than he'd been any other time. I knew I'd get booted out. I soon was. Next stop, the Children's Aid Society. They talked my half-sister Rachel, who had a farm outside Cornwall, into taking me. Her farm was a better home than the others I'd had, but I was still an outsider. I still felt what I'd felt for so many years – no real caring. There was bad blood between me and her son, who was a couple of years older than me. But the worst thing was her father-in-law, who also lived on the farm. If you ever wonder why women are fighting for their rights, he was the kind of man who'd be the cause of it. Rachel, as much as she might have wanted to keep me, was caught. Her son hated me; her father-in-law hated everyone, and she was living with a bunch of men who didn't give her no room to make no decisions. It was clear I'd have to leave.

That move was a specially sad one for me. I liked living on a farm, and even though it wasn't perfect, it was family, blood ties. Besides, the food was great. You got a root cellar full of barrels – barrels of pickles, barrels of sauerkraut, crocks of this and crocks of that. And Rachel's old man didn't begrudge me good meat-and-potatoes meals. Food has always been a big thing for me, a big comfort when I been down. So the food was good, I was with family, and I was even off crime – temporarily. Would you believe I even went to school practically every day? You know them two miles in blizzards that old-fashioned fathers tell their kids they had to walk? I walked them. Walked them to a one-room schoolhouse with eight grades and one teacher in a single classroom. You got this big black pot-belly wood stove and a bucket for drinking water, except it's always froze over first thing in the morning. The toilet's outside; I'm sure them country schools is where the expression about freezing your ass comes from. Well, I didn't get to freeze my ass nearly long enough before the CAS lady was ready to whip it.

'Well, Tony,' the CAS worker said to me in exasperation, 'what on earth are we going to do with you now?' That worker always called me Tony, not Anthony which I'd always insisted people call me. That day I decided to be called Tony.

Next they placed me on another farm. I hadn't got in no trouble with the law at Rachel's farm, so I guess they figured I'd straighten out if I was far enough away from the temptations of a city. To a degree, that was true, but to a degree it wasn't. By then I got stealing in me so bad, wasn't nothing going to stop me. This farm had a kid about my age; me and him loved each other about as much as me and my cousin did at Rachel's. I couldn't get along with nobody them days even if they were trying to be nice to me. The chip I was carrying around was too big for any friendships. If I wasn't picking fights, I was out looking for trouble.

This family didn't get a chance to throw me off their farm because I ran away too soon. Except I got lost in a swamp on a rainy fall day. Everyone was out looking for me for two days – the cops and farmers from all around – but they never did find me. It wasn't a fun two days. Cold and dark, muddy and wet. I had no food and I was walking in circles. When I finally got out of that bog, I found myself on a neighbour's farm.

'Where you been, Tony? Everyone's been searching for you.' I just shrugged. What could I say? 'Come on in and get something to eat. Then I'll take you back.'

'I ain't going back. I'm going to my brother's, to Little Joe's.'

The farmer tried to talk me out of my plan but eventually he gave

19 Rejection, Guilt, and Gangs

in and took me to Joe's farm. Once my married half-brother agreed, reluctantly, to take me, CAS gave its okay. But me and Joe had never got along before and we weren't destined to get along ever. Three months later I was back on the CAS doorstep, saying I needed another home.

Next stop, a detention home on a farm. It was run by a nice family – the only real nice family I ever had – the Seavers. Detention was sort of a group home with six other disturbed and delinquent boys like me. I could understand them, get along with them, and the Seavers was real sympathetic people. They fed us real good too – plain farm food, hearty and nourishing. Don't forget, food mattered a whole lot to me, maybe more than anything else in my life. You'd just have to glance once at me to see that; I was always a pudge. We laboured real hard on the farm, but I was a man-sized twelve-year-old – about five feet tall, 175 pounds – and could handle man-sized jobs like cutting hay with a horse-drawn mower. I liked the hard work but I didn't like getting up at sunrise to milk cows.

Give a boy a man's job and you got to expect something to go wrong now and then. It did. Once when I was cleaning the milk separator I got the discs all mixed up. I didn't realize the error and set about putting the machine back together again. When I turned it on I knew something was wrong, but before I could hit the power-off switch, the thing went berserk. Pieces scattering all over the place. Discs was flying around the shed like flying saucers. One a them lodged in the extractor, doing so much damage that the machine had to be replaced. The Seavers knew it was a honest mistake; they were real good about it, never even punished me. In return, I never stole nothing from them, though I did go on a few thieving binges while I was in detention.

Even though it didn't make a straight kid out of me, that time with the Seavers was important because it showed me that there are caring people in the world. It was important too because I saw my mother a few times in that period. I'd only seen her once before, when I was eleven and seen her from a distance. That time, they wouldn't let me inside the asylum, so I seen her from the lawn through a window on the second floor. She looked very tall and heavy. Two nurses were flanking her like guards, and I remember my aunt told me she looked bad because she just got through one of her scenes. At the time I didn't understand what 'scenes' meant, but I figured it was something awful. Later, I learned that her scenes consisted of smashing hospital windows with her bare fists in order to cut her wrists and bleed to death. Can you just imagine what hell that woman went through? I don't remember much more from that visit except how drab the building seemed, like all the prisons I was going to see later. I left feeling a little frightened and a lot depressed. The Seavers knew how upsetting any mention of my mother was for me, so they weren't happy when my uncle showed up a short time later to take me for another visit.

'Don't go, Tony. We're going to the drive-in tonight, and you won't be back in time.' Mrs Seavers tried to bribe me out of going partly because everyone was scared of mental sickness then, especially the French people. I loved the drive-in, but I couldn't be bribed; I felt I had to see my mother. That time they let me inside the asylum. Even though I was huge, my mother was huger; she practically plucked me up bodily and kissed me. We talked a bit in French – she only spoke French – but I don't recall what we said. I felt she cared for me, but I didn't know this woman; she was a stranger. So much a stranger, in fact, that I'd never go back to visit her when I grew up. Yet, strange as it may seem, my thoughts would always go to my mother when I'd get in trouble.

How much Tony's mother cared, how much she was aware of him, is an unanswered question. Certainly his family has differing recollections. Tony's half-sister Rachel recalls visits to the mental hospital.

'She never asked about Tony and she never asked to leave, to come home.'

Cécile (Brodeur) Jodoin recalls visits differently. 'She'd always mention Tony, always ask about him. And she always asked my father to take her home. After our visits she often went berserk. We'd hear her screaming and yelling as we left. And she often had scars on her hands and arms from trying to break windows to escape.'

Whatever she might have felt for me, I didn't feel nothing for her. Just felt numb, I guess. In the car going back to detention I said to my aunt: 'Ça ce pas ma mère. C'est toi qui est ma mère.' That was the whole conversation. In the silence I wrestled with my feelings.

My uncle had said I was the reason she was in that place. I couldn't figure it out. I couldn't understand what I had to do with it. I arrived at the Seavers feeling angry.

I guess they were right; I shouldn't have gone because it made me start stealing again. With a vengeance. Me and a friend stole some bikes and rode them to the river. We broke into a cottage, stole a row-boat and rowed out into the river, where we lost the oars. The cops found us hours later just drifting.

Cops. Always cops in my life. Even the Seavers had a son that was a detective on the Cornwall police force. He was okay, though, tried to talk me out of crime, warned me what was ahead. Not that I listened. People had tried everything to reform me. Nothing worked. Beatings sure didn't do nothing to discourage me; lectures made even less of an impression. A few times the Seavers' son took me down to the Cornwall jail and threw me in the cells for a few hours. The theory was I'd get a taste of what was in store for me and run the other way. Good theory, but nothing to do with real life. I'd already been the scare-tactic route, and I wasn't one bit scared off. I was too far gone. Jail didn't scare me; it seemed tame compared to some of the places I'd already been. Besides, I could count on three square meals in the bucket. So I'd leave this little visit to jail and run off to commit my next crime.

On impulse I ran away from the Seavers and broke into an abandoned house, a place that local kids considered haunted, and took up residence for four or five days. The season was heading for winter then, so it was real cold at night. No heat in the haunted house, of course. For a bedroll I ripped a blanket off a clothesline, and with my own body heat for insulation, that was going to have to do. Getting fed was no problem. Them days, if I couldn't grab what I wanted from the A&P store, I'd just back-door it, go around to restaurant kitchens, lift a pie or bread that was cooling on a window sill, or go right into the kitchen and run away with a roast hot from the oven. I wasn't scared of nothing. Getting cash was no problem neither. I snatched a purse with eighty dollars cash – a lot of money them days. Out looking for someplace to spend it, I ran into a friend.

'Let's go horseback riding,' I suggested.

'I can't, Tony, no money.'

'Here,' I offered, handing him forty dollars, 'take half of mine.' We had a great day riding around being wild on our rented ponies. I was thrown once but no big deal – except I discovered later that I lost my wallet on the toss.

'Hey, I lost my money, gimme some,' I said to my pal.

'No way. This is my money.' And off he rode. I couldn't believe what I was hearing. I gave him money. Then, when I needed help, he wouldn't give me some back. At that very moment's when I started distrusting everyone I had no good reason to place faith in.

I got caught a lot, sure, but I always done pretty good getting out of pinches. My luck was about to run out on my last day at the haunted house. See, when I'd be out stealing and fencing loot, I'd leave my blanket under the old-fashioned tub at the haunted house. One night, after a thieving day, I come back to find my blanket missing. I figured a rub or a wino took it. What am I going to do for warmth? Steal a replacement, of course. I went to the Cornwallis Hotel – it ain't there no more – to check out the cars. Sure enough, I spot a couple of blankets in a back seat. Just as I'm stealing away with my new bedroll, Constable Clark collars me. That was my first real bust – it earned me my first meeting with a judge. I guess I'd pushed the system too far and now it was going to push back. My childhood was over.

'Tony, I understand they've tried everything with you,' the judge said. 'The orphanage won't have you; the CAS can't place you; the detention home can't hold you, and your family can't put up with you. I have very little choice. I'm sending you to Alfred Training School for an indefinite term.'

Indefinite term; I knew what that meant. They could keep me there as long as the authorities wanted. A thirteen-year-old kid sentenced to an indefinite term. You think someone might have protested from the spectators' gallery. But no one was there for me. No one has ever been there for me, except maybe the Seavers. They must have cared a little because they stood in the driveway and waved goodbye when the brother from Alfred come to get me. They waved and Mrs Seavers even cried. I was all hurt and angry inside. 'At least this Alfred place can't be as bad as the orphanage,' I consoled myself. I was in for a surprise.

Alfred: Training School for Crime

2

Before I tell you about Alfred, about the brutality of the Catholic brothers, the homosexuality, hunger, and hard labour, you got to understand something about training schools. 'Training' schools is a good name for warehouses like Alfred where they store young offenders, because they do train you in them joints. Reformatories got nothing to do with reforming or rehabilitating youngsters, but they got everything to do with punishing and preparing kids for more crime. Training schools train you for crime. And I got quite the education.

While other kids were going through elementary school, I was going through detention. While other kids were in secondary school, I was in reform school. While other kids were in high school, I was in provincial jails. And when other kids went to colleges, I went to penitentiaries. So, like other kids, I went through an education system too, from detention homes to the Big House.

Straight kids learned to be good citizens, and I learned to be a good crook. We didn't have no teachers and textbooks like you got in school, but we had other inmates with more experience than any teacher and more information than any textbook. I had a real good library at Alfred – 120 other inmates. I was a quick learner.

The same boys that trained me at Alfred would teach me more later on because I'd keep bumping into them as I went through my twenty-two years' schooling in the so-called corrections system. Now, I wasn't learning much about reading, writing, and arithmetic, except enough to read street signs in rich neighbourhoods and write parole applications later on and count the money I stole. But I was learning how to graduate from petty pilfering to house prowling to safe-cracking. At Alfred, more experienced, older boys taught me how to spot a 'good house,' how to case it, how to tell if they got a dog and how to divert him with meat, how to break and enter without tools and without cutting my hands.

The higher the institution, the more advanced the lessons. At Alfred I learned how to house prowl; at Guelph Correctional I learned how to pick locks, and at St Vincent de Paul I learned how to crack safes. The entire prison system, bottom to top, is one big school training you for a life of crime. Prisons make it real easy to learn how to become a better and better criminal, but they make it real hard to learn how not to become a con. I know the public gets sold a bill of goods about all the programs they supposedly got in prisons for reforming and rehabilitating all us bad guys, but they're being fed a lie. Prisons got little to do with skills training for making it on the street like a square john. Jails are good for two things: locking so-called undesirables up, and setting them up for a life of crime.

Tony's jaundiced view of the corrections system is shared by most cons schooled inside. They snicker at the mere mention of 'corrections,' bristle at allusions to trades training, wince at questions about their literacy skills, and laugh at suggestions that there's any way out once you're in. Ron, a forty-three-year-old rounder, a veteran of the prison system, and a prison-rights activist, calls kids who wind up in the Alfreds of Canada 'victims of justice.' Ron coughs the tight, hurting hack of a man who smokes too much and cares too little about himself to stop. Hurt blue eyes stare angrily from the lined, leathery folds around them.

'It's almost as if there's a master plan. You see these young kids in school. Truants. They get labelled "bad." These "bad" kids get ostracized by kids from "good" homes, by their teachers, and by their families. Soon enough, the only thing they're good at is crime and getting caught.

'Once they're in the system, you know they're going to become victims of justice. They are going to be sent away under the guise of being corrected and rehabilitated when, in truth, they are going to be shaped into criminals. Trained, from training schools up, for a life of crime.

25 Training School for Crime

> *'If all these young, troubled, unloved, acting-out kids were actually schooled and helped, how would all the crime pimps live? Crime, remember, is a fantastic business, often more lucrative for the people on its fringes than for the criminals. Great for all the people who live off its avails – police, guards, probation and parole officers, judges, lawyers, locksmiths, and law professors.'*
>
> *And training schools, from the physical plant to the psychological climate, are perfect settings to set young offenders on a path of crime.*

I remember driving up the path towards Alfred, seeing an ugly, cold-looking, two-storey limestone building. It was an institution all right; it was no home for a young boy. 'Oh God, another place run by the church,' I thought to myself. I knew it was church-run because of the massive religious statue glaring down on approaching cars. Would these God-fearing keepers be as heartless as the nuns that worked me over in the orphanage? By now, I knew the church was something to fear.

I also knew that these were supposedly good times, that everyone was flush with post-war excitement. The church was out there regrouping the troops into prayer lines, praising the Lord for ending the war, and reuniting families. Everywhere you looked – billboards, comics, magazines, movies – all you seen was happy families. That had never been my scene, and driving up the path to Alfred, I figured a happy family was something I better forget forever.

Alfred looked like a big institutional farm because it had barns, sheds, pastures, and fields around the main building. Inside, the complex was divided up for big boys and little boys. Because of my age, thirteen, I should have been put with the little boys, but because of my size they put me with the big boys.

My dorm was a huge, unfriendly room with high ceilings. It had three smaller rooms in three of the corners. One was the living quarters for the dorm screw, Brother Leo. Another was a storeroom for his goodies, like candy and cigarettes. The third was a room for segregation. In my dorm there were about sixty boys lined up in single cots, real crowded. There was no such thing as privacy unless you got segregated for punishment, sent to the Room, that awful little box with bars in the corner of the dorm.

That's where Brother Leo threw you after he beat you for breaking any one of the endless rules we had to live by. He'd strap the boys with anything handy – like a bat or hockey stick or his fists – force you to put on a padded kimono, and leave you in that hole for days, sometimes even weeks at a time. Just bread and water and a pot for a toilet. When he thought you'd learned your lesson, he'd let you out. Imagine making a kid live like that!

The Room was practically my bedroom. That hole was my first run-in with the eight-by-ten world that lay ahead for me. When I was in the Room, I felt like the hate of the whole world was on top of me. I figured I deserved it, too. I was sure I was the worst kid in the world. I must have been. After all, I drove my mother crazy. Now I was doing things to make these men of God punish me.

What did Brother Leo punish me for? Any excuse he could find – and I gave him all he could want. I was always into something. One time I stole a big roast of beef and another time I swiped Brother Leo's private stash of cigarettes. They taught us to smoke at Alfred by giving the boys a ration of one smoke a day for good behaviour. Once I got hooked on that nicotine, one a day – when I was good and got it – wasn't enough. So I'd have to steal to get more smokes. Anyway, Leo was never short of excuses to get brutal with me. And I never backed down or apologized or spilled the details of my crimes. He'd beat me until I was blue, wanting to know where I hid my stash, like the stolen cigarettes, for instance, but I'd be half dead and he still wouldn't get a confession out of me.

There was one escapade he never got the pleasure of beating me for. Losing my virginity. A woman who worked cleaning in the administration building – she must have been in her early forties – well, she got fascinated by my big, handsome body. Before you knew it, we were in the broom closet exploring bodies. I was thirteen.

Losing my innocence and getting away with it was one thing, but losing at hockey and getting away with it was another story. The brothers were sports crazy, especially about ice hockey. Even though there wasn't much in the way of a school for us, we had two hockey rinks and we had to win in competitions with outside teams. Losing was a punishable crime. If you played a good game, meaning a winning game, you'd get treats, like pop or a little extra food. Since the food was poor and scarce, we were always hungry, so we competed very fierce. Often, we won. But when we lost, some of us would really get it. Many times I got hit over the head with a hockey stick by the good brother, or pummelled with his fists, or forced to bend over so he could strap me until my bare ass bled.

They thought we were full of demons, and beatings was a great way to drive them out of us. I saw more whippings at Alfred than at any pen in the country. Some of them brothers were so sadistic it was unreal. I can honestly say I feared for my life. I remember one day I was in the gym playing pool. I must have upset Brother Leo because he punched me, so hard it knocked me flat over the pool table. I was protecting my head, expecting his fists to work me over, when I heard this sharp crack. I took a peek and saw one of my buddies waving a pool cue. He had broken it across Leo's head when the brother was winding up to punch me out. My buddy got beat real bad for interfering, but maybe he saved me from a fatal blow. The Man was some hot that day, maybe hot enough to kill.

I dunno. Maybe some of that meanness came from the unnatural lives the brothers were living. It even drove them to what I think are unnatural acts – sex with the boys. Homosexuality was a real problem for the boys who didn't want to do what our warders wanted from us. There were a lot of pretty boys around and they were under a lot of pressure to put out. If they did, they got special favours and better treatment than the rest of us. If they didn't, they got special beatings and more abuse than the rest of us.

One kid I recall, this one brother was always after his body. The boy was always getting strapped because he'd never give in. This kid was in even more trouble than me and I was always scared for him. One day, when a small carnival came to Alfred, I saw his chance to escape.

'Listen,' I told him, 'you gotta run.'

'I know I have to get out of here, but how can I? I'm trapped,' he said.

'No, you're not. I got a plan. You got to sneak into the village just after supper, before count-up, and stow away with the circus.'

'It can't work,' the boy protested. 'Maybe I can get as far as the village, but I'll never be able to stay out because everyone will be searching for me.'

'You got to try,' I encouraged him. 'The carnival's leaving tonight – you can leave with them.'

I guess he was desperate enough to try my scheme. A bunch of us covered for him, and he actually made it. He made it – can you imagine? He's one of the few Alfred mates I never ran into again and never heard nothing about. Who knows? Maybe he escaped a life of crime, and maybe I helped him do it. I know I felt real good at the time about pushing him out of that hell-hole.

I ran away myself lots of times too. Hell, I was always on the run, trying out my latest foolproof escape plan. But I got caught every time and I got brutally beaten every time and I got the Room every time. They had a method for trapping go-boys. Soon as one of the warders saw a boy on the dash across the field, they'd round up a couple of truckloads of older kids and start the chase. One truck to the left, one to the right. The kid trapped, helpless. If he somehow managed to escape – make it across the field ahead of the trucks – the older boys had better track him down, because if they didn't, they'd be whipped real hard, punished as accomplices. Better an accomplice than a warder, I figured, so every time we were called up for tracking duty, I was automatically sent to the hole for refusing to help. Only me and a couple of other older boys took that position. Even as a youngster, I knew I could never be party to putting anyone away in an institution.

Food was always a big deal for me. It was so bad at Alfred – I was always hungry and always stealing. You got up in the morning to a bowl of cold grey porridge, real poor-house slop. Black tea was your juice. A couple of sandwiches – stale bread, hardly nothing inside – was lunch. For supper we either had beans or bologna, a small slice cut eight ways for eight boys. Bologna and bread and boiled potatoes and black tea. Some diet! While we were wolfing down this mean meal, the good brothers watched us from their raised platform at one end of the dining hall. They were up there eating real good – steak, stew, all kinds of mouth-watering stuff.

They had a habit in the dining hall of getting the boys to beg for their scraps. We'd stand there with outstretched arms, pleading with them. Favourites would almost always win. I think I got their leftovers once in three years!

Once a year, at Christmas time, they'd pretend to be good to us –

a turkey dinner. Big deal. They made us parade around the table admiring the roasted birds before we could sit down to eat. But we only got to be part of this absurd ritual after we plucked about five thousand of them birds for the brothers to sell. Christmas time is a bitch in any joint; that's when you feel the loneliest, the most abandoned, the most unloved. Christmas in the joint without attention from family makes you feel like you're the scum of the earth. Every year I'd get care packages from my dear aunt, from my half-sister Rachel, my cousin Hector Brodeur, and my father sometimes. Once, my aunt forced my uncle to come with her to visit me. I got the odd letter from the odd relative during the year. But that was it as far as contact with my family and the outside world was concerned. I was alone in Alfred and alone in every joint.

At Alfred we were supposed to be in school, but we were more often in the fields than in the classroom. In spite of the fact that some of the boys were as old as seventeen, the reformatory school only went to grade eight. I'd already passed eighth grade when I was in detention, but my first four months at Alfred, they stuck me in eighth grade again. It was a joke; the only subjects we studied were English and stamp collecting. Because I'd been a quick learner in my school days, I could already read and write passably good. By the time I got to Alfred my formal education was over. After those few months, they just put me out to work full time and made no pretence of educating me further. Even my four months in school, most weeks we only had about two days in the classroom, from nine to noon and then an hour and a half in the afternoon. But even that got cancelled if there were crops to plant or harvest, or if local farmers wanted cheap child labour for any other work. The keepers and the farmers saw us as useless juvenile delinquents not worthy of an education.

The brothers weren't concerned with education – they were concerned with hockey and homosexuality and profits and preaching mass. We had to go to mass every day, including Sunday, as well as high mass and benediction on Sundays. Being in the chapel was better than working or being whipped, but the religion part didn't do nothing for me. It was just force-feeding from unholy men, real hypocrites. Religion was a yoke around my neck. I couldn't wait to shuck it off. After the nuns at the orphanage and the brothers at

Alfred, I was as sour on religion as you can get, sure I'd never like or trust anyone from the church again.

Being preached at, beat on by the preachers, and set to hard labour – that was the routine at Alfred. The training school owned a lot of land. They grew different crops, root vegetables like potatoes and beets mostly. Child inmates did all the work. Whatever vegetables weren't used to feed us were sold on the open market. A lot of produce moved out of there, and the brothers seemed to have lots of money for their little indulgences like good food and liquor. The kids who did all the back-breaking work never seen no money and no rewards. We never experienced no normal childhood neither, none of the playfulness that should have been ours.

But we tried to get back at our keepers and have a little fun whatever ways we could. Tending turkeys – a major business venture at Alfred – was one chance we had to raise a little hell. You can't profitably sell birds with torn skins, so naturally we tried to rip the skin when we were plucking them squawkers. Me, I liked to free the birds that were hanging upside-down waiting to get their throats slit. It caused all kinds of confusion, and I loved to see the brothers running around frantic, trying to round up the turkeys.

I was always getting whacked across the back of my head in the turkey barn for some misdemeanour, but it was worth the good feeling I got from rebelling against the harshness of the place. My turkey rebellion was not confined to small-time crimes. I made a couple of big scores with them turkeys – with the encouragement of an 'honest businessman.' One of the local small farmers, who used to hire boys as day labourers, approached me one day.

'I see you have a lot of turkeys in there, Tony. It must be hard to keep an accurate count.'

'Yeah, so?' I knew what he was after, but I was going to make him say it.

'Any chance you could get me a few?'

'Depends. What's in it for me?'

'I'll give you a buck apiece for good birds.'

'How many do you want?'

'As many as you can get, son.'

We worked a deal – the numbers, delivery method, and times. It was easy. The boys had very little supervision in the turkey barns – guess the brothers didn't fancy the stench. Since we raised about thirty thousand turkeys a year, no one would miss the odd grand. It was easy to arrange a meet with the honest businessman on one of the many small bush roads on to the Alfred property. All you had to do was load four cages with four birds each on to a handcart and meet the buyer. I made six hundred on that scam before I got caught and whipped.

You might wonder why we didn't all run away from the barns since the holy screws didn't guard us too heavy there. In fact, the turkey barns and the community farms were the best spots for making a run for it. At first I did run away from the barn. After I seen the success they had tracking me and the others, and after the first year, when they used to tease me that my indefinite sentence might end if I stayed put, I ran less. Getting away was easy; staying away was almost impossible, and being brought back was a ticket to brutality.

Every whipping I got made me stronger, but it also made me want to rebel more. I was caught in a cycle I couldn't get out of. The more I rebelled, the worse they punished me, and the worse they punished me, the more I rebelled. Sooner or later, there was a good chance I'd get maimed or even killed, because these brothers didn't fool around.

One brother with an ounce of heart realized the danger I was in. Brother Irving knew Leo might finish me one day during one of his rages. To get me off the property, Brother Irving assigned me to work with the boys who slaved as farmhands for a dollar a day – money paid to our keepers, not to us. Sometimes they'd give us a dollar a week, but usually they kept all the pay.

At least the farmers didn't beat us; instead, they worked us almost to death. The occasional farmer treated us like human beings, but most of them made us feel like our place was with the animals in the barn – which is where we sometimes had to eat. And we didn't often get the good food served at the farmer's table. The brothers certainly didn't care how the farmers abused us, just so long as the money rolled in – about a hundred dollars a day at peak times – and we were kept alive.

I was fourteen years old, putting in the work day of a full-grown man, and a farmer at that. Like a farmer, I slaved on those farms all year 'round. I could plant, tend, and harvest crops. I could milk cows. I could cut a cord of wood a day. And I could hay – mow, rake, sticker, and stack – with just a team of horses. I'd be out in the haying fields from first light to last, day after day. Stubble would get under my clothes and itch like crazy, but I'd keep going. Sometimes the stuff wouldn't even wash off in the shower, so it would scratch me as I slept the dreamless sleep of exhaustion. I'd wake with skin red and cut as I dressed to face another harsh day.

Once in a while it wasn't such a harsh day because there'd be a farm bee. Farmers down there were pretty poor and couldn't afford to buy the expensive equipment they needed like threshing machines. So, for barter, they'd get some guy that owned a threshing machine and he'd work all the farms in the area, one after the other. All the farmers would move around with him, helping their neighbours get the threshing done. That's when they'd have a bee – everyone pitch in to finish the harvesting or whatever – as quick as possible so the machinery could move to the next farmer. Bees meant lots of help and lots of great food, like luscious lemon meringue pies, because the farmers' wives all tried to outdo each other.

Working on community farms also meant I had hired hands as field partners. I already understood that the community code was different from the inmate code, but some things worked on both sides of the wall. I didn't like to be pushed around inside or outside. But on one of the farms there was a hired hand, a Dutch guy, who didn't know that. One day we were both sent to the hayloft to move hay.

'You go up in the loft and spread the hay. I'll toss it up,' I told him.

'No,' he answered real cocky. 'You work. I'll watch.'

'C'mon.' I went over to where he was sitting and he stood up.

'It takes two to do this job. I can't throw it up and stop every few minutes to go up there and spread it.'

'Get to work,' he ordered. He stuck out his jaw and shoved my shoulder. 'I tell you what to do, and I say start pitching. Then spread it.'

I swung my pitchfork at him. He turned on his heels and took to the house to rat to the farmer. I figured I was in for big trouble. Surprise! The farmer was fair. He told the man that if he'd been up in the loft where he was supposed to be, there wouldn't have been no trouble.

It usually pays to stand up for yourself. I was learning that lesson. Even sometimes when you do, you still get taken advantage of, though. Sometimes you even like to be taken advantage of, like by a farmer's daughter, for example. I guess I was about fifteen by then and she must have been eighteen – an experienced older woman. Things started innocent enough, with her bringing me extra food, sandwiches and stuff, and just being nice. But then she started rubbing up against me, and pretty soon we were in the haystack. It got to be a regular habit. We were enjoying each other all over the farm – in fields of high grain, under the tractor, behind the barn. It was great fun for about four months, till one day in the hay-mow a shadow fell over us. It was her father.

'Get your clothes on, boy, and pack your gear.' When I came out with my bundle, he was waiting in his car. The farmer's daughter was nowhere in sight. That car ride was one of the longest I've ever had. The man never said a word, and I kept my mouth shut. We just sat in silence, bumping over the roads to Alfred.

I was sure there'd be a brutal reception at Alfred when the farmer reported. I had twenty rough minutes of suspense while he talked with the chief brother and I occupied a hard chair outside his office. Another surprise. No one mentioned the incident, and two weeks later I was on another farm.

The fun was over. No farmer's daughter to lighten my days. Just child slavery on one farm, then on the next. One day, when I was sixteen, I was working for one of the most miserable farmers. He had me out in the noonday sun picking strawberries while he watched from his shaded porch and sipped lemonade. I straightened up to wipe off some of the sweat running into my eyes and to decide if it was worth taking a sip of the warm water in my bucket. The brother in charge of the farm workers, Brother Justine, drove up in Alfred's black limo. He called me over.

'What's up?' I yelled. 'I got to keep working. I got to finish this field by the end of the day.' It was more of a large garden than a field really, but it was bloody big, and if it wasn't done, I would get a poor cousin's supper. I saw the farmer get up and stroll my way. After all, he didn't want any of his workers not earning the dollar he paid the school!

'What do you want?' the old grouch demanded of the brother. 'He's not done here yet.'

'Oh yes he is,' the brother answered. 'His time is up. He's going home.'

'Home,' I thought to myself. The word shocked me. It was news to me, but it couldn't have been better news. I'd done three years in that hell. A moment's jubilation surged through me. My indefinite sentence had come – after three years – to a definite end. I looked at the farmer and looked at the big silver milk pail of strawberries squatting on the ground. I stepped right into that pail and squashed those berries with all my might. It was a small blow back at a man who'd been so needlessly miserable to a young boy. It was just a gesture of revenge, the best I could come up with on the spur. As I walked towards the car, big red footprints behind me, the farmer hollered objections.

'Nervy kid' the farmer bitched. 'Send him back here – he owes for those berries.'

The brother didn't say nothing, which was surprising. Just held the car door open for me. When we got back to the dorm, it was real quiet because all the guys were out working in the fields or on some farm. I fast sorted through the bits and pieces I'd collected over three years, packed the few things I wanted to take, and distributed the rest on the boys' beds. I took my prized pea jacket that I bought from the old Jewish pedlar that used to come around to the farms, my one pair of pants, and my few pairs of socks. I didn't have no underwear because you had to buy shorts from your pocket money – two dollars a week – and I figured underwear was a luxury in that economy. I left a few envelopes, cigarettes, and any little things I knew the guys couldn't get inside. It wasn't that I was leaving friends; I was already a confirmed loner, but I liked almost everyone and almost everyone liked me. I had made the kind of surface friendships you need to survive institutions.

The brothers wished me well in an indifferent sort of a way, gave me a couple of dollars and a one-way bus ticket to Cornwall. I phoned my aunt to tell her I was coming home. Then they drove me to the bus terminal. I knew there wouldn't be no one to meet me at the station when I'd arrive. There'd never be anyone there for me when I'd get back from doing time.

Riding to Cornwall, I thought about my three years in hell. What had been the good of doing that time, of wasting my youth in an institution? Was I any the better for it? What did I have to call my own? I had a few clothes, a few dollars, and a smoking habit. I'd been overworked and underfed and was going out into the world pretty much unschooled. Unless I wanted to pluck turkeys or work as a labourer the rest of my life, I had no legal skills to sell.

But I had learned a few things about myself and few things about making it in the criminal world. Alfred confirmed what I already knew – I was a loner who'd never get close to no one. And I wasn't going to let no one push me around. At Alfred I learned to stand my ground. If you let anyone bully you, they'd never stop. I hadn't picked fights and I didn't like fighting, but when a boy would try to threaten me or a brother would try to control me, I stood up for myself, even if I knew I'd lose the fight. When I stood up for myself among the boys, I won respect and the bullies had moved on to weaker prey. I also saw how stubborn I'd been, a natural rebel. I bucked the system every chance I got and I hadn't buckled under even when punished.

Yeah, I learned lots at Alfred. How to cope with pain and hunger. How to be sneaky. How important friends and favours are. I had a buddy at Alfred used to take kids under his wing, show them how to survive the system. For his advice and help he earned a little money or a couple of smokes. This system of mutual favours exists throughout the penal system, and God help the man that doesn't pay his debts.

I also learned something else that would help me a lot in later years inside. Hard work. I wasn't afraid of it. And it is a good way to make time pass. Time is all you got when you're a con. Of course, I'd learned some skills necessary to move up a few rungs on the ladder of law-breakers. The only question was – did I want to keep breaking the law, or did I want to be a square john?

I was sixteen, feeling life had screwed me. It hadn't made me hate yet, but it had made me want a little revenge. I felt the world owed me something for all the time I'd done, for all the pain it had inflicted on me. 'Yeah, I guess I want to get even,' I heard myself confess in my head.

But I didn't know exactly how I was going to do that.

Detention Barracks: You're in the Army Now

3

After all the time I done, after all the pain I suffered, I wanted to be welcomed home. After all, I was still only a kid, starving for some love and affection after all that hate and rejection at Alfred. I might have known there'd be more rejection waiting for me in Cornwall. My uncle had decided I was a bad seed that should be planted far away from him. I was barely in his front door when he was suspecting me of doing something wrong.

'What is it this time, Tony? Did you escape from the training school?'

My aunt, always quick to my defence, butt in. 'Please don't say that. The boy didn't do anything wrong. I told you he'd been released and that he would be home.'

My uncle wasn't going to be taken in by any soft-hearted pleas. 'How do you know he's telling you the truth? Maybe he ran away and he's just hoodwinking us. I'm going to check. I'm going to phone Alfred. Then we'll know for sure.'

When my uncle left the room to call, Aunt Alma embraced me, her eyes all dewy with apology for her husband and happiness for me being out and being home. She always loved me and accepted me; she was the only one I could ever count on to be there. Uncle Alphonse calmed down a bit when he realized my time was all done. Him and my aunt argued over my staying with them, till Alphonse finally gave in.

'All right, he can stay for a while. But he's got to get a job and he's got to stay out of trouble with the law. I can't afford to feed his big appetite, and I don't want any more police at the door. Besides, it's time he learned how to make an honest living. One slip-up and he's leaving.'

Me and my aunt both sighed with relief. But I also realized that if I wanted to stay at their house, I'd have to abandon my revenge plans for the moment. Next day I went to visit my father. Hard to tell whether he was glad to see me or not. It was like he had nothing to do with me, like I was some distant relative. There was no bond between us, but no tension, neither. He didn't care and he didn't not care. Or maybe he did feel something and he just didn't know how to show it. I guess I must have mattered a smidgen because he did help me get a job with the city.

The work was exactly what Alfred had trained me for – labour. I dug ditches, graded roads, and dug more ditches. Them days, most of the labouring jobs was done by hand. It was back-breaking work for heart-breaking pay; I might just as well have stayed at Alfred. The same slaving grind. Not that I'm lazy, never was. But I was young and hot and full of sap. I didn't know what I wanted to do with my life, but I knew it was something more exciting than eating dust and drinking beer.

Even though I was tempted to pitch that pick and run, I stuck with it, scared what I'd do if I gave up the straight life. All the shit they threw at me at Alfred made me wonder – a little –whether crime pays. Maybe I should tough it out on the city chain gang, give the square life a chance? I told myself over and over that I had to try. 'I have to try. I have to try.'

For three months I told myself I had to try. And I did try. I was doing good trying, too, till my delicate-balanced world started to fall apart. What happened? My uncle claimed ten dollars was missing from his pants pocket. Naturally, he accused me of stealing it. He was wrong; this once I was innocent. I protested against his accusations; he protested against my innocence.

'I know you did it, Tony. I don't care how much you deny it.'

'I didn't steal no money. I'm innocent.'

'This is the deal. You want to stay in my house? Fine. Just pay me two dollars a week for five weeks until your debt is paid and you can stay. Otherwise, you leave.'

'I didn't rob you and I ain't payin' you back.'
'Goodbye, Tony.'

Once a thief, always a thief. Was that how the world would treat me? I was going to learn that every ex-con faces that dilemma all his life. The world don't believe in change. They won't let you change, they won't help you change, and they won't believe you if you really do change.

My father hadn't changed. I realized that when I tried living with him again. He still didn't know how to be a father or a friend. He let me stay with him, but there was too much water under the bridge for us to make a go of it. He had his lifestyle set – hard work, hard drinking, and hard womanizing. I was just cramping his style. Seeing how unwelcome I was everywhere made me withdraw into myself. I saw that I had to withdraw bodily too, go someplace where I couldn't even hope anyone cared about me.

The army. A perfect choice. Don't get me wrong. I wasn't keen for combat, just keen to get out of Cornwall. I wasn't thinking about the Korean War, just my personal war to find a place I fitted in.

I fled Cornwall, ran away from the pain of trying to make it with my family and the hopelessness of trying to make me into a square john. I was going to enlist in Ottawa, and although I never really thought it through, I didn't feel like I was signing up for a straight life. That's not to say I was plotting to rob the army. The only thing on my mind was how I was going to get in, since in 1952 I was only seventeen. While I was figuring how to join up, most guys my age was into girls and music, hanging around fountains and jukeboxes listening to Hank Williams croon *Your Cheatin' Heart*.

Getting enlisted wasn't as hard as I thought, though I did have to manipulate my father to sign papers. I got sworn in and sent to Camp Petawawa for basic training. First thing they taught me was my service number. They drill you so damn hard that I still remember that number: sc18057. I was in the Royal Canadian Regiment, Second Battalion. Most of basic training was a drag – drills on everything that didn't matter to me, like perfectly pressed clothes and perfectly polished buttons.

What mattered to me was money. The army was not the place to get it – not in wages, that is. A meagre living, yes, but a real living, no way. I wasn't into living meagre, and I had all the imagination and skill to ensure I could live good. I stole. It was the simple solution. I just picked up anything that wasn't tied down – like army-issue boots and shirts – and sold it outside the barracks. But that kind of petty theft wasn't very profitable. The poor stealing from the poor and selling to the slightly less poor. There had to be better opportunities for a talented guy in the forces.

There was. Pay-parade day. First, let me tell you about pay parade. The army loves rituals. For example, when they called your name on payday, you marched to a desk, pulled off your tam, signed for your pay, placed your money in your tam, put your tam back on, saluted, and marched off the field. When you were clear, you'd get the cash out of your tam and put it in your pocket. A lot of fanfare for very little money. But a lot of guys were getting that very little money the same day – a good day to grab some of it while they were flush.

How? Simple. I went out and bought a crown and anchor game that used dice instead of a wheel. It had a snazzy green felt layout and everything. Then I put out the word that there's a game in our barracks. I started the game at a buck a throw, with me playing the house. A couple of hours later, I'd be a bit ahead, and I'd raise the stakes to two dollars a shot. Later, I'd raise the stakes again to five dollars. This jump would eliminate all the cheapskates and encourage all the gamblers. Then I'd make some serious money. For a while, it was a sweepstakes for me, till our sarge got wind of my little operation.

'I hear you're running a little game, McGilvary. You know you can't do that without a licence from the Sergeant's Society.'

'How much does that cost?' I knew what was coming.

'Only 25 per cent.'

'All right.'

Cutting the sarge into your action is one system you can't buck in the army. Petty though their rank, they had the power to make your life miserable without even trying. So I paid my protection money and shut my mouth. Surprisingly, he even helped business a little.

'McGilvary, we aren't pulling in as much as we could. From now on we'll move from barracks to barracks, hook a lot more soldiers.'

Sarge had the right idea. The take was getting big and his greed was catching up with the purse. 'Time to pay up for my good advice, McGilvary. Your licence will cost 50 per cent.'

So I've got a full partner. Okay. But when he got even greedier, demanding 60 per cent, I went out of business. Sarge bought his own outfit and got some sucker to run it for 10 per cent.

During my gambling phase I was also busy going AWOL from time to time. I'd just take off for a bit and find myself a party in town. Sometimes I'd get caught and confined to barracks, but I was incorrigible. My kind of partying requires money, so I needed a new angle to generate the kind of funds that would keep my social life active. While considering possible scams, I went back to petty theft just to keep some change in my pocket.

I was still working on fresh angles when I somehow finished basic and advanced training at Petawawa. Then we got shipped to Fort Churchill, Manitoba, on winter-survival schemes. They taught us how to survive the cold, sleeping in tents and igloos we built ourselves. We got used as guinea pigs to test new clothing and new weapons. We'd play war games, with one battalion setting camp and the other trying to penetrate it, and things like that.

One time on one of these schemes I forgot to wear my jock strap. I could feel that icy cold seeping into my crotch. Guess what happened – I froze my dick! It was very embarrassing when the nurse had to dip it into a pan of snow and manipulate it to thaw. As if the humiliation wasn't enough, I got twenty-one days CB – confined to barracks – and a hundred-dollar fine. They thought I deliberately froze my penis to escape a thirty-day scheme coming up. Imagine! Picture the man that would choose this method to get out of work!

Fort Churchill was a booming place, more than just another army camp. There was a US base to support the radar station, a bunch of surveyors that was mapping the north, a civilian town, and an Eskimo village. Lots of traffic – trucks and planes, even Bob Hope doing a US show. To me, traffic and people means market – market for theft and market for sale of hot goods. For example, three barracks woke up one morning to discover their flight boots missing. Someone had snuck in overnight and removed them from beside the bunks of the sleeping soldiers. So much for guards! The boots found their way to various parties interested in warm feet.

Canadian army flight boots were noted for warmth – even American soldiers wanted them.

A lot of army issue developed legs and walked away while I was there. Turned out you could buy keys from certain responsible people. Considering the value of what was locked away, the price of those keys – about two months' pay, roughly two hundred dollars – was cheap. Of course, you couldn't keep the keys, but I learned at Alfred how to make impressions. What walked? Liquor from the dorms, blankets from the quartermaster's store, even a five-ton truck full of beef. Even in a small place like Churchill, it's no problem dumping five tons of beef.

I was accused of numerous thefts but never charged because there was no proof. Besides being suspected of stealing, I was always in trouble for my attitude. Don't get me wrong. I loved the army, and I could perform: march, shoot, maintain my gun, everything they wanted except press my clothes right. I have to admit; I was a slob. I still am a slob. I always will be a slob. In the army that's a crime worse than stealing. I'd show up for inspection or parade in a ring-around-the-collar shirt and pants that looked like they'd been in the trenches. I was so hopeless that Sergeant Valence was ordered to keep me in barracks.

Valence was a good guy; he'd warn me a couple days in advance of a parade that I'd better get my clothes to the cleaners. Many times he kept me out of trouble, and he found a good use for me – platoon scrounger. Whenever the platoon needed something, tents or supplies that weren't arriving after being requisitioned, he'd send me out. I always found what he wanted; he never asked where or how. Stealing from other units was a way a life. Of course he'd never tell me to steal. Rather, he'd say, 'Boy, this platoon could really use another five duffel bags. Don't know where I can get them.' He'd let out a sigh. 'Guess I'm going to have to fight the quartermaster for them again.' Another sigh, then he'd walk away.

Next day the gear would land in his path. We neither of us said nothing. When we went on schemes, I was the one to go after the supplies from the air drop. I always made sure to get a couple extra K-rations for the platoon. Ensuring full bellies, especially mine, was one of my specialties, which is why I never got my adult weight below 225 and sometimes made it closer to 300.

43 You're in the Army Now

It's not surprising that I'd get accused of stealing from time to time. But once I was accused of stealing from another soldier that slept in the same room with me. Stealing, especially from a bunkmate, was a serious crime in the army. They were certain I did it, so certain that they kept me in detention for two days till I could be brought up before a major. Because he had no proof, the major let me off. Sarge Valence was waiting for me when I came out.

'Tony, I know you didn't do it. I know you wouldn't steal from someone you slept with.' I didn't say nothing. I didn't have to. He was absolutely right. He didn't know it was the con's code I was observing, but I knew it.

The food in Churchill was okay, but for first-class eats you had to go to the American mess. We had better gear; they had better chow. I was into food, not uniforms, so I found a hefty American soldier that wanted to drink in our canteen because we had stronger beer. We'd swap uniforms and trade places. It was against the rules, of course, to eat or drink in the other force's mess. Everything was against the bloody rules.

Always ordering us around – something I've been subject to all my life, and always hated. This time we were ordered to move on, to London, Ontario, and the Wolsely Barracks. At least the weather was a welcome change from the cold, barren tundra. And London was civilized compared to Churchill. More women. Up north there was only one woman to every ten men. In Churchill the barracks were ancient, while in London they were brand new, had all the conveniences.

The barracks was surrounded by a fence with guard posts. Every unit pulled guard duty in twenty-four-hour shifts. Not bad, really, because there were a lot of guys on each shift, so you could spell each other off, maybe only work two hours with four off till your turn came again. Only rough thing about guard duty was inspection. They got madder and madder at me because I seemed to be getting dirtier and dirtier. My clothes were baggy, my hair was scraggly, my beard was prickly. Only my rifle was spotless.

One captain was always riding me hard. Riding all of us, really. 'Just wait, you SOB, I'll get you,' I swore to myself. One night when I was standing guard on the front gate, he came rolling in dead drunk.

44 Square John

'What's the password?' I demanded.
'I don't know. Let me in.' He was weaving from side to side.
'Sorry sir, I need the password.'
'I forget the damn password. Let me in now. You know who I am.'
He was furious, screaming and yelling and making a huge ruckus. I was determined. I wouldn't let him in. Eventually Sergeant Valence heard the noise and came to investigate.
'What's going on here?'
'He doesn't know the password, sir.'
Sarge suddenly realized that the drunk was our captain. 'My God,' he said, fear shaking his voice, 'let him in.'
'I can't. He doesn't have the password. You want him in, you take the responsibility.'
'Okay, okay, just let him in.' I opened the gate.
That little stunt made me feel good, but it also got me up on the carpet – in front of the colonel this time. He listened to my story; then he said, 'Not good, McGilvary. You made a big mistake.'
'Yes sir.'
'What mistake did you make?'
'I didn't shoot him, sir?' The captain gasped. The colonel smiled.
'That's right. Now, why didn't you?'
'They didn't issue us any bullets, sir.' I kept an absolutely straight face. It worked. They let me go, but I knew they'd be on me more than ever, and I knew my untidiness would do me in.
Sure enough, I was soon thrown off parade. As punishment, I was put in charge of cleaning duty. Little did they suspect how I could turn that twist to my advantage. New barracks means new washers and dryers. They disappeared during my short – very short, only two days – stint on cleaning duty. I found out about the case of the disappearing laundry room just as I was getting a dice game rolling.
'Tony!' Sarge Valence stormed in on our game. 'Come with me.'
We went down to the laundry room. It was empty. Washers, dryers, everything, even the ironing boards were gone. I was the prime suspect, of course. They were puzzled about how the scam went down. Where was the stuff? Was it still on the base? I had certain ideas about how the play might have gone down. The army

45 You're in the Army Now

never has enough imagination to figure how crooked trusted men can be. If you have one man on the rear gate and he isn't too honest, stealing a laundry room is a snap. Four men could strip the room and load the stuff on a truck easy, then drive out past a paid-off guard. Sell the hot washers, pay the blind-eyed guard a percentage, then split the rest even. A piece of cake. The army couldn't figure that one out; they turned the base upside-down looking for a long-gone laundry. No one ever got charged.

Army life was boring me, not enough of a challenge, too easy to rip off. I requested a transfer to Korea. Don't get me wrong; I had no idea what the Korean War was all about, and I didn't want to fight. I just wanted rich black-market opportunities. They rejected my application because of my young age, seventeen. Then the crunch came when I was CB for a couple of days while my buddies were getting seventy-two-hour passes. I wasn't staying behind. So, I just left, to hell with passes.

I knew, of course, that they'd be on my tail, so I didn't go home. Instead, I went to Sudbury and got a job through an employment agency. I worked three months at Canada Bread taking hot bread from ovens, till one day I got word that two MPs were at my cousin's house looking for me. I hopped the next bread-delivery truck to North Bay. From there, I hitched to Winnipeg.

I don't care what anyone says – there's a lot of coincidence in life. I was just hanging out in Winnipeg when I felt a hand on my shoulder – a sergeant who knew me, and who knew I was AWOL. He threw me in Number Eight Detention Barracks. They rode you hard in there. The barracks had to be kept spotless. You had to shine your shoe-polish tin so you could use it as a shaving mirror. To check the standard of your work, they even did a white-glove inspection. One speck of dirt on them gloves and you were in deep trouble. They loved punishments, especially to see you double-timing it around the parade square wearing a seventy-five-pound backpack and holding a rifle high over your head. You couldn't stop till they allowed it; they never did. You just ran till you dropped. One day I was scrubbing the corridor with a toothbrush when one of the sergeants come in.

'Let's go, McGilvary.'
'Where we going?'

'You're leaving.'

'Leaving?' I couldn't understand this. I'd only been in two weeks; I had two and a half months left on my ninety-day sentence. They put me in a regular barracks. No explanation. Some days they let me go into Winnipeg, other days not. They ran me past a bunch of psychiatrists and psychologists and gave me a bunch of tests. For three months, this unexplained nonsense went on.

Then, just as mysteriously, they let me go. They gave me a misconduct discharge, a train ticket to Toronto, some meal vouchers for the train, and some vouchers for civilian clothes from the Bay. I was pleased but perplexed. My interrupted but approximately eleven-month career as a soldier was over. I was eighteen. What had I learned in the army? Only one lesson that mattered: I'd always be able to make a living – my criminal skills were now sharp enough for that. And that's what I would do with my life – be a criminal. By then, it was simply doing what came naturally.

Life on the Carnival Circuit

4

I left Winnipeg so broke I couldn't take Laura, my native girlfriend, with me, but in a vague sort of way I imagined I'd send for her later. At the time I hopped a train, I didn't know she was pregnant with my first kid – at least, the first I knew about. I had empty pockets when I boarded that train, but they were sure bulging when I got off in Toronto. Somebody would get a surprise when he reached in his pocket for his wallet.

For the first few days I just wandered around the city enjoying my freedom and freely spending the money I stole. On girls and partying. It ran out pretty quick, so I had to figure a way to make some more. Just as I was considering a career in house prowling, I ran into a guy I knew from Alfred. My whole life I'd be running into cons I knew from other crimes and prisons. That's how an outlaw gets started again once he's back on the street. Anyhow, I ran into this bandit buddy, and he said to me, 'Let's join the circus.' He knows about some carnival in Ottawa – the Bernard and Barry Shows.

Why not, I thought. I liked the idea of carnival life; it seemed the perfect choice for a rogue and a rover like me. We hitched to Ottawa, and I can remember me and my buddy walking past a bakery just after we arrived. You know that smell that comes from bakeries when the bread's in the oven – irresistible!

'Want somethin' ta eat?' I ask my pal, my plan to steal fresh bread already decided.

'Sure. But we don't have any money.'

'Who needs money ta eat?' I answer. 'I just gotta have some a that bread we're smellin'.'

Next thing you know, we're in a park greedily stuffing ourselves with white bread warm from the oven. Even without butter – I was in too much of a hurry to stop to steal butter and jam – it was delicious. When we finished our little picnic, we headed off in search of the carnival. That same afternoon we found it and hired on. They put me in the cookhouse washing dishes and peeling potatoes. Them days there were no electric peelers or cutters; my hands was all the automatic equipment they needed.

I felt free as a bird – a sensation I would always get on the carnivals. Carnival people are my kind of people; they're nothing like the bad reputation they got. Like Tony Tamarino, the cookhouse concessionaire. A concessionaire is a guy that rents space on the fairgrounds from the show owner. He rents so he can put up his rides or games and make a fast buck. Tony T took a real liking to me. A hard little Italian he was, about five-foot ten, stocky, with a bit of a gut. He was gruff on the outside but he had a good heart on the inside.

Tony T came up in the streets, like a lot of carnival people, but he never had no trouble with the law. He was smart, street smart, self-taught. Sure he drank a lot, and swore a lot but he had more smarts than it seemed, and more kindness than you'd expect from a carnie. He's the one that taught me never to let anyone on the midway go away hungry – even if he couldn't pay for the food.

Besides the cookhouse, Tony T ran the food and booze concessions on the carnival train – the dressed-up boxcars that moved the show from town to town. The four guys working the concessions for him were cheating. When he got to trust me, to see what a hard worker I was, he asked if I wanted to take over working the concessions for a third of the profit.

You bet I wanted them. There was everything on that train you could imagine – food, beer, even slot machines. I'd organize and sell the packaged food and cold beer, cooled with mountains of ice. Running the boxcar concessions meant hard work, but it also meant big money – provided I almost never slept. If you slept too much, your inventory would disappear, so I was awake and counting all the time. When we got to the next spot the carnival was playing and Tony T saw how much more money he made because I never beat him – never stole no booze, not even one sandwich – he made me his head waiter.

On the move I'd run the concessions; on the grounds I'd be the grill-man, cooking burgers and dogs. The life was very hard but very rewarding. Them days, a cookhouse was a big tent, the centre of life for carnies, ride boys, and joinees, the local guys that hired on in every town we played from southern Ontario to Halifax. Getting that cookhouse tent in the air on a hot day, you suffered. It was a framed joint, stood up by itself. Once you got it standing, you'd build a wooden floor. Once the floor was laid, you'd bring in your appliances. We had ice-cooled fridges and a big gas-powered grill about forty inches square. There'd be big dining tables to set up in the centre of the floor. We were feeding about two hundred people, not exactly your average-size dinner party. Don't forget that anywhere from a week to two weeks later we'd have to take it all down, load it all up on trucks, then unload the trucks into boxcars. Sometimes as soon as the next day, in the next town we were playing, we'd have to unload the boxcars into trucks, then unload the trucks at the site and set the whole thing up again. The carnival is no playground for wimps.

Working the cookhouse is one of the most slaving jobs you ever want to have. I'd work from seven in the morning till two the next morning. Then, if there was a crap game going, I might get in on that. It could be five before I went to bed. The nights I slept five hours, those were a good night's sleep. I slept in a sleeping bag on a fold-out army cot on the cookhouse floor. Except for the owners and some of the permanent carnies, like the freak show people who owned their own trailers, everyone else either slept in the tents they worked or, if they had a bit of money, they'd sleep in motels.

Besides being brawny to handle the back-breaking work, I also had to be a bouncer and a mother hen. Why? Because when you'd get everyone in there, the odd flare-up was bound to happen. Carnival people are very hot, easy to temper but easy to cool, too. Then you'd get the ride boys, just street urchins, poor kids with no one and nothing. They needed a mother, and even though I was only nineteen, I'd often be a big-hearted fat mamma to them.

They'd confide their problems, borrow the odd buck, that kind of thing.

Mostly they counted on me to keep them fed good. On our huge grill you could cook about a hundred burgers at a time and still have room to pile them up and keep them warm. The air was always thick with the smell of onions frying. A real fast-food joint – hot and noisy and greasy. I remember some of them wieners with not too much affection. We used to buy them in bulk and salt them down to preserve them. By the time I cooked them, they could be pretty green. I can remember scraping all that green glop off real careful, though, before grilling them.

Experimenting. I was into experimenting in the kitchen; I loved to make new things. Someone asked if I could make dumplings. My mouth watered at the word. I remembered the delicious dumplings that Hector Brodeur's wife, Thérèse, used to make for me in Cornwall.

Hector and Thérèse won't forget the dumplings either. Ordinarily a phone call from a friend requesting a recipe would be a non-memorable event. But Tony's phone calls to family and friends are never unremarkable. He has a knack for turning non-events into the stuff that stories are made of. Hector recalls a morning the phone awakened him at four-thirty. He laughs good-humouredly at the memory.

'Oui. Allo,' he said fearfully, 'qu'est-ce qui ce passe?'

'It's me, Tony. How ya doin,' Hector?'

'He didn't even wait for me to answer, didn't apologize for calling in the middle of the night, nothing, just went on like it was normal.' By now Hector is laughing so hard he can barely finish the story.

'"Listen, I need a recipe for dumplings ... Is Thérèse there?"

'"Of course she's here. It's four-thirty in the morning. Where else would she be?"

'"That late?" Tony sounded surprised. "I'm in the cookhouse with some of the carnival people, we're in Ottawa, and they won't believe that I can get a recipe for the best dumplings in the world. Ask Thérèse to get it for me, will you. I'll wait."

'By now she was awake. "It's Tony. He needs your recipe for dumplings. If you go downstairs and get it, I'll read it to him."

'So she did and I did and Tony said "Thanks. Goodbye." Like it was the

most normal thing in the world to call for recipes at four-thirty in the morning. We had a good laugh and went back to sleep.

'That wasn't the only time. He did the same thing another time much later when he was with a carnival in Florida. That time he wanted the recipe for pineapple upside-down cake at three a.m. I don't think Tony knows how to use a phone before midnight.

'Not all the late calls were for recipes, either.' Hector grins a boyish grin, slightly naughty. 'Sometimes he'd call us from a party at a hotel somewhere. He'd put his girlfriends on the phone. One time – I think they were in Kingston – one of the girls begged me to join them.

'"I can't. I'm a married man."

'"What difference does that make?" she answered.

'"It makes a lot of difference to my wife."

'Tony was always good for a lot of laughs. He'd get lonely, I guess, and just think to call us. So he'd phone. Didn't matter where he was, what he was doing, or what time it was.

'He's not very good for knocking at doors much earlier than midnight, either. I can't tell you how many times he's arrived on our doorstep at two or three in the morning. We got used to it after a while and we always had his bed ready for him, especially during the carnival's off-season. He'd get a job – easily; Tony was always one to find jobs easily. But he'd leave them and us fast enough. We'd wake up one morning two or three weeks later and he'd be gone without a word or a note. That's Tony.'

I sure convinced those guys that I could make the world's best dumplings. In fact, I got famous on the midway for them. One day Miranda, the wife of the two-headed man, came to the cookhouse. 'My husband would really like to taste those dumplings, Tony,' she tells me.

I knew why he sent Miranda. Henry, the two-headed man, didn't socialize with no one except his family – his wife and his two beautiful, normal kids. Ordinarily he never left his trailer; if you were going to see him, you were going to pay to see him. He was so scared of people's reactions he even put a high tarpaulin around his trailer for complete privacy. Miranda came back many times for more dumplings. So one day when I'd made a fresh batch I delivered them myself. Surprisingly, they let me come into their trailer.

I didn't flinch when I first saw him up close, but my eyes went sympathetic. 'I know what you're thinking, Tony, but please don't feel sorry for me,' he said. It was hard not to feel pity – he looked worse than the Elephant Man. At first I thought he had two heads, but it was actually one with a cleave that went about a third of the way down his head. He had two separate faces, two eyes – one on each face – two nostrils, holes really, one on each face. He had two mouths that overlapped at the corner. Him and me got to be friends. He was real intelligent, always reading books. I always liked being around him because he was a nice man and he knew so much. Eventually, he told me his story, about how his family had sold him to the circus, just left him on the midway, him thinking he was lost and they'd find him. He told me about his upbringing. He was treated like an animal – caged, often left in dark rooms, beaten, starved, put on display for people to pay and gawk. Finally, he was able to free himself from his keeper, but he still ended up a carnival side-show. It was the only work he could get. He wasn't bitter or nothing. Educated himself, had this wonderful family, and rose right above his treatment. Henry wasn't the only freak show on the B&B carnival. There were ten of them under one roof: alligator man, monkey girl, fat lady – I can't remember the rest.

Getting to be friends with Henry was one of the good things about my first season with B&B Shows. I loved my life that year, but then I always love feeling free, being someplace where I fit in, where the people like me. Whenever life is like that, I stay straight. I never had no trouble with the law when I was on the carnival.

When the season ended in October, I went back to my uncle's in Cornwall. There was a letter waiting from Laura, my native girlfriend in Winnipeg. Said she had my baby boy and named him Michael Anthony. So, on the spur, I went to Winnipeg to find her, only she wasn't living in the same place and she didn't leave no forwarding address and there was no address on the letter and I couldn't find any mutual friends. I just couldn't find her. I never did see or hear about Laura or my kid again. Guess he's in his thirties now.

That winter in Winnipeg was pretty uneventful. Just stealing, getting by, hanging out with rounders and roamers, the real lost causes. I felt pretty empty. When the carnival season reopened, I was relieved to get out of Winnipeg and get back to the B&B Shows. We played Cornwall that year, so all the Brodeurs came to the midway with their kids. It felt so good to see them. I had so little family I felt connected with that just the sight of their faces made me feel like a regular human being.

Everyone in Tony's family remembers his generosity. In speaking of it, they always refer to carnival times, when he tossed teddy bears to them and their kids.
  '"Here's a winner," he'd shout, the minute he saw us coming. Then he'd throw teddy bears at all of us,' Anita Brodeur recalls.
  'Yes, as soon as he spotted us coming up the midway,' Hector adds, 'he'd be gathering up the biggest and best prizes to give to my twins. And he'd make a lot of noise about it, sure could embarrass you. But you couldn't be mad at him because he was so generous. Whenever he visited us, he'd always fill the fridge with expensive groceries.'

Carnival life was as good to me that season as the one before. I loved the people and I loved the atmosphere – the music from the merry-go-round, the smells from the grab joints selling candy floss and candy apples, caramel corn and popcorn, and fountain juice. I liked the smells and the excitement, all the bustle and all the noise.
  You got to know carnival people to understand. They're hard-working but they're also fun-loving people. They're gamblers, happy gamblers, you might say, but they're also lonely because they're isolated, living in a self-contained community that's always on the move. So it makes them a close family, and that's what I never had. Carnies are always helping one another and caring for one another. They're definitely out for a buck – who ain't? – but they don't want to hurt nobody. Like me, I never wanted to hurt nobody. Maybe because we were alike – outsiders – they always took a liking to me and let me into their circle.
  They're not all crooked like their reputation. Sure, there was rats in the pile and always someone running some gaff, but when the owners caught them, they'd usually get thrown off the show. Yet the world sees carnies as a pack of thieves; they carry the same

stigma as ex-cons. Innocent or guilty, you're always the first one blamed and the last one to get a break.

I'm not saying there were no rackets; a lot of carnival life is just borderline legal, and some of it used to be outright illegal. The government had flying squads of special police to raid us. They'd get flown into a town where the carnival was playing; the local police would pick them up at the airfield; then they'd join forces to swoop down on the carnival to bust up the rackets. I remember one time they busted B&B. All the flatties – the guys running the gambling joints – came tearing into the cookhouse and sat down.

'Give us food, Tony. Fast!' one of them ordered.

'What ya orderin'?' I asked.

'It doesn't matter. Anything. Just make it fast!'

I threw a pile of steaks on that grill and gave them all rare meat. They were eating real innocent when the cops came in. You see, the law got to catch you in the act or they can't charge, so all the concessionaires just ran to the cookhouse when someone alerted them to the raid. I was running one of the rackets myself, the G-top, that's the after-hours gambling joint for the carnies. I turned the cookhouse into a G-top after the show closed at midnight. We'd play dice and cards and sell a little booze. Shoot enough dice, the house is bound to win. Sell enough booze, you also end up in the money. I was splitting the take with Tony Tamarino. A typical night, I'd make $150.

There were good reasons to have a G-top. First of all, it kept the carnival people amused, so they wouldn't go into the town and ball it up, raise hell and get in trouble. Trouble for individual carnies always meant trouble for the show, maybe orders to leave town. Second, it kept the ride boys broke, so they wouldn't leave the show and they also wouldn't go into the towns where townspeople would make them feel so unwelcome.

Because we lived so close, like a small travelling community, we had to have certain rules. It's a bit like the con community inside – you have your own values, a code that's different from the community code. Like the girls on the show, for instance, the ones in the girlie shows. Them girlie shows, incidentally, was real innocent. If those girls did what they do today on videos, even on TV, the carnival owners would have been put away for twenty years!

Anyway, those girls could not be hookers. No way. If they got caught hooking, they'd be forced to leave the show.

Also, if a carnival guy hooked up with a carnival girl and the girl took a fancy to another man, she couldn't do nothing about it. She'd have to leave the show rather than live with a new man while the first one still wanted her. There was no discrimination – the same rule applied to the men. The rules only applied to people living on the show. But there were lots of short romances with local girls. I had my share of them. Girls are always fascinated by carnival life, just like they're drawn to cons. Life in the fast and risky lane, I guess. They think it's exciting being around racy men. Funny thing was that a lot of them girls that hooked up with the carnies, they'd be the ones the town thought were just perfect. Believe me, they were no angels; they knew how to let their hair down. I fell in love with every second broad. Some of them stayed with me for a few towns, just for a while. We'd shack up in the cookhouse, sleep together on the cookhouse floor. It was a bit crowded for two in my army cot, especially with me weighing over two hundred pounds.

I wasn't the marrying kind, but a lot of carnies were. When a carnival couple married, the rule was that the ceremony must take place on the ferris wheel. When anyone died, the ferris wheel seats had to be draped in black.

Lots of rules – like when I wanted to switch concessions, go to work for another concessionaire who offered me more money than I was making with Tony T at the cookhouse. The rule is that you can't switch that season unless you have permission from the concessionaire you're working for. I remember asking Tony T for permission.

'I have a chance to be an agent, to run my own concession. I'd like a crack at it.' He didn't look pleased. 'I've served you good, never beat you for a buck, so gimme a shot at it.'

Tony T was reluctant, but he gave in because he liked me and he knew I was ambitious and he didn't want to hold me back. Since I got permission, I took a concession for Solly Leroy running his budgie wheel. That's where you got all these caged budgies for prizes. The mark spins a crown-and-anchor wheel. If it stops on white, he wins a comb; if it stops on red, he wins a budgie bird. I became a real firecracker agent. I knew how to attract the crowds.

You'd never believe how much money I made because people wanted to win a budgie!

I learned another rule. I learned to holler 'Hey rube' when a mark lost a lot of money and was getting hot, like he might attack me. Not that I couldn't defend myself – I was a big guy, and I looked mean enough to discourage most people who thought about attacking. But the owners didn't want no trouble, no bad publicity, no fights. So if you thought trouble was brewing and it couldn't be handled without fists, you'd holler 'Hey rube' to attract some help from agents working other concessions. Sometimes it would turn out that the concessionaire was at fault, that he was cheating the mark; in those cases the owner would give the money back to the mark and often kick the agent off the show. Don't forget, it's a big show and you get all types of agents who might join for just a town or two. We might have forty concessions on a show the size of B&B – that means about fourteen rides, maybe eight adult rides and six kiddie rides.

I found the rules easy to live by. It was my kind of life. I was nineteen. It was 1954, a big year, the year transistor radios first blared down on the marks as they strolled the midway. I'd hum along to *Three Coins in a Fountain*, *The Naughty Lady of Shady Lane*, and my favourite, *Sh-Boom, Sh-Boom*.

Most of the time I felt great. In my element, on the margins of the law, living with marginal people like me. I felt free, and whenever I feel that way, I don't get in no trouble. I had gotten through my second season with B&B, but late fall was closing in, so the show would soon be closing. I started to feel restless, scared of getting into trouble and going to jail once I'd leave the carnival.

Beachcombing in Vancouver

5

I was scared of getting back into scamming and ending up in a slammer somewhere, and my mind was scrambling for something to keep me busy and straight between carnival seasons. Don't know why exactly, but I hit on the idea of a winter in Vancouver. I got this urge; I felt I just had to get out there. Maybe I figured the mountains and the ocean would cleanse me of the criminal longings that were never far from my mind. Underworld or straight world, at least I'd be warm in Vancouver instead of freezing my buns in Ontario. Anyway, I was set on going west, so I asked a carnie from Vancouver if I could drive out with him. Bingo ran a side-show with trained lions, a midget bull, a dog that sang, and other little animals that did silly things. End of season, he'd pack up his menagerie and his wife and head home.

Bingo was pleased to take me along because I could help him take care of the animals. I was pleased too till I saw my bed – just a few scrawny bars away from restless lions. The sound of their roars and the look of their puss – I thought I was having nightmares till I realized I wasn't dreaming; I was seeing the real thing. Not the prettiest sight to have sleeping next to you! By the time our little caravan reached Vancouver, I was ready for a good night's sleep.

I had it at Walter Hay's place over on Twig Island. Walter, another carnie buddy, had a nice family living in a nice float-house, and they were nice enough to take me in. Guess they didn't figure I'd stay almost two years. Walter was an old hand at beachcombing, his between-carnival-seasons trade. I didn't know much about beachcombing, but Walter assured me you could make a good buck and have a good life.

'Beachcombing is definitely for you, Tony,' Walter argued.

'Yeah? Convince me.'

'It's very exciting. It's dangerous because you always have to outwit logs that could crush your boat, or logs that could bury you if you fall in the river. And like the carnivals, it's partly legal and partly not.' Walter laughed a knowing laugh. 'I'm sure you'll like the least-legal bits best.' The man knew me. 'Besides, you'll like the beachcombers, especially some of their daughters and their beach parties.'

It was an easy sell. It meant staying with Walter, which kept me connected with carnival people. It meant I'd learn a new trade. I've always been eager to learn new things, especially things you could apply to making money.

Now, you must understand that we were talking about running around on logs that were rolling down a river, and I was about 235 pounds at the time. But my weight never stopped me from doing nothing – except squeezing through the occasional milkbox as a kid. It wasn't going to hamper me one bit from flying over those logs. Almost the first time I tried it, that first week on the Fraser River – education week, I called it – it came easy. I was as fleet of foot as any man half my size.

Walter schooled me in a row-boat. He taught me to spot good logs, the Douglas firs and yellow cedars, the ones that would fetch the best price. He taught me about the logs you could take legal – the ones floating free down the Fraser or grounded on the shore – legal salvage logs you could sell to the mills for a pittance. And then he schooled me in the ways of stealing logs that weren't legal for the taking. There were basically two ways of doing it. Either you could free logs from the sections being hauled down the Fraser by tugboats, or you could free them from the stockpiled sections chained to the shoreline along the river. Them stockpiles sometimes run as long as ten miles.

Sometimes storms would do the work of freeing them, heave the logs up in the air and set them coursing down the river. They were the legal salvage logs most of the beachcombers were looking for, because the majority of beachcombers were working legal. There was no money in working legal – it didn't take me long to figure that out. Salvage logs resold to the mills that owned them were only worth three bucks apiece. Those same logs sold at thirty-five dollars a thousand foot square feet if you stole them and sold them as hot merchandise to mills that ignored the mill number stamped on the logs. With three to five thousand feet in them logs, you could grab maybe a hundred and fifty on average for a hot log. Legal, that same log was selling for three miserable bucks! Obviously, I was more interested in selling them hot.

The real test of whether I could cut this trade came when I had to try running across the boom log. The boom's the key log in the chain of top logs that holds the sections. I had to run along it in the dark of night with a cold black river flowing inches below my bare feet. From the first day I never wore the spiked boots the loggers use. I didn't need them. Just my bare feet and raw nerve were enough. I not only got into the habit of bare feet but also the habit of wearing nothing but rolled-up jeans. I liked to feel free, not caught by clothes. What I was trying to do in my half-naked state was set some of them logs free from their section being hauled downriver by tugboats from the logging camps.

This is how we'd do it. Walter would row me alongside the boom log. I'd transfer from our boat to the boom log, carrying my work tools with me – a peavey and a pipe pole. A peavey is like a three-foot-long pick handle with a loose, giant hook at the butt end. That hook bites into a log so that when you apply pressure to the handle, the log rolls. A pipe pole is a skinny, twelve-foot-long pipe, pointed at the end, and it's got a clamp and a hook at the end also. If you happen to fall in the water and you're carrying your pipe pole the right way – at a right angle to your body – it can save your life. How? By hooking over logs and allowing you to hoist yourself up out of the water before your head goes under. If you didn't have a pipe pole and you fell in, you'd be a goner because them logs just closes up above your head.

Anyway, I'd balance myself with one foot on the boom log and one foot on the log I was stealing. By putting some weight on the log I was stealing and working it with my peavey, I could force it under the boom log and set it free-floating. I'd free maybe two logs before transferring back to the row-boat. The logs would be running down the river; we'd catch up with them, grab them with our pipe poles and bring them alongside the boat so we could dog them.

Dogging means driving a spike into the log so we could drag that log behind us. You drive them spikes in with a heavy, two-headed hammer. The spike, or dog, as we call it, is about five inches long, and it's on a cable. You could put a large number of dogs – fifty to a hundred – on a cable. But the number of logs you could dog depended on how much power your boat had. Obviously, a row-boat got no power, so we could only take two logs and row with all our might to get them logs to the mill.

I forgot to mention that there is one other way of stealing logs. Just open that section by smashing the boom chain from the boom log. Once the boom chain is unleashed, it's like opening a corral fence; all the horses come teeming out. But doing it that way wasn't a hot idea because it would alert the mills to theft. They'd never notice one or two logs missing from each section, but they'd always notice a missing section.

Sometimes I was stealing faster than I could sell, so I needed places to stash my hot logs. I'd build my own framework with boom logs, and Walter and me would stash our logs in our home-made section tied off his float-house. There were always boom logs being hauled down the river by tugboats, so I'd rob them same as any other. There was one hitch, though. I'd have to carry a 99-pound boom chain around my neck, along with the usual 15 to 20 pounds worth of peavey and pipe pole. Picture it – a 235-pound barefoot butterball balancing on two boom logs, carrying about 120 pounds and all in the dark of night. Them days, I wasn't scared of nothing.

But where else could I hide hot logs? That was easy. Just slip the odd log into the stockpiled sections lining the shores of the Fraser. Tuck them in behind all the mill-owned logs. That way, they looked like company logs. I knew the mill schedules, and I made sure to get my logs out before the mills moved sections for cutting.

It didn't take long for Walter and me to grab lots of money selling hot logs to shaky mills. See, every log has a mill number to indicate its company owner. But the shady mills would blur that mark by pounding the mill number with a couple of sledgehammer blows.

Then they'd cut that wood real fast and lose it in the ready-to-sell lumber piles.

When I was still a rookie, out nights selling logs on my own, the mills would try to underscale the logs, rip me off. To stop the mills cheating me, I learned how to do the scaling myself. Dishonourable thieves always bugged me. Just because I was selling them hot merchandise didn't give them licence to rob me. So I played the field till I got in with a mill that didn't try to underscale and that also agreed to pay me thirty-five dollars a thousand feet. Most of the logs I was stealing had three to four thousand feet of lumber. I was bagging a good penny.

It didn't take long before we had enough money to move up from our row-boat to a fourteen-foot skiff. It only had a two-horsepower motor to go putt, putt, putt down the river, but even with that little bit of power, we could dog and haul seven or eight logs. Two weeks at that pace, we earned enough bread to buy a twenty-eight-foot, 99s Marine–horsepower fishing boat with four bunks – king of the beachcombing vessels. The owner wanted thirty-five hundred for it, big money in them days. I gave him the cash I had in my pocket, about one thousand dollars, and agreed to pay the rest over six months, with 5 per cent interest. That night I stole twenty-four logs running with the current, making the money to pay him off. It didn't take no six months. That beauty of a boat could pull twelve or fourteen logs against a current. We were in the money now.

Walter was right; I loved the life. It was rough and risky and attracted a real earthy kind of people. Most of the beachcombers were honest men with square-john jobs. River rats, people who'd spent their whole life on the river – fishermen beachcombing in off-season, sawmill boom men moonlighting, guys like that. There were hardly any criminals beachcombing, very few renegades like me. Even guys like Walter who were into robbing logs would never steal on dry land, would never rob another man. Most of them were older too, over forty and even fifty. At nineteen I was half the age of the average beachcomber. But the 90 per cent working legal and the 10 per cent dealing hot, we had this in common – guts enough for adventure and danger. Don't forget, them beachcombers, if they had seaworthy boats, would be out on the Pacific at the first sight of a storm. Storms meant logs flying – maybe ten feet in the air – flying out of booms, and they wanted to be there to grab them. It was a dangerous game, not one your ordinary citizen would play.

Legal and illegal beachcomber alike, you were always battling nature, human and Mother nature. One night in a big storm, two sections of logs broke loose from the Imperial Mills stockpile. They came crashing against a boom log right near Walter's float-house. In that blinding rain, the Fraser heaving like a stormy ocean, I was out there with a cable of dogs, dogging logs. If you'd seen me that wild night, the way I was riding them logs, you would have thought I was Hopalong Cassidy. Some of them shot out of the waves like a bullet. Next day, when the river calmed, two tugboats come from Imperial Mills. I saw the captains undoing the dogs. Shotgun in hand, I went outside.

'Ya got some plans for my logs, gentlemen?'

'C'mon, man, put that gun away. You know the logs belong to Imperial Mills. Look, our mill number is stamped on them. We won't charge you, we'll just take what belongs to us.' They didn't look the least bit scared, real calm. I shot a blast into the logs. That jolted them. Now, they were ready to take me seriously.

'Can't say it's been a pleasure seein' ya. How 'bout I close my eyes and ya disappear.'

I did and they did, but I knew this little gambit wasn't over. I sat guarding my booty with Walter's shotgun, waiting for the mill to make its next move. Before you know it, a mill representative in a three-piece suit shows up. Now, a suit man's a very unusual sight to see when the mill is dealing with beachcombers.

He holds up his hand like he's carrying an imaginary white flag.

'Can we talk, sir?'

'Yeah, we can talk 'bout you buyin' my logs. These here are salvage logs and you know it. I took 'em fair 'n' square. They run away from your booms in the storm. Ya want 'em back, ya pay salvage rates.'

He blustered and bellowed for a while. I just stuck to my guns, including my shotgun. Eventually, he agreed to pay salvage rates – three dollars for regular logs, four for boom logs, five for top logs, plus five dollars for boom chains. I made a nice hunk of money and I made it fair and square.

So I could play the legal beachcomber too, but mostly I was to scamming. The beachcombers that appealed most to me were the ones working my angle – the shifty angle. They might have been legal-side some days, but basically they were outlaws and pirates. They were living fast – fast boats, fast fists, fast women, and a fast buck foremost on their minds. They were always ready for a fight. Often two or more beachcombers would spot the same log and go for it with a vengeance. The log might end up floating away while the beachcombers would be getting at each other's throats over who was the owner of that log. There was a lot of jumping from boat to boat on the fast-moving night river, a lot of blows exchanged.

When they weren't fighting, they were loving. Their wild beach parties would start out innocent enough, but soon the mood would change. Usually, they'd start with a corn roast on a deserted beach along one of the islands off Vancouver. Word would go out that there's a party tonight. Every beachcomber would grab a case of hard stuff plus four or five cases of beer and arrive at the site already gassed up. We'd light a big bonfire under a forty-gallon cleaned-out oilcan, to boil the corn. If you were watching from a boat offshore, the firelight would outline couples dancing and drinking and making out. Girls would appear from nowhere. Girls were as much a pushover for beachcombers as they were for cons and carnies. That same thrill of associating with the fast life, I guess.

In spite of my bulk, I was quite the stud them days, although I never got romantically attached to no one. Easy come, easy go, that was my motto. But the girls got real attached to my money, and whenever I had a temporary girlfriend, I was temporarily out of cash. I spent it all. I'd buy them whatever they fancied – fancy clothes, fur coats, flashy diamonds, you name it. You'll never find a woman to complain I skimped when it came to buying what she wanted. I always was like that; I loved women and I loved pleasing them, even if they took me to the cleaners. At the beachcomber parties I was forever meeting new women to help spend my money. They were quite the parties.

I think the beachcombers liked the fights best; there were always lots of them. In fact, some of the parties were off limits to women because the men held them for the purpose of drinking, playing poker, and sparring. Nasty brawls. I stayed clear of the fistworks much as I could, but I'd always defend myself if someone came looking for trouble. You'd be lucky to survive one of them parties without a cracked head. Beachcombers weren't fragile people that feared getting hurt. They were living a pirate's life – life on the line everyday. If they were dogging a log in raging torrents of water, it might smash up their boats and maim them; if they were stealing the cops might get them, and if the law didn't get them, another beachcomber would.

I came up in the old school, where there was honour among thieves. But there wasn't much of that among beachcombers working illegally. They'd rob from anybody they could, including each other. At first that bothered me because the con code was already inbred in me. I knew you were loyal to your own. But once I got over the disappointment, I got better at their game than any seasoned beachcomber. And in a strange kind of way they respected you if you were able to steal from them. To them, it was the mark of a successful man.

I remember the night I first realized that they weren't honourable thieves. A shotgun blast almost blew me out of my bed in the float-house. I ran outside in my shorts to see Walter blasting a boat to hell. This beachcomber I recognized was making a fast get-away before Walter could hit the fuel tank and set his boat ablaze. That's when Walter told me it was common practice for beachcombers to rob each other. I didn't like it, but if that was the code, I'd live by it. And live by it I did. Except I only stole from the ones that tried to rob us first. I never grabbed nothing from a beachcomber that had scruples, only the ones that had none and proved it by trying to rip us off.

I wasn't more than six or eight months into the life when it wasn't enough to occupy my conniving mind. I was ready to expand. So, one by one, I developed some sidelines. Boom chains was my first. The mills used to pile them up on the docks, just inviting trouble. Under the cover of nightfall I'd row a little dory under the wharfs. Quiet as a water rat, I'd just reach up and pull them into my boat by the handful. I had to be careful, though, because they weighed ninety-nine pounds and could make an awful thud when they hit the bottom of the boat. By the time my little adventure was over, the row-boat would be so full of boom chains that it was practically sinking. Hot, the chains were only worth five bucks apiece, but they were an easy steal and an easy sell.

My second sideline was stealing goods off the back of supply barges at night. Cases of liquor, especially. That was easy too. It took two men and two drop nets. We'd just come up behind the barges in the fourteen-foot skiff. One of us – me, usually – would climb aboard and fill a drop net with goodies. While one was being lowered and unloaded, I'd fill the other one up. We'd pile that skiff so high there'd be no more than one inch of water-line left when we quit. We'd never get caught because all eyes were up front, including the eyes of the tugboat pilots. Tugboats were pulling the barges. It was dark, too, and the supplies were piled so high they'd never spot us. Besides, there was always the friendly BC fog to give us extra cover.

My third sideline was just a time-filler. It was legal. I'd work days as a boom man or a tail sawyer or a green chain man at the Japanese Imperial saw mill. It was worth the hard work because they paid top money. It was just occasional day work for me, gave me a little taste of the square life – which, at every bite, made me gag.

My fourth sideline was more fun. I was a bouncer at a night club in Vancouver. There were three of us: me, I was the gringo bouncer; then there was a black guy and a Chinese guy. We were working a place with dancers and strippers that attracted a lot of uptown types slumming downtown. The patrons would get pretty drunk and rowdy. I never spent a night there without a beef; usually, there were six or seven. Eventually I gave up that job because I didn't like having to be violent, even with a drunk. And I especially didn't like that they wanted to hurt me. It's always open season on bouncers. My boss at the club knew I was a beachcomber moonlighting. He knew I was always watching the clock because I was timing the tides. Beachcombing was my priority. Around two a.m. I'd announce that I was leaving, time for me to go to my real work. I'd probably been bouncing since ten. Luckily, sleep was not something I needed a lot of. Usually, I'd catch a few hours early morning or midday. Or not at all. There were just too many profitable and exciting things to do.

Like another of my sidelines, duck hunting. There's a twelve-mile marsh at one end of Sea Gull Island – they call it Sea Island now. The marsh is just at the mouth of the Fraser River. Walter knew that marsh like it was his home. Duck season, the hunters would wait along the edge of the marsh, wait on dry land like good law-abiding citizens. You aren't allowed to shoot ducks from boats. Nevertheless, we'd take our little skiff deep into the marsh where we'd be hidden by dense marsh grass, sometimes as high as twelve feet, and miles of them hot-dog-like things, bull rushes. The ducks and geese would be hiding in there too, a couple of miles thick. I'd be shotgun and Walter would be pilot.

Ducks and geese were so thick we'd be bumping into them with the boat as we slid along silent and slow. When we were in a good position, I'd start shooting. At the sound of the gun going off them ducks and geese would scatter, just soar out of that marsh, so many of them they'd make a blanket between us and the sky. I'd keep shooting, and they'd keep falling by the dozens. When our massacre was over, the boat would be piled high with dead ducks. Poor suckers, they never had a chance. But they sure squawked and squealed in protest. The noise was deafening, but never loud enough to drown out the sound of the game warden's fast boat coming after us. The game warden never had a chance, neither. No one knew that marsh like Walter; he'd steer us to a safe hiding spot till the warden gave up searching. We never got caught, not once.

It was all too good. Too long a stretch – just over two years – without trouble from the law. I should have suspected my time was up. Yet I was still a little surprised when the mounties interrupted our evening meal one night. They took me away from the table where I was enjoying a great feed of salmon with Walter, his wife, and their two kids. The back of a cop car, the inside of a cop shop – familiar territory I hated to be seeing again.

'We've been hearing a lot about your activities this past year, Mr McGilvary, like your little run-in with Imperial Mills.'

'Wait a minute, there, that was legal,' I protested.

'Maybe that was. But save your song of innocence. We know you're up to lots of illegal dealings too. You're in a tough spot, McGilvary. Some of the beachcombers want you out of here because you're too brazen, too greedy. And we want you out of here for the same reason. Too many people on both sides of the law aren't happy to have you around.'

Here come the threats – I know cop talk.

'We just brought you in for this little chat so you'll know we're on to you. Starting right now, we're going to be on your ass twenty-four hours a day. We'll get you, McGilvary, mark my words.' He moved his fat face nearer to mine, to make sure I was getting the point. 'Now, get out of here.'

I'm always happy to walk quietly away from large men carrying big guns. Beachcombing was a good score, but the game was up. I decided to take their advice and get out of town. I took a cab back to Walter's. Sad but resigned, I went to my room to collect my things. I had a cupboard full of expensive clothes; I liked buying expensive, tailor-made duds to impress the ladies. And there was some cash, about ten thousand dollars stashed in socks under my mattress. I always banked in socks because I knew how easy banks could be robbed. I told Walter he could have my share of the boat and all the gear, and I gave him four thousand cash to fix up his float-house. I stuffed the rest of the bread in my pockets, stuffed some clothes in a suitcase, and headed for the train station. I bought a ticket to Toronto.

I remember pulling out of the station, my eyes tearing at my last glimpses of Vancouver, my mind racing over the events of two years. I had been happy. I had been free. I had been part of a loving family. Nothing had moved me more than seeing Walter's dedication to his family. My mind had run wild with fantasies about one day having a family like his.

Yes, I had been happy. The river had been my friend. How many times had it sprayed my face, soaked my body, filled my soul, and let me know a little peace? Plenty. It had given me plenty. I knew you paid for everything in this life. I'd had a good stretch. How soon would I be paying?

Doing Crime, Doing Time

6

Instead of making an uninterrupted journey to Toronto, I got off the train in Winnipeg, lonesome for the girls I knew there in my AWOL days. Besides finding girls, I found trouble – my first bit in a real jail, Headingly Correctional. It's not a pretty memory; I even got ugly scars to remind me.

This is how it happened. I partied a little and spent a lot till my money ran out. It runs out fast when you're buying liquor by the case and enjoying women by the dozens. Probably pretty hard for an ordinary working john to understand how I could blow all my bread on a fast fling with fast broads. But bandits don't think about tomorrow; they live for the moment. Tomorrow you'll do some business, and tomorrow will take care of itself. Like every outlaw, I wasn't into saving, so soon I had no money, not even enough for my room. I got so low I had to hawk my fancy clothes. I went from having six thousand cash and a valise of tailor-made duds to being a vagrant, practically overnight. On the street, everything I own in the world on my back, and plotting my next scam – a scam I never got to pull because I got picked up on a vagrancy charge and hit with a twenty-four-hour get-out-of-town floater. When I didn't leave town, they threw me in Headingly.

My first time in the slammer, and I had to arrive in 1956, when a riot was going down! Guys smashing their toilets and sinks. Naturally, I felt obliged to get in on the act. For my contributions – smashing my toilet and sink in the range cell – I was thrown in the hole, where, in the spirit of the riot, I blocked my toilet and sink. By then the riot had wound down and most of the guys had given in, but I was too high on rebelling to back down. Stubborn, maybe stupidly stubborn, was something I was beginning to see in myself.

The screws hauled me out of that hole and, using handcuffs, hung me by my wrists from a grille close to the ceiling so I was dangling on my tiptoes. That practice, I learned, was routine torture them days. Ask any old-timers that done time in Headingly – they'll remember. In fact, you don't have to go back that far. Just check the Winnipeg newspapers from 1985. There were lots of guard-brutality charges that grew out of a 1983 riot. The authorities investigated and the media ran an exposé on how malicious guards have often hung young offenders by their wrists.

I should have beat it out of town when I had my chance; it would have saved me six miserable months and the scarred wrists that remind me of Headingly even today. That bucket wasn't a pretty place. I knew it from the minute I got checked into that government hotel. The minute they close the door to the outside world behind you, you know it's going to be bad. You lose all your individuality, starting with the humiliating check-in. First, you have to undress in front of everybody – guards, other new fish, and inmates working reception. Then you got to walk into the showers in front of everybody. When you come out, they spray you with disinfectant – in front of everybody. Then they give you prison clothes – not designer fashions, believe me. Dark-coloured cottons like workmen wear, plus work boots and a jojo, that's a three-quarter-length smock coat. Then there's the fingerprinting and the mug shots, and finally your assignment to the fish corridor, the range for guys first coming in.

At Headingly I saw things I'd see and experience over and over in my career as a criminal. I discovered that there are all kinds of guards, just like there are all kinds of people. There are guards that want to help you – a few – and guards that don't care about you, don't care about nothing except the pay cheque – they're the majority. Then there are sadistic-as-hell guards. Prison is their opportunity to flex their big muscles and small minds, to beat up on powerless people.

I also found out that conniving is a way a life inside for cons, just like it's their life on the street. We were always breaking some rule, defying some authority, plotting to beat the Man. Always trying to get away with something and always ready to go to the hole for any small infraction. Like stealing food, for instance. At Headingly they had two-gallon jugs of coffee on every table in the dining hall, but we weren't allowed to have coffee on the ranges. Coffee and cigarettes, you must understand, are the Coke and chips of life for men inside. You always got to have one or the other, or both. So we'd work in groups to smuggle them jugs back to the ranges. To re-heat the coffee we'd roll toilet paper into doughnuts about twenty layers thick. When you light it, it burns maybe four or five minutes, producing a good flame. Men inside, deprived of basic things, are very inventive. A con's a con, no matter where he is. Inside, on the street, it don't matter.

Six months in Headingly was more than enough. I was given an unconditional probation for busting the plumbing in the hole and given a Toronto train ticket by the John Howard Society. Everyone just wanted me out of town. I left Winnipeg a little wiser in criminal ways and a lot angrier and more frustrated than before.

I think I felt hate for the first time. I remember the fire in my belly and the burning in my brain. I was going to get even for my tortured wrists.

That thirst for revenge! That's why I couldn't get off the train and into stealing fast enough. From Union Station I made a couple of calls, looking for the rounders I was collecting as friends through my tour of orphanage, foster placements, detention home, training school, detention barracks, carnival, and beachcombing. When you're a bandit, you run with others living outside the law. You know where they hang out in every city; it's easy to make a contact. I easily got hold of one such guy. He immediately invited me over to his place.

'Just in time, Tony,' he greeted me at the door. 'We're pulling a big score tonight.'

'Count me in.'

I was up for pulling a B&E that night. It net us fifteen cases of cigarettes. There's fifty cartons in a case. Them days we were getting seventy-five bucks a case. After we pulled the job and fenced the loot, we went on a party. I met this hooker broad known as Shirley the Machine. You can guess why she was called that! Shirley was a twenty-dollar hooker, making three to four hundred dollars a day. I don't need to tell you how many johns she got to do for that kind of bread.

I liked Shirley. We decided to team up. I wanted her to quit hooking because I knew I'd be stealing enough to keep us both. But she was real insecure, needed a lot of men appreciating her, so she decided to keep to her trade. I never took any money from her; she did the work, so she should keep the money. We stayed together a couple of months. Two months was pretty much my longest time with any woman.

I was stealing very heavy. I'd break into anything I could – house or store – and steal anything that wasn't tied down. But I wasn't altogether happy with house prowling. It can be scary. Sometimes they got attack dogs in rich homes. Also, I didn't like breaking into a man's house, making his family feel vulnerable, even though I knew they'd make more on the insurance than the value of the stolen goods. Much as I was never comfortable house prowling, I did it a lot because it was easy and the money was fast. Just pick up a TV real easy-like and turn it around the same night for fifty, maybe seventy bucks. Usually I'd commit my crimes between seven and ten at night, then hawk the goods within two hours.

Fencing merchandise was the easiest part of crime, though you hardly ever got a fair price. Them days a fence would pay 25 per cent of wholesale cost. In my early days on the crime beat I was an easy mark for fences because I never knew wholesale prices. So they'd be buying diamonds from me at 5 and 10 per cent of what they owed me. Fences are real robbers. First I rob some poor sucker; then the fence robs me. But, not satisfied at robbing once, he robs twice – underpays me and overcharges the poor sucker that buys the hot merchandise.

You might wonder what kind of guys these fences are. They're the 'honest' citizens who make crime a booming business. Mostly they're store owners – variety, furniture, or clothing shops. Most of them have never been charged. They go to church on Sunday; they give to charities; they belong to service clubs. Very upright citizens, pillar-of-the-community types. They're very careful and well connected, and they can usually buy, talk, or lawyer their way out of a jam.

After robbing and being robbed, I could be downtown by midnight looking for other rounders and looking for more action. Looking to join the late shift. There was always action to find if you knew where to search. Dundas and Jarvis area had lots of joints crawling with ex-cons, would-be cons, rubs, winos, and hookers – that whole marginal community that's awake while the rest of Toronto sleeps. We used to hang out at Spot One, Norm's Grill, the Butterfly Restaurant, and the Brown Derby on Yonge. The type of crowd in them joints – it was like being inside on the outside. Parolees are told not to associate with other cons. Now, tell me, who else are we supposed to associate with? Who else do we know? Who else wants us? Cons are like everyone else – we like to be around our own kind.

And being around them, I'd naturally hear their plans – plans I sometimes wanted to be part of. My reputation as a house prowler was such that I was in big demand. Everyone was always wanting me to join their team. I had so many offers that I could pick and choose, but mostly I chose because I was into crime as a full-time passion, twenty-four hours a day. Even though I worked with others, I always preferred working alone – always been happiest as a loner.

Sure, I ran into a lot of jackpots. When you're as active as I was, the cops are always on you, and you're bound to get pinched sooner or later. I could always feel it when sooner was coming; I'd always know when my time on the street was getting short. One night after a B&E my partner and me was making our get-away. The cops came out of nowhere, and suddenly we were in a car chase. We ditched the car and ran, the cops shooting at us. My partner got caught; I escaped. He never squealed, but I had a feeling I was through. My feeling was right, because one night not long after three of us went on a job. There was nothing in the house worth taking. I was pissed off because we left empty-handed, so I decided to pull another job alone. I did. I cleaned out the jewellery from a fancy Etobicoke house. Six cops were waiting for me outside. My time was up.

I waited in the Don Jail for my trial. When I went to trial, the judge said to me, 'We know you broke into two houses that night, and we know you had partners; they were with you in the first house. Tell us their names, Mr McGilvary, and the Court will consider a suspended sentence.'

'There was no one with me, Your Honour.'

'Very well. You leave me no choice – one year in Guelph Correctional.'

I was still a kid, really, only just twenty-one, but my path seemed set. Here I was being sent to yet another institution, another jail. Would I commit crimes and live in institutions my whole life? That's what I was wondering while the blue goose – a converted school bus big enough to transport thirty prisoners – took me, shackled and handcuffed, from the Don to Guelph.

After the humiliating check-in and the mandatory six weeks on the fish corridor, I joined the prison population. I was assigned to the butcher shop, where a real crazy bugger of a guard by the name of Deacon trained us to cut meat. They were so strict you couldn't fart without being detected. If you wanted to go to the john, they'd fan you going out and coming back. Those searches really did prevent us stealing meat and knives.

It wasn't just strict in the butcher shop. The whole joint was strict, and mean. It stands out in my memory as one of the more brutal places I've been. You were always being dragged to the hole by six or seven guards that wanted to get you in isolation before the population would erupt. It was a very volatile environment, the guys ready to riot the minute they witnessed any flare-up between inmates or between guards and inmates, the guards eager to beat on you every time no one was looking. That hole they were forever condemning you to was a real punishment – no more than a dug-out cellar with cells. Rats running wild. It wasn't fit for a human being. Guelph was the kind of place that would make you or break you, either make you so hot you'd want revenge forever or make you so scared of prison life that you'd go straight. I wanted revenge forever.

Because I was accustomed to cruelty, I could take it at Guelph, but I felt sorry for square johns doing time, not just at Guelph but in every prison. They couldn't take it; they had no background for taking it. I did time with lots of straights over the years – everything from a priest that killed his girlfriend to a stock broker that sold fake stocks in fraudulent companies. Doctors, lawyers, cops, judges – pillar-of-the-community inmates, they can grasp the administration's rules, but they can't come to terms with the con code.

They go through hell inside. And unless they're Harold Ballard, they don't get preferential treatment. In my experience the screws treated everyone the same. In all my years inside I never saw one case of special treatment, though I heard endless tales about the cushy way Ballard got treated. Straights doing time can't relate to the lifestyle inside, can't make peace with being caged, and can't accept the con code. They don't know how to keep to themselves, to see nothing, hear nothing, talk about nothing. They don't know how to protect themselves from the dangers, like wolves that prey on weak, scared cons. They don't understand that you mustn't trust no one, mustn't injure anyone's feelings, and mustn't lose at gambling any debts you can't pay. Squares don't know how to wheel and deal to stay alive.

Some people literally died in that place. Like Bruce, my buddy in the butcher shop. He was doing a bit for cattle rustling. Bruce had this little pimple on his face, nicked it shaving. I saw it was blistering, so I complained to the prison doctor and pushed Bruce to get it treated. The medics put a little salve on it, but he kept complaining. Soon his whole face blew up, you couldn't even see his eyes. I insisted that they take him to a proper hospital outside the joint, but they didn't. Bruce died in the prison infirmary, some kind of blood poisoning, I figured. All I know is the man died from inadequate medical attention. The inquest into his death was a whitewash, blamed the whole thing on an unexplained 'act of God.' I spoke at that inquest, but they didn't pay no attention to my accusations. Indifferent prison officials killed that man, and doctors that didn't care killed that man, and the attitude that inmates aren't human beings deserving decent medical treatment killed that man.

Not everything that happened in Guelph was quite so terrible. I do remember one funny incident. It was while I was working as the night baker – I changed jobs a few times at Guelph. We had a lieutenant there we called 'Flashlight Freddie' because he was always shining his flashlight at night. One night, me and another guy was horsing around in the bakery, hefting thirty-pound pails of water at each other. The lights were out and I was hiding, waiting for my prey. I heard what I assumed were my buddy's footsteps. I was standing on a stool ready to empty a bucket of water over his head. Whoosh! I poured the thing over him. I heard a cursing bellow.

'Je ... sus! What the fuck! Who did this! You're going to the hole.'

Freddie flashed his light. By the time he got it shining, I was already in the locker room pulling off my kitchen whites and pulling on my prison blues so I could get lost in the population. You've never seen a fat man change so fast! Meanwhile, I could hear Freddie roaring around, cursing and making threats, swearing he'd find the bastard who done it to him. They even called a line-up that night, but he never did find me out. If he had, I would have been in the hole thirty days on bread and water.

Speaking of food reminds me that I also worked in the kitchens, both the kitchen that fed the cons and the staff kitchen. I always tried to be around food preparation because you ate better. One of my jobs was feeding the buller gang – the real bad guys that spent their time moving rock. They were pretty hard rocks themselves, segregated from the rest of us. They were guys you'd want as friends, not enemies, so I used food to bribe them. Meal times, I had to prepare and deliver steam wagons to their range. Instead of the regulation one scoop of potato, I'd give them two. The staff man caught me.

'One scoop, Tony, you know the rules.'

'Yes, sir.'

But I went right back to my tricks, winning the buller's respect by going against the Man. Little by little, I'd sneak them treats – a little more meat from the stew, a little more bread. They sure could put away that bread; they were already allowed six slices to a meal!

The buller gang got to like me, so they asked me to play floor hockey on one of their teams. When one player swiped me across the side of my head, I hit back – in the crotch. For them that's reason enough to kill, and I'm sure this guy would have, except another guy from the buller gang saved me. He hollered, 'Don't do it, man, he's the guy that feeds us.' Saved by a few scoops of potatoes!

There were always brawls going on for some petty reason. Put that many men – about a thousand – in an over-crowded, over-disciplined environment, deny them any pleasure, and you're sure to make them fighting angry. In those conditions any excuse is good enough to vent their rage and spend their energy. I was never one for violence, never aggressed on no one, just protected myself when attacked. Once I was attacked over the *Story of O*. Dirty books were taboo in prisons, but we always managed to get them. I borrowed the *Story of O* from another inmate. I was reading it real slow, savouring all the juicy bits. One day the owner came to me.

'I want the book back, Tony. I got another friend who wants to read it now.'

'He can read it when I'm finished, and I ain't finished yet.' I knew this could be considered a provocation in prison, a routine type of incident to start a brawl, so I readied myself for the consequences.

'You don't give me that book, man, I'll tear it out of your hands.' He was winding up for a blow.

'You touch this book an' I'll tear it up myself,' I said, knowing then that we'd exchange blows for sure.

'You try to tear that up, I'll punch you in the mouth.'

I tore the book up before he could reach me with his fists. He did what he said he'd do — punched me in the mouth. The battle was on. We brawled on top of the tables, under the tables, over the sink. The kitchen staff just watched, betting on the winner.

'McGilvary will kill him!'

'No way. Rourke will win.'

No one got to kill no one because a half-decent sergeant decided to break it up. He was so decent he didn't even send us to the hole. Remember, we were brawling over a silly paperback, but that's the kind of tension in a prison. Men kill for less, just because they think someone looks at them funny. But it isn't funny. It's a very dangerous and violent life, a life I was eager to get a rest from. I'd be leaving soon enough when my ten months and eight days was up — that's how much time you do on a year's sentence.

Something happened just before my release at the end of 1956. This guy, Eddy, got real drunk on home brew, stuff we'd made from fermenting yeast, canned tomatoes, potato peelings, rice, raisins, and sugar for three days. Eddy was real romantic, always writing love letters to his wife, and to his girlfriend. This particular night he mixed them up, put the letters in the wrong envelopes. When his wife got the letter intended for the girlfriend, she was ready to divorce him. Eddy actually loved her a lot — he'd had five kids with her — but he also loved the girlfriend, just couldn't give her up. His wife came first, and he was real scared she'd file for the divorce she was threatening. He knew I'd be back on the street soon, so he came to talk to me.

'Tony, can you do me a favour? Can you go to Parkdale, go to my wife, tell her anything you can think of to stop her from divorcing me? You're a good con man, a smooth talker. If anyone can convince her, you can.' The man had tears in his eyes, his voice real pleading.

'I'll try, Eddy. I'll do my best.'

After my release, the first thing I done in Toronto was knock on her door. She was home.

'Excuse me for disturbing you but I just came from Guelph this mornin'. I promised your husband I'd visit you.' If she'd listen, I didn't have a clue what I'd say.

'That dirty ...' she shook her head, tears filling her eyes. 'After all these years of me waiting for him in jail. Him with his girlfriend on the side. I trusted him. What a fool ...' She was breathless and sobbing hard. 'I don't want to talk about him. The rotten, two-timing bastard.'

The door was closing in my face. I had to push against it to keep it slightly ajar.

'Please, let me explain. It's not like you think. Please listen.' She didn't open the door, but she didn't slam it either. I knew she was vulnerable, still cared, hadn't made up her mind for sure.

'You know what prison life is like,' I said plaintively. 'You know what guys inside are capable of, how mean they can be if they got a vendetta.'

'Vendetta! What are you talking about? What has a vendetta got to do with Eddy two-timing me?'

'Open that door, lady, let me in,' I was thinking, but I stayed on the porch and pleaded, making up the con as I went along.

'You're blaming an innocent man that loves you, blaming him for nothing.'

'Innocent, my foot. What are you talking about?'

I figured I had her then.

'Eddy made a few enemies in Guelph. That's normal. But one of his enemies is a real slime that happens ta be a forger. He wrote the letter, not Eddy. He knows how much Eddy loves ya an' he knew how ta hurt him.'

She opened the door then. I couldn't read the look on her face. Disbelief? Curiosity? I talked fast, more about the forger and the vendetta.

'You think I'm born yesterday? You think I'll buy that baloney? There were certain things in that letter, personal things, only Eddy would know.'

'Of course there was. He had ta make the letter convincin' so he pretended ta be Eddy's friend for a while to gather information. Cons are very clever, ya know.'

She thought for a minute. I wasn't sure which way it would go.

'Would you like to come in?'

'Thank you, no. I don't go into another man's home while he's in jail.'

That impressed her. We chatted a bit more. When I left she was willing to consider that maybe my rendition was true. First thing I did when I left there was arrange for word to Eddy to give him the story I used. I found out sometime later that they stayed together.

How was I feeling, being on the street again? I think I had an attitude: doing time didn't mean nothing – it was all a farce, a farce I had no strong feelings about giving up, though a rest interested me in a big way. I was going to keep playing the game. I didn't think about going straight. I thought about my next score.

Certainly, after Guelph, I was better equipped to pull it. Guelph had been my high-schooling. I'd learned some very useful stuff, especially foolproof methods for jimmying windows and doors. I had a few more names of fences and cons, a few more phone numbers to get me started again. That mattered because I was released on short bread – a mere twelve bucks in my pocket, the standard release cash payment. I hadn't been paid for my kitchen work at Guelph and I'd gone in without front money, the cash the prison admin banks for you while you're inside. All I ever got inside was free tobacco.

Little did I suspect I wouldn't have to worry long about poverty because I'd only be on the street a month. January 1957. I spent that month in Montreal helping Westmount residents find excuses to collect on their hefty insurance policies. I helped a few store owners that way, too. One night I pulled a job with two guys, robbed a furrier. We had a car full of furs when a police cruiser pulled us over. The other two jumped out real obedient, spread-eagled themselves for a search. Me, I jumped out and fled in a hail of bullets. I outsmarted the cops by hiding in an apartment building till they left the area and assumed I'd left the area too. Free of the fuzz, first thing I did was phone the families of the arrested guys to tell them their men needed help. Same night, I went back to stealing. Two days later I got busted on a house prowl.

I was charged and sentenced in French a language I'd stopped using and was beginning to forget. Besides, the judge was speaking real Paris French and I only knew real patois. I remember standing in court smiling because I understood the judge to say 'cinq mois.' I was stunned, but relieved at a short sentence. The guard standing near me must have realized my confusion. He nodded his head. 'Pas de cause à sourir,' he whispered. Then he mouthed, 'Cinq ans, pas cinq mois. Five years in St Vincent de Paul – get it smart guy?' It registered. Panic. Five years in the Big House with the bad reputation. I only just turned twenty-two and I was going into the worst joint in the country – for five years.

Incorrigible Crook: Bordeaux and St Vincent de Paul

7

Them days, the mid-fifties, Montreal's Bordeaux Jail was used as a reception centre for prisoners going to St Vincent de Paul, a maximum-security joint in Montreal. Some reception! The place looks like it was built in the medievals. Cells with big steel doors and tiny peep-holes. The stench of must and urine stickin' to your nostrils. An ugly place. Even the sewer rats seemed a special breed of ugly. Wasn't a day I didn't see families of them rats running the yard, some of them mothers as big as a foot long and three pounds apiece. Bordeaux was just the right kind of depressing environment for hangings. They done one when I was there. You want to feel a black, angry mood falling over a place, you got to be in a jail when the hangman's on the job. It's not the right place for a twenty-two-year old kid that never got a break and never got no help staying out of trouble.

It was bad enough just being in that hell-hole for hardened criminals, but it got worse – fast. My first day, they threw me in the hole. I didn't do nothing to earn the privilege. They were overcrowded, so they solved the space shortage by sticking the overflow in the cooler. That's one hole I'll never forget. Mostly, I'll never forget the rats. They come up out of the sewers via the toilets. That's why they gave us wooden covers for the toilets – to keep the rats from getting out into the cells. As extra insurance to keep them rats out of the cells, they even gave us small slate slabs to put on top of the wooden covers. It's a rare thing for prisons to put stones in inmate hands, but we needed something to secure the toilet covers. Besides, slate flakes real easy, so it's no good as a weapon.

Sometimes you got to remove the slate and wood to use the can. But you couldn't sit on the rim; you had to squat on it and pilot your offerings in while keeping an eye for the rats. Many inmates got bitten on the ass while they were taking a crap!

There was no yard time to give us some air or a break from the twenty-four-hour confinement in cells. Only time we ever got out was cleaning time. For that hour a day every range looked like a market square, the amount of noise and trading that was going down. Books was a big item of trade. It might be hard for a square john to understand, but I seen men practically kill each other over a pocketbook. The tension in Bordeaux was a constant centimetre short of an exploding fuse.

Sometimes it exploded. Personally, I never seen nothing at Bordeaux, but prison trains you to convenient blindness. Besides, violence flares and fades very fast. A shank sinks into flesh fast, furtive, and quiet. All in a moment's loss of control. Or maybe there's a short scuffle in the centre of a fast-formed crowd that disperses soon as a con lies bleeding on the concrete floor. Nobody sees nothing – even if they do hear the pipe or the shiv hit the ground. You may be blind but you aren't dead, so you feel the constant threat of annihilation.

Twenty-four hour-confinement alone is enough to make men lose their grip. But we had more to contend with than just confinement. Many inmates there were doing the bitch. That means they had indefinite sentences, like I had at Alfred. They never knew when they'd be getting out; they never knew when or if the prison authorities would decide they was fit to live on the street again. Nothing worse for an inmate than an indefinite sentence.

The tension was also aggravated because other men were awaiting sentencing; they didn't know what kind of time they were going to get. That wait before sentencing is a very hard number for every inmate. I remember how it felt inside me before I got my sentence. How many cold mornings did that paddy-wagon ferry me to court? How many times was my case remanded – delayed – before that five-year shocker finally got delivered? Those cold mornings huddled shivering with the others, silent and scared, staring through the darkness at the paddy-wagon floor as we got dragged to court – that's a bleak memory etched permanent in the minds of many cons. It's like being cattle going to slaughter.

At Bordeaux you also got the guards to deal with – mean as they come but hungry for money, so they'd run you whatever you wanted – mickeys, dope, whatever. It was the easiest place I ever been in to get anything you needed from the outside, and the only joint where the guards were running most of it.

Only good thing I got to say about Bordeaux is beans. The only place where cons would choose beans over steak, the only joint where you got grown men fighting over seconds of beans. Great beans, fèves au lard, French style. Lots of molasses, lots of pork fat, and lots of gas. But it didn't matter in Bordeaux; farts was the sweetest smell around.

Even with the reputation St Vincent got as the toughest joint in the country, after three months at Bordeaux I was relieved to be shipped there. The whole bit I done at Bordeaux, I don't remember feeling nothing but anger. Yes, I should be punished for my crimes, but I was only a thief – I never harmed no one. The prospect of five years in maximum for a young man – that seemed to me a far greater crime than mine. But I knew I'd get back at 'them' one day. If I was paying an unjust price, 'they' were going to pay too. I don't know if in my head at the time I called what I was thinking 'revenge,' but it was the feeling that kept me going. I certainly never gave a moment's thought to going straight.

Revenge and escape, that's what I was thinking about when they unloaded me at St Vincent de Paul. I repeated the name slowly in my head – 'St Vincent de Paul.' I couldn't help smiling. I wondered how many people would feel joy at the mere mention of his saintly name? After all, he was a seventeenth-century Jesuit priest that worked with the poor, set up hospices at a time when there wasn't nothing in the way of social services. A Mother Teresa type. He must have been quite a guy because most parishes today have a society in his name. Strange how a name can conjure up such different images for people. At the mention of that particular saint, I will never think of anything holy or sacred.

St Vincent makes me think of hell-holes, of desperate over-crowding – 1,150 inmates. It makes me laugh when I hear inmates today complain about overcrowding when you got four or five hundred guys in a joint. It's a rich neighbourhood, like Rosedale spacing these days, compared to poor-neighbourhood Regent Park spacing in my day. Packed like sardines, cells so tiny you had to chain your cot to the wall just for room to stand. A bare lightbulb dangling from the ceiling. No window, just one down the corridor maybe twenty feet from my cell. The usual bucket toilet. Cut-up newspaper for toilet paper.

My first day at St Vincent I didn't get much time to size up the joint because I was rushed off for my first visit to the hole. It didn't take a whole lot to earn it. Some guy comes up to me in the yard; obviously he sees that I'm a new fish.

'Here man, take these.' He hands me a case of Coke – Coca Cola, not cocaine; cocaine wasn't in them days – and a carton of cigarettes.

'What are you giving me this stuff for?' I ask, knowing full well what it's about.

'For nothing, man. Just take it and enjoy it.'

'No way. No wolf gonna prey on me.' I gave him back the stuff. I knew it was a good opportunity to establish my reputation as a man that could defend himself, that didn't want nothing to do with homosexuality, and didn't need no protection. So I grabbed one of the Cokes and bopped him over the head with it. No sooner had that bottle hit its target than the guards was on me, guns pointing. Before I know it, I'm in the damper. Hole sweet home!

It had a wooden bed and a wooden pillow. I was stripped to shorts and only got one coarse blanket at night to fight the cold. Two buckets – one for drinking water, one for a toilet. The cuisine was not French: three slices of bread and water for breakfast, porridge and a scoop of potatoes for lunch, three slices of bread again for supper. Once every four days, they'd give you a solid meal. For reading you had a Bible – that was it. Them days, I couldn't stomach the church, let alone feel desperate enough to read a Bible.

In five hellish years at St Vincent I did a total of maybe five months in the hellish hole. What other misdemeanours earned me time in segregation? One time I struck a guard that was riding me.

Touch or even offend a guard and that's automatic hole time. Another time I got into a fight with an inmate. We both went down for that brawl. Ironic, though – we come out of the hole friends after communicating from our separate segregation cells through the walls with a prison tapping code. A third time, they thought I was going to attack a guard with a knife, so they threw me in. There was no chance I'd actually do it since I never was that kind of violent. I just wanted to defend myself, so I threatened him because I was at the boiling point with this particular screw. He was on me all the time. No reason, just decided he didn't like my face and he was going to get me. One day he calls to me, 'Hey, mother ...' He definitely had a gun in his hand.

'Don't call *me* mother!' I snapped back. I was working in the kitchen and a knife was handy, so I moved my hand in its direction. I'd barely touched it before guns from every direction were pointing at my head. And don't imagine they wouldn't have just shot me dead on the spot if I'd grabbed that knife and raised my hand. You got to understand how much tension tightened the atmosphere in that place; I never been closer to so much raw emotion, festering, always threatening to bust through the thin surface. You always felt things could explode at any moment, things including yourself. The actual violence wasn't that extensive, but the potential for it was red hot. What kept it from going off was the Man – his guns, his presence. St Vincent was very heavily guarded by men as mean and ugly as they come.

They never addressed you by name, only by number. 'Get over here 1684' meant they were calling me. They never addressed you unless they absolutely had to. By the same token, an inmate never talked to a guard unless he absolutely had to. Almost always, when you were out of your cell, there was a mean guard with a big gun trained on you. For major infractions like slugging a guard, they'd bend you over, haul your pants down, and whack you ten times with a heavy strap. Very humiliating for a grown man.

The tension they created made it inevitable that the joint would be fist city, guys fighting at every opportunity. It also made stabbings and killings inevitable. In the five years I done, two men died in that kind of violence, inmate to inmate or guard to inmate. Shivings was a dime a dozen. Suicides – men driven by guards to beyond coping – was more: seven while I was there.

The guys were always trying to get back at the screws, but it was very hard to get any revenge. One inmate figured a clever angle to hit back at this one guard. The inmate was mad because this screw constantly picked on his friend, to the point where the friend overdosed just to escape the persecution. Offed himself to get away from a guard! Anyway, the angry inmate worked in the shoe-repair shop. When the guard in question brought his boots in for resoling, the guy put lye in the sole. Eventually that lye ate through the leather insole and burned the screw's feet. It was small revenge, but it was sweet.

With the overcrowding and the guns and the confinement to cells, the environment was so cruel that inmates were desperate to get away, get high, get stoned, get drunk, whatever. There must have been drugs or booze at all times in every third cell in that joint. There probably wasn't a prisoner in there that wasn't on something. You had to get high; it was the only way to survive. Goofballs, tuinals, seconals, dexadrine, black beauties – you name it, we got it. Uppers and downers. But there wasn't much grass and hash. Them days, weed meant tobacco. How did we get all the drugs? As you'd suspect, the guards brought some of it in, but 1,150 cons don't need guards to run dope; we could figure how to do it ourselves. Good as they were at searches, we could still outsmart them at running in drugs with delivery trucks and visitors.

I was never much of a druggie or a drunk – just the odd pill to stay awake or go to sleep, or the odd drink to kill the emptiness of life inside. But at St Vincent I got more interested in staying high. You could even get drugs legal, easily con the prison doctor into doling out the dolls. I conveniently developed a convincing case of migraine headaches worth one tuinal a day and the occasional rest in the prison hospital. I saved up my drugs for long weekends, when I didn't have to work the usual six-hour day. We were only allowed out of our cells on to the range or into the yard a half-day Saturday and Sunday, and you could refuse to leave the cell if you wanted. So I'd store the pills in a hole I drilled in my cupboard. I covered that hole with plastic putty painted the colour of the cupboard. Come a long weekend, I'd ask to stay in my cell, where I'd get so high I'd fly three days straight, so blotto I couldn't even walk. But after I seen one friend die from an overdose, I gave up the heavy drug-taking.

I remember one time before I quit. A shipment of goofballs come in waterlogged, ruined, so the runner gave it to the men working in the stone shed, my work site at the time. We was eating the stuff by the spoonful. They carried thirty-two guys out of that shed; one of them never got up again. I'll never forget the fear on the guard's face as he stalked us from his cage in the stone shed. When he saw all the men freaking out on the drugs, even his shotgun and his cage didn't seem enough protection from our wrath. The screw started screaming for help.

After that incident and my friend's death, I had it with drugs, went back to the old-fashioned method of staying high – brew. Getting a steady supply of alcohol in that pen was a breeze – from the TB ward! Up on the fourth floor of the Dome – that's what we called the main building – there was about twenty-five inmates in 1957 with TB. That was just after that big polio epidemic that killed or crippled thousands of Canadians. A new drug had been introduced to fight TB too, but I guess it wasn't no good because TB was still killing lots of people. Having TB entitled them sick guys to get rubbing alcohol for rubbing themselves down everyday. But having TB prohibited them from getting tobacco. Being sick didn't prevent them from wanting smokes, however. So they wanted tobacco and we wanted alcohol. That's why we swapped regularly, using what we called the horse. It's just a long string with a piece of iron at the end to give it weight. They'd tie the rubbing-alcohol bottles to the line and lower it down to the different ranges. The ranges were grouped around a central open core that went right up to the ceiling of the Dome, making it easy to pass things back and forth. The bottles come down on the horse; tobacco went up on it. We'd mix the rubbing alcohol with water, half and half, then add it to Coke. Even with water and Coke, you still had to twist your nose to swallow back the terrible taste. But it was a good high.

We traded tobacco for lots of stuff from the sick guys, things like canned fruit and shampoo, treats they got that we couldn't get. No one ever thought nothing about touching the stuff they were handling. In prison, life is day to day, fear is constant, death and disease are always lurking. You just don't think about it; you don't think about nothing except surviving this one day.

The TB ward wasn't my only source for juice. I also made the best coconut rum you ever tasted. To explain how I did it, first I've got to tell you about my vegetable garden. I kept this little plot about three feet square in the prison yard. Supposedly it was for growing tomatoes. But the tomatoes was camouflage for coconuts buried under the plants. This is how I done it. Christmas time, they'd hand out coconuts to the inmates. It was supposed to be a special treat, except most of the cons didn't even know how to eat coconut and they weren't interested. So these coconuts would just lie around. In the cell next to mine an old-timer doing life on a murder rap told me his formula for making coconut rum. Punch holes in the shell; pour out the milk; fill the coconut with heavy-duty molasses poured through a funnel; seal the holes with dock tape, and hide the coconuts for thirty days. Voila! Heavenly coconut rum.

I'd scour the range for coconut donations. Because I had a reputation as an eater, the guys just thought I was into coconut meat. Don't forget, everyone's into their own weird trip in prison, and no one thinks nothing of strange behaviour or habits. Since the cons had no use for their coconuts, they'd give them to me, figuring on a return favour some day. It was quite a sight – this jelly-belly rolling around the range with arms full of coconuts. Everyone used to laugh at me; they wouldn't have laughed if they knew what I had in mind. Getting a regular supply of coconuts came to be an obsession, since we normally only got them at Christmas. But they were cheap, so sometimes when I'd ask the kitchen staff, they'd buy some. I had guards running them in for me too; they were convinced I was a coconut addict. Getting molasses was the easy part. Cake and molasses was a staple dessert; all I had to do was bribe a kitchen inmate-worker to save me a jug from time to time.

Secrets are impossible to keep in prison, so eventually other guys got wind of the coconut caper. Before you know it, inmates are developing a taste for coconuts – and in the summer for gardening. The prison authorities was too dense to catch on at first, but if they dug up the yard, they'd find a grove, coconuts side by side, row on row. And they'd find them in a few mattresses as well, besides other hiding places. Eventually, they did catch on, and that was the end of easy coconuts.

The coconut caper had been too good to be true anyway because nothing was easy in that joint, including the work. We didn't toil long hours – only six a day – but we toiled hard hours. What do you think we earned for our labours? Twenty-one cents a day! That's right – twenty-one cents per day. I started in the kitchen and quickly graduated to the quarry. They said they were kicking me out of the kitchen because too much sardines and beef was missing from my shifts. Ain't any wonder that food went missing. The meals in that joint was terrible lousy, and there was never enough food. To make matters worse, you ate all your meals alone in your cell, so you didn't have any good company to distract you from the bad taste. Worse yet, the food was served on metal trays instead of real dishes. The trays had compartments like a tinfoil TV dinner. Horrible institutional. No wonder everyone was stealing and conniving just to get enough to eat. As you know, I got a special place in my heart for food, so I was anxious to lift every extra bit I could. I'd say one-third of all the food that come in that pen was stole by inmates; many of them then sold or bartered it to other inmates.

Unfortunately, I lost my inside track on food theft when I got booted from the kitchen on to the rock pile. Just like the image old movies portray of inmates – on a chain-gang breaking rock under the noonday sun or the freezing rain, lots of guards riding shotgun and pushing you hard the minute you quit or try to talk to a buddy.

All I could think about was escape. It didn't matter how poor my chances of getting away. It didn't matter how bad the punishment of getting caught. It didn't even matter if they shot me. I had to run. 'Go boy! Go boy!' kept playing in my brain. It's a song that every inmate sings to himself. Lots try to escape; a few make it. During my time at St Vincent there were too many escape attempts to count. I remember one attempt when three guys tied up the hobby-craft officer and left him naked. At a shift change they conned the guard into letting them into the tower. Them days, the door to the tower was inside, not outside. Once inside the tower they tackled that guard, grabbed his shotgun, and jumped the wall. One guy broke his ankle and got caught right away. The other two made it to downtown Montreal before they got picked up. The typical story of a botched escape. But you feel like you got to try.

One rainy day only six months into my five-year sentence I decided, on the spur, to make my move. We were riding the rails in one of them little open boxcars en route to the quarry. Armed guards were trotting alongside on their horses. I leapt off the train and started running fast as possible. But the long grass was wet and slippery, kept snagging my feet and slowing me down. I didn't have a chance, of course, not with horses chasing me, but I couldn't stop myself from trying. At that stage I just couldn't adjust to the idea of spending five years living like I was living. I could hear the other guys in the background cheering me on. 'Go boy, go boy, go boy.' The chanting helped, but the wet grass beat me. In a matter a minutes I was lying in it surrounded by nervous horses and riled guards. I was staring into the barrel of guns pointing down at me from every direction. They beat on me and threw me in the cooler. But I never let it get me down.

After thirty days of talking to my toes I was released and reassigned to the stone shed. That's where all the rock that the chain-gang breaks on the quarry gets made into different things, like bird-baths and monuments for the government. It's also the one spot in the joint reserved for real hard rocks, the most dangerous and incorrigible criminals. My escape attempt, as poorly planned and executed as it was – just a spontaneous act of desperation, really – that attempt earned me the reputation as a hardened case.

Fifty-two guys was working in the stone shed, each at his own station working his own piece of rock. One end of the big rough room was a cage, the guard's station. He'd pace in there all day, hugging his shotgun and looking for any excuse to train it on one of us. I'm sure he felt pretty menaced even with the protection of his cage and his gun.

In spite of its reputation as the work-site for hardened convicts, the stone shed was actually a good assignment because nobody bothered you. Besides, you were outside the prison building although inside the penitentiary walls. It was the best location for robbing delivery trucks. Once the guards knew me, knew I was a loner and not a trouble-maker, they used to let me tool my rock outside the shed. The yard was the least-supervised area. One day a rookie delivery man drives a Coke truck into the yard.

'Can you tell me how to get to the chief keeper's office?' he asks, leaning out of the driver's window.

'Yeah. You'll have to leave the truck here and walk over – it's a bit of a distance.' Then I give him directions, what you might call the long way around.

Totally unsuspecting, he leaves the truck and heads in the direction my hand is pointing. Other cons working in the yard are on to my scam. The greenhorn driver is barely around the first corner when a gang of guys descends on the truck. They got laundry carts, wheelbarrows, and small wagons. You never seen a truck unloaded so fast. We were passing bottles through the bars like a regular assembly line. Empty cases strewn on the ground all around the truck. We're already back at work pretending everything's normal when the chief keeper comes tearing into the yard with the rookie, looking bewildered, in tow.

You might wonder why all the excitement about Coca-Cola. Coke was a luxury. Most of the guys had very little money. Besides, it was an event, a way to rip off the Man, exercise our conning instincts, and create a little excitement to break the deadly routine.

The Coke truck was a snap; emptying a meat truck was a little more complicated, especially when you got a delivery man that knew our tricks. But we could outsmart him. We had a crane in the yard for moving the rocks delivered from the quarry into the stone shed. Sometimes, when the meat truck drove into the yard and the screw was too lazy to come out of his cage in the shed, he'd just holler us an order to carry the sides of beef into the joint. That was our signal to put the crane on beef duty. Just drop the thing over the truck. The guys would load the sides of beef on to their shoulders as usual, then start walking like they're headed for the kitchen. Except one or two sides of beef would disappear before it reached the kitchen door. We'd hook it on the crane and lift it away real fast to where other guys were waiting with knives to cut and fast distribute that meat.

You might wonder what we could do with raw meat that wasn't exactly the cut for steak tartare. Cook it, of course. On sardine-can stoves. All you need is a sardine can, some asbestos, a few screws, an element wire, and an electric cord. You could steal most of the supplies from the kitchen and the tailor shop or bribe a guard to buy you an element wire. My sardine-can burner worked like a charm – wasn't anything I couldn't cook on it. Practically every second inmate had a stove like this.

Cooking was one of my pastimes in the joint. I got famous for pigeon stew. One day I was sitting outside the stone shed daydreaming, staring aimlessly at the pigeons. Something I read about pigeon pot pie came to mind, so I started undressing the pigeons with my eyes, wondering how I could catch them birds. I mentioned it to the old-timer that taught me about coconut rum. 'Any idea how I can trap pigeons? I got this idea to make pigeon stew.'

He turned up his nose in disgust. 'Forget the pigeons, Tony. They're diseased and scrawny. You don't want to eat them.'

'I do want them. If I'm not worried about catching TB from the guys on fourth, I'm sure as hell not worried about what I might catch from pigeons.'

He wasn't convinced, but he made a suggestion anyway. 'There's old screen windows lying all over the yard – perfect for constructing a trap.'

He was right. Just like the butter boxes we used as kids for trapping squirrels. Before you know it, I was expert at trapping nine or ten pigeons a day. The guard couldn't care less; he'd rather see me slitting pigeon throat than going after his or after another inmate's. They liked inmates that were busy with hobbies. After trapping the pigeons, I'd wring their necks, bleed them from the mouth, cut them into little bite-size pieces, and cook them for stew. The rest of the ingredients, like potatoes and carrots, I'd get a kitchen inmate to steal. That was easy. I even had every spice they got in the kitchen. Inmates were satisfied to get a little taste, which I'd send around using the horse and a lidded container we had for such purposes.

Cooking wasn't my favourite pastime. Making teddy bears was. Plush toys was a very popular sale item inside because guys could send them to their kids. I even made up my own pattern for miniature teddies, which I hand-produced three to a box for six bucks. Three teddies with bow-ties, that was my specialty. Why teddy bears? Them days, there was only certain crafts you could do in maximum. Tying flies, which I would have preferred, was out, because the flies could be used as weapons, so it was much easier to con the Man into crafts that required soft materials, like making plush cushions. There was already a big production in teddies going on in the joint, but the makers were producing large-size bears. Because I didn't have the front money to buy the supplies I needed to start producing big bears, I came up with the idea to scale them down. Three months in Bordeaux, where you had to buy your smokes and your books and you got no pay for work, wiped out the little bankroll I went in with. Sure, I could borrow twenty-five bucks from the St Vincent inmate fund to get started in a hobby-craft, but I still wouldn't have enough capital for a lot of supplies.

I borrowed patterns from a couple of the guys that were into teddy bears. Using a ruler and callipers, drawing on butcher paper I stole from the kitchen, I scaled the design down to a range of small sizes. I gave each size a number, copied them on to Bristol board – stolen from the art class – and then made patterns to those sizes. I just figured it out on my own, like I done with almost everything I learned. My most miniature bear was about six inches, both ways.

I used the twenty-five dollars to order my first plush, then stole or bartered my other start-up materials. I needed stuffing. That was easy. I could pick that up in sheets, socks, and shirts from the laundry room, as well as cast-offs from guys moving to other ranges or getting released. Ribbon. That was harder. I stole my first lot one time when I had to go to the front for some bureaucratic routine. I lifted the braided ribbon holding back the long heavy curtains. I leaned on an inmate tailor for thread and needles. Actually, I never done much sewing myself, because before long I got him to do the sewing by machine for me. He was an addict that would do anything for goofballs, or the money to buy them. So between sewing pants for the Man he'd stitch teddies for me, and I'd pay him from my earnings. I also needed packaging boxes so guys could send the bears to their people at home. Pies used to get delivered from the bakery in boxes with cellophane tops; the bakery name wasn't even stamped on them because for prisons the suppliers never did the fancy things they done for regular commercial outlets. I traded a kitchen inmate-worker tobacco for boxes. He'd even flatten them and make sure they were real clean before passing them in piles of twenty through my cell bars.

The cell-block man – he's a staff guy – of course he knew what I was doing. And it wouldn't take much figuring to realize my production was far outstripping the materials I'd ordered. But that I might be stealing a lot of stuff didn't bother him in the least. Incidentally, I never stole so much as a thread from another inmate. You only steal from the Man – every con knows that. Screws only cared that inmates stayed out of trouble and out of their faces. As long as I was busy running my little business, there was less chance I'd be busy making trouble.

So making the bears was no problem. Selling them was even more fun. Saturday and Sunday, when the yard was up, I'd be out there at my little makeshift stall hawking – along with about 150 other salesmen. Everybody's got something to add to the flea market – maybe porcelain dolls with fancy satin dresses or petit point blue boys or punch cushions in multi-coloured plush. A square john would see a weird scene if he had a window on yard days – all these tough-looking characters with tattoos, cigarettes dangling from the sides of their mouths, bargaining hard for teddy bears and cushions, walking around with stuffed animals in their armpits. And the conversations weren't what you'd expect from tough guys, neither. 'Tu fait ça, Tony? C'est beau. C'est bien beau.' But cons, when they're inside, are very sentimental people: they never forget a birthday or anniversary; they're always sending presents to their kids and to their wives and their girlfriends, often both.

The guys would sign front money – their cash held by the prison administration – over to me in payment. I'd bring the authorization forms to the hobby officer, who'd transfer their money into my account up front. Then I'd use that money to pay the inmates on my assembly line and to pay the hobby officer for supplies I couldn't steal inside. I developed quite a following for my teddy bears. I could barely keep up with the demand. I got lots of special orders too, guys that wanted certain colour combinations or wanted their initials sewn on. It was hard to steal enough supplies fast enough or get supplies from outside fast enough of materials that was hard to find inside, like teddy bear eyes. But new sources always appeared.

One day the chaplain's assistant, an inmate, invited me to tea in the chapel. He got me permission to visit by claiming the chaplain wanted to talk to me, which he didn't. The assistant wanted to order some teddies for his grandchildren.

'Sure thing. I'll make ya four boxes, won't even charge ya. Sort of a return favour for getting me up here, off the range.' The guy was pleased. I was conniving. 'Terrible shame those plush drapes behind the altar are so dirty at the bottom. Guess the cleaner must get them wet when he washes the floors,' I say real innocent, like cleanliness is a big concern of mine.

'You're right, Tony. I never noticed that before, tell you the truth.'

'Makes the chapel look shabby,' I add, just to sharpen my point. 'Why don't you shorten them drapes, just cut off the bottoms and sew a nice hem?'

'Good idea. The chaplain will appreciate that.'

'Don't throw out the dirty plush, though. I can dye it and use it for my teddy bears.'

My few remarks started a process that you wouldn't believe. I got real friendly with the assistant and I kept going back for more plush. He'd shorten the drapes – don't forget they're hanging the full length of a thirty foot wall – a few inches at a time till they looked ridiculously short. One day I say to him, 'I think you need new drapes.'

'We sure do; these drapes look awful. The chaplain's been mentioning that we should do something about them.'

'I think cream would be the most suitable colour for this room,' I add with conviction, realizing cream would be the most suitable for dyeing different colours.

The assistant ordered almost double the material the tailor would need to make new drapes, gave me the surplus. You won't believe this, but shortly after they were installed, soon as the bottoms was a little grungy, I was back for more – and he gave me more. The assistant got to be a real expert on hand-sewn hems. Luckily, I was released before the new drapes got noticeably short!

Teddy bear production was more or less my daytime hobby when I wasn't working the stone shed, my work-site for most of the five years. By night I often played chess. Two guys in separate cells with separate chess-boards, using the horse to communicate our moves. It's a good thing chess is a slow game anyway!

Nighttime was a little eerie in the joint. I can still imagine the large window down the corridor from my cell. It acted like a big TV screen reflecting the goings-on in the different cells – one guy reading, another listening to the radio, someone crying, someone else dancing with his broom. I used to watch a coloured guy that straightened his hair with lye, then wrapped it in a turban to set. I was most fascinated by this one prison artist that made statues non-stop. This lifer was so talented that the guards never obstructed him. They even helped him get supplies so they could get these statues off him. His production was so big that he designed and built his own drying kiln from plywood and sun-lamps. That artist worked day and night in his cell making statues – from earth I brought him from the stone shed and eventually from clay he bought through the hobby officer. He could make anything. Quebec being French and Catholic, his saints were real popular. He'd make the Virgin, moose, bears, gorillas, everything. His images were all religious or fierce. I think he might have had one of them dual complexions, or whatever you call them.

I was never short of things to do. Once I accepted that I had to do the time, I made the best of it. I got down and depressed from time to time, sure, that's natural, but I never let it drag me under to thoughts of suicide. The blues would hit and I'd strike back by burying myself in hobbies and scams, like lotteries and little bookie lines I ran in the joint. Besides, I always had a stash of food – peanut butter, sardines, unfortunately no Cheese Whiz, which was my favourite – to console me in low moments. The food may have been rotten and sparse in the joint, but I got fatter. I always manage to get fatter.

The times I felt loneliest was when the other guys had visitors. I used to listen when they called out the names of guys that got people waiting to see them. They never called my name. Except once. Who could be here to see me, I wondered? My uncle, Alphonse. He made no bones about the fact he didn't want to be there. I guess he made a death-bed promise to my aunt that he'd visit me in St Vincent. I was too busy grieving the loss of my dear aunt to pay much attention when he told me he'd take me in when I was released. Not that he wanted me – just another death-bed promise. Catholics can be very religious, especially French Catholics. He couldn't violate a promise made to a dying woman. I only got to see Uncle Alphonse, but all the other Brodeurs were out in the car, sad that they couldn't get in. My cousin Anita even tried to convince the front desk that she was my sister in order to get admitted. But the prison authorities were heartless – not even one break for a young man doing five years that never had one visitor before his last year.

In 1961, shortly after Alphonse's unhappy visit, I was released, thirty-two dollars in my pocket and a million dollars' worth of revenge in my heart.

From Burwash Prison to Bootlegging, Brothels, and Boosting

8

I remember the cold, dreary day I was released from St Vincent because I kept the blue goose waiting while I ran around the prison wall to find a particular tree. Those five years inside I'd played handball against a thirty-foot perimeter wall. I'd seen the top of a particular maple tree every time I played, but I couldn't see its base. 'One of these days, you mother, I'll piss on your trunk,' I used to say to myself, dreaming of the day I'd be released. So first thing I did on release was keep my promise to a tree.

I remember feeling very angry, but not about anything special. Just angry. There was no one outside waiting for me, no one to help me out or help me get straight. So my thoughts right away went to thieving. I was thinking about it all the time we were driving to Gare Centrale, the train station. How was I going to make some fast bread?

I had no intention of going to Cornwall with empty pockets. So first thing I had to do was dump the guard driving the paddy wagon. You knew the guy didn't want to stick around, even though he was supposed to stick with you till you were on the train. I made out I was real excited to be going home. Once the screw felt sure I'd be taking that train, he was gone in a flash. So was I.

Uptown Montreal. I was twenty-six years old, with thirty-two dollars in my pocket. I got a four-dollar room. In them days there were four-dollar rooms, not the Ritz, mind you, but good enough, especially for what I had in mind. By next morning I had $1,700 in my pocket — and don't ask me how I got it. Now, I was ready to go home.

Guess I was thinking about going straight because I got a job at Fraser and Brace in Cornwall on an outfit doing steel reinforcing at construction sites. Before two months were up my feet got itchy and my uncle was riding me. I couldn't make a go of it. No way was I ready to be a square john. So I went to Toronto and joined Peter March Amusements as a roughie — the guy that puts up the tents and gets everything ready for the agents to come in. Them days, the games were a little shaky and the agents were a little shaky too, so a roughie had to be an all-round bouncer. First day on the show I got into a beef. Think I got fired and rehired three times that day. But that's carnival life — very hot. The carnival had always been a good life for me, and again I was happy taking care of five concessions, partying it up, and making good bread, seventy-five dollars a day.

In Elliot Lake we had a riot. A couple of miners got beat playing the razzle dazzle, one of them games where marbles got to get into certain holes. So these guys got hot, so hot that they rounded up a gang of other miners, most of them already been beat at the game. These rowdies start tearing down the ferris wheel. At the time I was looking after the fish-bowl booth for a gentleman gone to the gents. So naturally I used the ammunition at hand. I start pitching bowls full of gold-fish at the rampaging miners. When the mounties arrived, one of them — to me he looked like he was six-foot eight and three hundred pounds of muscle — picked me up by the back of my head like I was a feather. I must have been 250 pounds then. Next thing I knew, I was in jail, but the old man, Peter March senior, bailed me out.

Very soon after I did him another favour. I was wearing a brand-new set of clothes, sitting pretty on a concession counter, flirting with some girls, when I heard someone yell 'Fire!' The octopus ride was ablaze. I rushed over, shovelled earth and sand till it was out. Man, did I look a mess! All my natty clothes covered with mud. I was standing there feeling tired and miserable when Peter March, in his big grey caddie, came rolling up the midway.

'Get in, son, we're going downtown to buy you some new clothes.'

Over two thousand dollars' worth of new threads, would you

believe it? Them days, I was into clothes, a real spiffy dresser, so it was a great day for me. Besides, I knew I was in good with the old man, and when you're a con, you're always thinking about your contacts and about debts people owe you. Might come in handy one day.

I finished out that season, May to October, as a roughie and a cat-rack man. I was in charge of the G-top too, the after-hours gambling joint for the carnival people. We sold beer and whiskey, played tipboards and punchboards, and had a few crap tables. I got a piece of all the action, so it was a real nice season for me. And like all the times I've been on the carnival, I didn't get into no trouble.

But trouble for me was never far away. Just days after I came back to Toronto, I got ratted out on a B&E in Forest Hill. My driver got caught, so he ratted on me to save himself from a sentence. He was a cab driver, a square john that developed a taste for fast money. That's how he got into being my driver. He'd park out front of the house I was robbing; nobody would suspect a thing. I should have known better than to be scoring with a square partner because you can never expect squares to observe the con code, keep their mouth shut. As I could have predicted, he sang and I got a year in Burwash Prison near Sudbury.

When they brought all the new fish into the main camp at Burwash, a sergeant came to look us over.

'I need a baker for Camp Bison,' he said.

Camp Bison. I was thinking. I knew I had two buddies there, so up went the hand.

'I'm a baker,' I claimed. Truth was, I'd never baked a cookie in my life.

'Okay, McGilvary, you're the new baker. Let's go.'

That night I was in the kitchen, ordered to make four thousand hermit cookies for breakfast. I whispered to my buddy, 'I don't know how to bake.'

'Just follow the recipe,' he advised me.

Well, I did, and they came out beautiful. Spooks, the staff cook, was all impressed. Proud, like he made them himself. He was the kind of guy that was scared of his own shadow, scared of making a mistake, always wanting to impress his superiors. He warned me that the head man would be in to check the cookies.

And when the head man walked in, who was it but Scotty. I knew Scotty at Guelph when he was just an ordinary cook. I guess he worked his way up through the system just like I did, only on another track. He was in charge of all the kitchens in all the camps at Burwash. Scotty was a short little Scotsman with just a few curls on his head and a real go-getter attitude.

He tasted a cookie. 'They're terrific. You've got the job, McGilvary.' Then he went bragging all over the camp about the terrific baker he's got and how he knew me when I was a terrific cook at Guelph.

I was terrific, all right. Terrifically drunk, as soon as I could be. The opportunity came that first day. A stock truck arrived with a case of vanilla extract. I grabbed that box fast and hid it behind the other supplies. To make sure it was the real stuff and not the artificial vanilla they usually send to prisons, I lit a spoonful. Pure blue flame – alcohol. I felt real glad to have a baker's job.

Me and the guys on my range, we drank vanilla extract with coke and ice all night. I really got sloshed, and I was plenty sloshed next day, when I had to bake sixteen big cakes in pans about three feet by two and a half feet.

I had a helper who was drunk as me and had about the same amount of baking experience – none. I can remember us staring down into the batter swirling around in the Hobart mixer. We were both dizzy, mesmerized by the swirl. I was holding a ten-pound can of baking powder.

'Tony, d'ya s'pose we put enough baking powder in?'

'I dunno. We put in what the recipe called for. Guess that's enough ... maybe we could add just a pinch.' I tossed in a tablespoon, fascinated to watch the white powder get sucked into the swelling grey batter.

'Maybe just a pinch more,' my buddy suggested.

'Okay.'

We were having so much fun watching the powder drown in the waves of batter that we kept adding pinches. Instead of tossing in tablespoons of the stuff, I started shaking the can. In the final toss, I emptied the rest of the ten-pound can into the batter.

Spooks was always checking on me and sticking his nose into the oven. The cakes were starting to rise.

'Real nice, Tony, they're coming along fine.'

Ten minutes later, the cakes had risen even with the top of the pans.

'You're a fantastic baker, Tony. They're right on.'

Fifteen minutes later, the pans were overflowing, batter pouring everywhere. Spooks opened the oven door to investigate. 'See what you're doin' by openin' the door,' I said to him. 'You're screwin' up the works.'

I wasn't too worried. I was gassed up, still sipping away at the vanilla. Suddenly, there was a rapid series of loud noises. Bang! Bang! Bang! The pans were empty and the oven was a huge mess. That was my introduction to the bake shop and my exit from the bake shop. Into the hole for ten days. It wasn't as bad as some I've seen, but a hole's a hole. They call it the hole for a reason. One thing, there was no toilet, just a hole in the floor. You had to be a bombardier to spot it. You got one rotten mattress and one dirty pillow. You were allowed one book a day. You got your food through a slot in the door – three slices of white bread or maybe cold porridge for breakfast, a slab of cold bean loaf for lunch, and more bread for supper. Every third day you got full meals like the rest of the population.

After ten days I got back into the kitchen because of my reputation as a cook. Mostly I cooked home brew. While it was fermenting in two five-gallon milk cans, we hid it in the back of the stove. To get the cans in there, we had to unscrew two hundred miserable tiny little screws and then screw them back in. That's a lot of manoeuvring for ten gallons of brew, but in prison it's worth it. Gives you something to connive about and something to do, and it lets you get drunk, which is the best way to make time pass.

After six quiet months in the kitchen I got assigned to a bush gang. Me and two other guys had to cut thirty logs a day with swede saws, but I didn't do none of the sawing. I was on coffee detail, and I sharpened the saws and axes. Usually the guys worked fast enough to finish their quota in the morning, so afternoons we'd sit around a big bonfire. I'd snare a few rabbits, skin them, and cook them over the fire. Soon enough I was stealing potatoes and carrots, salt and pepper, and making rabbit stews. Before long all the work gangs were coming to our fire. They'd add stuff they were stealing – some chicken, a beefsteak. Those stews were the best of Burwash. Otherwise, it was pretty boring, especially for a guy like me who had already done time in a penitentiary.

In 1961, after ten months and two days, with twelve dollars in my pocket, they released me and put me on a train headed for Toronto at one in the morning. When I arrived, I went to a rooming house at 508 Parliament Street. It belonged to Jeannette, an old carnival friend. I was feeling sick of jail, just wanted to stay on the street for a while. So I had to pick a line of work that would only get me a fine or a light sentence if I got caught.

After I bought some food – hamburger, bread, milk, macaroni, and margarine at two bucks for the lot – I had six bucks left. That money paid for eight bottles of cheap wine. At two a.m. I walked from my room to Dundas and Pembroke, feeling pretty heavy because I had the wine bottles in pockets I sewed inside my army coat. I made sixteen bucks for bootlegging the eight bottles to rubs in Norm's Grill. Four dollars went for cigarettes and food, the rest on more booze. By the third night I added whiskey to my travelling coat store, and by Friday night, just five nights after my release from Burwash, I was on the street bootlegging three cases of wine, five bottles of whiskey, and I had money in my pocket. Making money has never been a problem for me.

But it was too long a walk from Parliament to the street corners and joints where I sold the booze, and too many trips a night to haul it all. It wasn't safe. Sooner or later I'd get busted. So I started looking for a safe place to store my stuff. On Pembroke I found a filthy dump with five bedrooms for a hundred dollars a month. It had a garage that opened right into the house. Perfect for my purposes. No one would know my business. Not that it really mattered. There was something hopping in just about every house on that street anyways. Kept the cops a-bopping.

I needed a runner to sell the booze for me, a runner who wasn't a drinker. I'd give him twenty-five cents a bottle plus a free room. If he got pinched, I could bail him out once because the fine was only a hundred dollars for a first conviction. But it was three hundred for the second time, so I only kept a runner till he got busted once. They were easy to replace, lots of small-time hoods downtown who'd do anything for a buck.

I had a place, I had a runner. Then I had to get the fleabag fixed up. I rounded up some hooker broads, told them I was opening a pad and I needed some girls to clean the joint up. That was easy. Then I went to the Salvation Army to buy beds – with very solid springs. I didn't have enough money for dressers or chairs or anything fancy, but beds was all we really needed to get started. The Sally Ann truck delivered a whole load of beds – guess they thought they were furnishing an orphanage.

No girls under twenty. No pimps. Those were the rules. I was just running a trick pad, a quickie hotel with heavy protection for the girls. The trick paid the girl, and he paid the rent. Usually twenty bucks for her services and five for my room.

I had seventeen girls working out of there. Half of them were heroine junkies; the other half were alcoholics. They'd do maybe twenty tricks a night. If they were in those bedrooms more than fifteen minutes, I was at the door.

'What's takin' so long? Ya don't need more than fifteen minutes. Hurry it up.'

It wasn't just a bawdy house. It was a bar too. I sold drinks to the girls and their johns before and after. Inside of two weeks I had the place furnished nice – drapes, the works. Then one of the girls moved in, paid rent. She wasn't into men – she went for women – but she was a prostitute all the same. Me, I got involved with one of the hookers, but she kept her money, and her tricks paid for a room just like the other girls. Business is business. Love comes afterwards.

Romantic love may have taken second place to business, but family love occupied a special place in Tony's priorities. He always felt attached to the Brodeur children he grew up with, especially to Anita, who was closest to him in age. During Tony's brothel period Anita inherited some money. She decided to live a little high in the big city; she called Tony from Cornwall to say she was on her way to town.

'Tony was at the train station to meet me. I was a little shocked to see him greeting me in bare feet, but glad to see him anyway.' Anita laughs at the memory of her barefoot host whose only pair of shoes was at the shoemaker getting resoled.

'He brought me to what he called "his place." I thought it was a bit strange seeing all the traffic that passed behind the curtain separating his living

quarters from the entrance. I thought it might be hookers, but I was too shy and too scared of the answer to ask.

'We didn't stay there long before Tony took me to a nice motel room. He knew I was scared to be all alone in the city, so he got some guy to sit outside my room all night.

'My God, when I think of it now; he took me to a whorehouse!' Anita blushes, can barely speak the word. Whorehouse.

I didn't want to bring her there, but I had to go back to the house to get my shoes. I'd asked one of the girls to rush over to the shoemaker and fetch them while I was out meeting Anita. I knew about the inheritance that was bringing her to town. Most of the family was grubbing for them bucks, but I never bummed a dime. I really cared about my family. Only way I had to show it was never asking for nothing and doing what small favours I could – like staking a bodyguard outside her motel-room door.

I kept that house going about a year. Twice the cops tried to bust me using marked bills, but it didn't work. One night I heard a knock at the door. I answered it.

'Yeah, wha'd'ya want?' I said to one of my girls and her trick.

'We want to rent a room,' said the hooker broad.

'Sorry, I don't rent rooms.'

All the girls had keys, so I knew she was telling me her trick was a cop. My time was up. I knew it. They were probably watching the house, and they'd eventually make me. If they had to, they'd frame me. So I got all the girls and some of their johns to come to the pad.

'It's a party, everyone. Food and drinks are on the house,' I announced.

That party cleaned the place out. When there was no more booze and no more food, I made another announcement.

'Help yourself, girls. Anything ya want, take it outta here. I'm closin' down.'

They were making phone calls; trucks were arriving; furniture was moving like it was dollar day at Woolco furniture department. Before it was over, I was long gone. The cops, I heard, arrived about an hour after I left.

I stayed low in Cornwall for a while. Even got respectable. On a spur decision I married Teresa, a childhood friend. I was thirty and she was thirty-nine. She was so square that we didn't sleep together till after we got married. Teresa was a widow. Her husband had died three weeks after they married, leaving her pregnant with a daughter. She had put all her love on that kid, made her into a spoiled doll. And she planned to control me too, straighten me out. Women always think they can do that. I guess I was sort of thinking about changing, too, because I got a square job for a while. But before long I threw the shovel and workboots ten feet in the air, packed my bags, and split. The draw of the wild life was still too strong for me.

When I went back to the life, Teresa was pregnant with our son, my second Michael Anthony. I left her to raise him alone, just like she had had to do with her daughter.

My life has always been spicy, always action packed. I liked it that way. I still do. And I certainly got my fill of fast thrills in my next career: boosting – we call it clouting, too. It's a very risky form of shoplifting. You might clean out a delivery truck while the driver's grabbing a coffee. In broad daylight. Or you might clean out a delivery truck while it's moving! Yes, while it's moving, driving down the highway. I'll tell you about that later.

One day I was unloading cigarette cartons from a salesman's station wagon, piling the cartons on the sidewalk. The guy came out of the restaurant screaming.

'Hey! Those are my cigarettes,' he hollered at me.

'Are ya sure?' I hollered back, looking a little perplexed.

'Yeah, they're mine.' He was getting angry.

'Okay, sorry,' I said.

I handed him the cartons; he loaded them back in the wagon, looking a little confused all the while.

'That's it,' I said. Then I turned slowly and walked away calmly. I was sure the guy was staring at my back. First corner I came to, I turned and ran like hell. I was a big man but I could move. Them days, I was pretty damn brazen, lifting so many cartons of cigarettes I almost thought it was legal.

John Wilson, past co-ordinator of a Toronto HELP *office, was a crony in crime with Tony. A trim man greying nicely under his navy newsboy cap, John runs his hand over his neat salt and pepper beard. Straightens his very navy, very businesslike suit.*

'I came across Tony when I was wired on heroine, and working the clout. I was stealing cigarettes off trucks, and even though it was my long suit as a clout man, Tony was better. He was one of the best clout men in the city at that time.

'Tony usually worked with a crew — a high-powered one, big money makers, the kind who put a lot of support money into the drug trade. But I never heard of him being involved in any drug deals. His reputation was as a grinder — out all day working the clout and out all night working the locks. He was excellent at that too.'

Working the clout meant big challenge and high risk, watchwords for Tony the con. He loves to talk about his spiciest bit of boosting — his night raids on moving trucks.

We had a contraption about four feet high to hold me on the front hood of a car, a moving car. If you can picture in your mind or look up in a library book how they trap wild animals in Africa, well, that's what we framed up on our hood. The same thing hunters in Africa put on the front of their jeeps.

It was my idea, even built it myself. I knew we were missing scores by not getting into trucks while they were moving. I knew we could steal more on the highway than at the truck stop. So, with this contraption, I figured out how to solve the problem.

Anyway, I would be in this rig, holding long stretchy elastic cords. We'd be on a dark highway at night driving fifty to sixty miles an hour, without lights and maybe a foot behind a big delivery truck. It was my job to reach across, snap the seal, bust the lock, and latch the door open with the elastic cords so I could transfer into the truck.

Shit, we'd be bumper to bumper when I had to make that transfer. If the driver slowed or came to a sudden stop, I'd be a dead sucker. The driver couldn't see us in his rear-view mirror because we were too close on his tail, no headlights on and darkness for a cover.

When I made the transfer, it was very risky stunt-man stuff. If the goods were stacked right to the door — like stuff in cases, maybe cigarettes — I'd have no standing room inside. Loose goods like fur coats were better because there'd be more room in the back of the truck. Once in with the goods, I'd hurl them to the side of the road. On a dark night them flying goods were too much of a blur for the driver to see, especially if he wasn't suspecting nothing. Partners in a second vehicle, a pick-up truck, would collect the stuff by the roadside.

When I would finish unloading, the driver in my car had to get real close to the truck in order to get me safely back on the hood. I just grabbed hold of the gadget. The elastic cord was rigged so it wouldn't flap when I let go. Instead, the van door would close. Then we'd take off, meet the pick-up vehicle later, fence the loot fast, and split the bread.

I did that real dangerous kind of boosting four times only. One time, my last boost, was some joke! I risked my life for a truckload of Bibles, would you believe it? Of course, I didn't know the delivery van was hauling Gideon Bibles till I transferred into the back. When I realized what they were carrying, I started to howl. What else could I do but laugh? What could I do with hot Bibles – donate them to motels so travelling salesmen could have a boring read in the crapper? I decided to leave them be, just transferred back into the get-away car. Right after the Bible caper, I gave up clouting. I don't know exactly why I quit. Maybe the hand of God reached out from them pages and put the fear in my conscience. I just got scared of the game.

One day in that same Toronto period another bandit asked me if I'd strip the goods from a store after he picked the locks. Okay, I told him. So we broke into this men's wear store in a shopping centre on a Sunday morning. After piling a bunch of suits into what looked like laundry piles all tied up in sheets I brought along, I threw them outside the door to load into a station wagon.

People going by on their way to and from church didn't suspect a thing; they figured we worked in the store, were taking inventory or something. As I walked in and out with my bundles, I'd wave or smile to anyone whose eye I caught. It was an easy heist, and even easier to fence the suits. For a two-hundred-dollar suit I averaged thirty-five dollars. My partner got a cut.

I did a few more jobs with this partner, but he was a drinker, and drinkers aren't reliable. I couldn't count on him to show up or do things right. Learn lock picking myself, that was the only solution. Since I knew a locksmith, I was able to get some old cylinders and locks. And I bought a set of picks. For a week I did nothing but practice – practice till my hands were bleeding sometimes. But by the end of that week I was able to open ten locks in ten minutes. Ready to do the whole job myself, and I did, many a time.

Lock picking is no mystery. You just get a package of picks, a comb case, they call it. Just the basics – your riffle, your tension bars, your lion's tooth and double lion's tooth, half-moon and double half-moon. I used to use a medium lion's tooth and a double lion's tooth for holding and catching. With this equipment, even an amateur can learn, inside of three days, to open 25 per cent of all conventional locks. But he must remember that the tension bar can be your enemy or your friend – too much pressure is no good. You need just the right amount of pressure and you need just the right amount of practice. Today, it's more complicated, of course. They're using laser beams to pick locks now.

As a rookie, I did okay, but I would have lots of chances later on to get even better. That's what prisons are for, to better your trade. My education in lock picking actually began in Guelph when I was a kid. To have enough to eat, you had to learn to break into the pantry without the Man knowing you'd gotten in there to steal peanut butter.

The best time of day for lock picks is six or seven in the morning, when working people are on the streets. They never suspect nothing; they think you're the store owner. With the traffic in the streets, you blend in. Another good time is just after closing, minutes after the owner locks up, because he probably won't be coming back right away, it's still light, and there's lots of activity around. People think all crime takes place in the dark of night, but they're wrong.

No matter when you commit crime, day or night, sooner or later a habitual criminal will get caught. Sometimes you even get caught when you're clean or innocent. I remember the time a police cruiser spotted me in my car and started chasing. For a change, I had nothing hot in the car, but when you're a con and the cops are on your tail, you don't stop to ask them why. So I gave it the gas. We were zooming around the back alleys and laneways over near Pape. It was a real car-chase scene, just like you see in the cop shows.

How was I going to get out of this jackpot? I decided I had a better chance if I ditched the car and ran. Except I was going too fast to stop quickly, and in trying to hide the car in an empty garage, I ended up going through the garage's back wall. Guess where I came out? The back of a cop shop, right in the parking lot. 'Christ, Tony, you sure don't have far to go to get arrested,' an officer who knew me said. I got a four-hundred-dollar fine for wilful damage, but my lawyer got me back out on the street that same day. Soon after that incident I got nailed one night trying to bust into a store, but I beat that rap too. I knew they were on me then because I kept getting charges. By the time that round of thieving and arrests was over, I'd been out on five bails.

You might wonder where the bail money comes from. Different people put up the bread, including every criminal's partner – the honest businessman. It's a straightforward business arrangement: you have to pay them 10 per cent interest on the bails as soon as you're back on the street. You also have to make your lawyer money very fast because lawyers like to suck your blood too. Going to jail a lot is very expensive.

I was out on that fifth bail – an appeal against a one-year definite and one-year indefinite sentence – when I got into one hell of a jackpot. Opening Bell pay-phone boxes. I could open one in fifteen seconds, which really surprised Bell because they thought no one could crack their babies. Bell bosses even came to visit me in the Don Jail. They wanted me to squeal how I done it. If I'd told them, I knew I'd get a lighter sentence because important people – that means rich people and big companies – can always influence the courts. But I told them nothing. Heard they changed the locks on their pay phones after that.

Seven years for vault breaking, that's what the Bell business cost me. I was twenty-seven years old. I'd been on the street almost two years. I thought about the five-year bit I'd already done at the Big House. It had seemed like forever. Seven years would be worse. It loomed ahead like an eternity. Little did I suspect it would take me fifteen years to serve it.

Seven-Year Sentence on a Fifteen-Year Instalment Plan

9

From petit point to plumbing – hobby crafts and trades, as we call them in the joint – man, was I about to get my fill in the next fifteen years. First, there was upholstering for three months at Kingston Pen, the reception centre for guys on their way to Joyceville. Three months of pounding furniture tacks. Then I was transferred to the fish corridor at Joyceville. Every time you go into a joint, you must do six weeks on what we call the fish corridor. For new fish, about to be fried. Them six weeks are boring for a habitual con like me. I don't need no indoctrinating. I could indoctrinate the indoctrinators. But the administration is usually real strict about those six weeks.

Except I had friends inside and they were spreading my reputation as a good cook around the joint. I was just six hours on the fish corridor when the staff cook came looking for me.

'I hear you're a hot cook, McGilvary.'

'Yeah, that's me.'

'Pack your gear, we're going to the kitchen,' he ordered.

So here I was, already part of the general prison population. It was like home to me, a familiar environment. At that time Joyceville was like an old man's home. Everybody did their own thing – hobbies mostly. No upheavals, no stabbings, no riots. Very tame, especially compared to the fifties. Ask anyone who did time in the sixties and seventies at Joyceville.

John Wilson, who used to be a Toronto HELP *co-ordinator, did time with Tony. He agrees about the atmosphere at Joyceville.*

'It was pretty loose. The environment was very relaxed, not like the fifties, when it was them against us and you were locked up sixteen hours a day. If a screw tried to talk to you in those days, you'd blow at him. "You don't have any right to say anything to me except to give me a direct order."

'By the sixties, however, they were getting into what they called "social development" – friendly officers, upgrading courses, lessons in relating to squares. Mostly it was mellow because of the drugs. The guards turned a blind eye. They'd come on my range, tell me to alert the guys to count-up time. I'd holler "Count up, let's put them (drugs) away." Then the guards would come in.

'The authorities knew drugs helped keep the lid on. They didn't want a return of the violence that plagued Joyceville in the fifties, so they just turned their heads to what we were doing. And it was easy to do what we were doing – moving drugs in and around the institution. Everyone thinks guards help inmates get drugs. Yes, there are a few who do, but we don't need them to help us. Cons are clever enough to devise ingenious ways to move the stuff.

'You put down a play, wait maybe a week for one guy to do his part – maybe Peter the inmate plumber, who'll collect the bombers or smoke from the pipe chase in the ladies' washroom after our friends stash them there on visits. That's part of what keeps our conniving skills sharp, and pulling off an ingenious play, co-ordinating the players, waiting for the pay-off, that's what makes prison bearable.

'Tony wasn't into drugs. Brews and hobbies were his thing.'

My first hobby was plaster of Paris – which I mostly used for plugging up sinks. I bought the occasional bag of plaster and stole the rest from the carpentry shop. I also stole handfuls of knives and forks from the kitchen for reinforcing statues. I got pretty good at making statues, everything from plaques of animal heads for hanging on walls, to matadors, to what do you call that woman with no arms – Venus? I made quite a few of her. Once the prison priest asked me to make sheep for the Nativity scene. So I did. Black sheep, like us, black sheep of the society. He didn't appreciate my art.

I really got into this hobby thing. Lots of guys in the joint do because there isn't anything else worthwhile to make time pass. When I got tired of statues, I went on to copper enamelling and then to petit point. It's kind of funny, I guess, to think about all these hardened criminals in a maximum-security joint, some of them big guys like me, sitting around stitching pretty pictures.

Petit point was one of the most popular hobby-crafts because it requires so much concentration. I did a one-thread Shepherd's Idyll with over a million stitches. It took almost a year to complete it. You're using a magnifying glass and you're bent over three, four hours at a time. I also made blue boys and pinkies – she goes with Blue Boy.

Between hobbies and reading, I could make the time pass. At that time I was into history, reading everything I could get my hands on about Hitler. That sonofabitch should have been hung as soon as he got started. I'm not a violent man, but I would gladly have blown that bastard away. People like him shouldn't be allowed to live; they're the real criminals. But with all my reading, I couldn't figure out why he was able to rook all them people. And them believing him. I just can't understand that.

After my Hitler period, I got into rabbits. Couldn't talk to me about anything else. Somebody would say 'How you doing, Tony?' and I'd answer with a lecture on rabbits. 'D'ya know that the lop rabbit's got an ear span of twenty-eight inches? It weighs four and a half pounds and it's sold as a pet. Except we can't get them here in Canada. Your Flemish giants can grow up to eighteen pounds; your New Zealand white rabbits can go up to twenty pounds.' Not too many inmates were interested in the breeds and diseases of rabbits, but I told them anyway.

For the first three years of my sentence I was working in the kitchen, which is a great place to be because you can get food and make brews. Brews are a heat score – you always get charged if you get pinched – but it's worth trying to fool the Man. They watch you all the time, but they aren't always too smart.

For example, when you make bread. The staff cook will come in with the yeast; he'll melt it in the sugar-water and add it to the dough. He controls the yeast because he doesn't want you getting any for brew. What the Man doesn't realize is that all you got to do is take some of the dough with the yeast in it. It doesn't take much to get sugar bubbling – all you need are two or three seeds, and it doesn't matter if they're in dough.

Also, in the kitchen you're in a good position to do favours for other inmates. Like the guys that were always coming up to me in the halls.

'Tony, I haven't had a steak in so long, I feel like I'm not human anymore,' some guy would say.

'Okay, I'll see what I can do,' I'd promise.

Maybe this guy worked in the plumbing shop, for instance, so I'd knock off a tap and tell the staff man to get a plumber. Meantime, on butchering day I'd have stashed a steak in a stash place I got in the fridge. When the guy came to fix the taps, he'd carry a large tool-box, partly empty in the bottom. He'd distract the staff while I'd throw the steak in the box, probably with a pound of butter, too. Once the guy got food up on the range and into the common room, where we had illegal hot plates, no one would ask questions. That's inmate turf.

If you got caught, and often we did, you'd probably go to the cooler. One or two of the screws would just throw the steak back in the fridge and forget the incident, but most of them went by the book.

Also, from the kitchen I was able to do other things to make life a bit more civilized for the guys. Like eggs, for example. At Joyceville inmates eat in the common rooms with maybe thirty guys to each room. Breakfast would go upstairs on steamers. By the time you'd get your eggs, they'd be dry and cold and almost nobody would eat them. By the end of a serving you'd be throwing out maybe fifty rubbery eggs. Besides, lots of guys don't eat breakfast – they just want a cup of coffee.

So one day I grabbed a staff chef, sat him down at my desk in the vegetable room, where it's nice and quiet after the potato peelers are off. I always had a pot of coffee brewing there.

I asked the chef, 'How many eggs d'ya buy a week?'

'About 3,200,' he told me.

'And how many d'ya t'row away?' I continued.

He said, 'About 2,500.'

'What if I got a way to cut your losses?'

As I kept talking, his ears got bigger. Two days later the head staff cook of all the pens was sitting at my desk. Within no time raw eggs were being sent up to the common rooms and guys were cooking them themselves, the way they like them and when they felt like eating eggs, maybe at night in a fried-egg sandwich. At first this egg thing was a big deal. Guys would be stashing eggs in the fridge in cups marked with their names. When the novelty wore off they'd leave the eggs in flats in the fridge and help themselves when they wanted. Today that's a common practice in prisons that have common rooms.

After three quiet years in Joyceville I made a parole in 1965 to Cornwall. I broke it almost the same day by going to Toronto and committing a crime. I stole something or other, I can't remember what. I didn't even have time to roam the streets of Yorkville, which was fast becoming *the* counter-culture neighbourhood of Canada. I heard them streets were full of suburb kids into drugs and sex and rock 'n' roll – kind of an uptown version of what downtown always been, but without the glamour reputation. Difference between the Yorkville druggies and the Dundas druggies was choice. The Yorkville rebels could go home when they got rebelling out of their systems. Most of the people I knew had no homes to go to, or, if they did, they were only worth running away from. Anyway, within a month I was back in Joyceville.

For good behaviour in the joint you earn good time, so much off your sentence, up to 25 per cent. When you break parole you lose all your good time. Since I'd already done three years on a seven-year sentence, I'd probably earned six months good time by then. I lost that when I goofed up on parole. When you go back in you got to do that time – in my case, the six months good time I'd earned – plus the new time you get sentenced for for the latest crime.

Going back after parole is real bad. You're blaming everybody. One person you forget to blame is yourself. I was hot at everybody. I refused to go back into the kitchen. I stuck it out on the fish corridor for six weeks, then went to the work board for an assignment. A job in the plumbing shop was advertised. Now, that could be interesting.

Food, as always, being a big thing for me, I had to arrange trips to the kitchen. That was easy. I'd just get the inmate cook to jigger the sink. When the plumbers were called, I was always ready with a large tool-box – the old trick, only now I was collecting on favours I'd done other inmates. Since I learned nothing about plumbing, the staff plumber would use me like a nurse in surgery. Hammer. Screwdriver. Pipe. Wrench. While I was handing scalpels to the doc, my buddy was filling my tool-box. I think the staff plumber suspected something because he'd always say, 'The kitchen again! What the hell's the matter there?' But I still got away with it time and again.

That staff plumber was a pretty relaxed guy. When we'd go outside to the pumphouse, he'd let me fish in the Rideau River while he worked. I put together a tackle box and rigged a rod with alder branches. It was real nice.

But it changed. The staff changed. The new plumber, he had an attitude that spelled trouble for me. I wasn't going to crawl back to the kitchen, however, so I fixed it that they'd come crawling to me. I put a bug in an inmate's ear that Tony is unsatisfied with the plumbing shop and he's thinking about becoming a carpenter. Two days later the staff cook was in the shop convincing me to come back to the kitchen. I finally gave in.

For the next stretch I was a cook, working hard in the kitchen twelve hours a day. Then the passes started. I got a four-hour escorted pass and then an eight-hour escorted pass, but I couldn't do nothing with them. I just strolled around the river and around Kingston with a guard. Them days I wasn't into strolling; I was into girls. Since I had no girlfriend at the time, I couldn't do what most inmates would try on an escorted pass – convince the screw to stay outside a motel room. There were none of them conjugal visits in my time, and a man's got his needs. It's natural.

Both my escorts were by-the-book men anyway, screws that follow the rules. In some ways, though, they're the best guards. Why? Because they're consistent. The manual is their bible. Say they caught me with a brew. They'd charge me, take me in front of the warden, and the warden would probably punish me with time in the hole. You get no breaks from a book man, but you also know what to expect from that type of screw. You could always tell a book man – all spit and polish, with their shoes shined just so. If they got a hanky in their pocket, I bet it's folded over three times. Prima donnas. Screws with ambitions. As I went through the system I'd see them achieve their ambitions, become keepers and chief keepers, real fat cats. The majority of guards are book men.

Dangerous screws are the ones that make their own rules, that don't observe the manual. One day they'll turn a blind eye if they see you stealing from the kitchen, for example, but next day they'll arrest you for the same misdemeanour. This unpredictable type is usually out to be friends with everybody, to look good in everyone's eyes. He's probably scared of himself and scared of the job. This same screw that's been kind one time and cruel the next is likely the man you'll meet on the goon squad, the team that drags cons to the hole when things get hot inside.

There's a third type of guard, the guy that really cares. Like the truly sadistic screws, they're a minority, but unlike the goons that like to beat on you, they can be a help. Maybe they'll do you a favour, like bring in something you want from outside. I don't mean contraband; I mean a book or materials you need for hobby-crafts. But don't confuse these caring types with so-called 'living-unit officers'; they're just screws out of uniform. Civilian clothes don't make them any more humane.

The ratio of screws to cons is almost one to one when you consider all the staff, whether or not they are actually guards. To a con, everyone that works inside, everyone free to go home at night, is a guard. And if you doubt that all the staff are guards, just see how people line up during a riot. It's them and us, and it doesn't matter what their official title is.

I always treated guards like human beings. I'd ask them 'How's the wife and kids?' But there was a purpose to being nice. I wanted them on my side. I might need them one day. So I was always preparing them – for what I didn't know, but for something.

As I mentioned, most of the guards were book men, just doing a job to grab a buck. They just wanted to keep the peace. But even in Joyceville, with its old-folks' home atmosphere, there were a few exceptions. I seen three sadistic guards drag an inmate to the hole, and I saw them strike him bad, just out of meanness. And I witnessed groups of guards beating up on inmates. Sometimes a screw would beat an inmate while other guards watched.

At Millhaven, where it's very rough, where cons hate cons and screws hate cons, violence is commonplace. It's brutal on both sides, cons killing cons and screws killing cons, not that they ever get charged. It's so violent in Millhaven that soon as a little scuffle breaks, out come the dogs and gas. I hear Joyceville is getting more like that now, but in my time it was a tame place.

That unexciting stint lasted about two years, till I made a pass to Ottawa. This is how it works. You apply for a pass. If you've been on good behaviour for a while, and if they know you aren't a violent type, you usually get it. But your classification officer does a 'community assessment' on the people you're visiting on pass to make sure they're upstanding types. Usually, the only solid citizens a con knows is someone he buys. And there's always somebody ready to be bought – mostly fences and businessmen, respectable citizens on the criminal fringe who've never been busted. These guys will do a con a favour because you'll owe him – maybe a good deal on hot merchandise.

Remember, cons couldn't live without honest square johns and right-thinking citizens.

So I sent word out on the prison grapevine that I'm applying for a pass to Ottawa. And I got word back on the grapevine that another inmate out on a pass had a family for me. I got passed the name and number and a few particulars, enough to convince my classification officer that it was legit. Then he did the assessment. A few weeks later the officer visited me.

'Real nice people, Tony, you have some good friends out there. You made the pass.'

Con friends were waiting for me when I got off the bus in Ottawa. First thing I did was call the nice family, thank them very much for their kindness, and tell them I'd drop by next day. I wanted to check this family out in case I needed them again. Then I was ready to party it up. Ball it up after all that time without a woman. Luckily, I got connections who owned a massage parlour with nine girls working, or maybe I should say nine working girls. The owners set me loose for about eight hours. I got massaged, all right, even my ears.

Next day I visited the family, brought Crown Royal for the man and flowers for the wife. We chatted a bit; then I split to do more partying and to do a favour for another inmate. Normally on a pass

I'd commit a crime and stay on the run, but this time I decided I'd go back because I had a message to deliver to a buddy inside and I promised to deliver it personally. A message involving his woman in Ottawa. He needed the information I got for him so he could make an important decision. Hadn't have been for that favour, I wouldn't have gone back. Loyalty, don't forget, is part of the con's code.

That bit was just a revolving door, though. I wasn't back in three months when I made another pass to the same family. Twelve days later I got caught breaking into a store. The same old routine. Lost my good time, got another sentence, went back to the fish corridor.

That was the first time I started to get angry with myself, not for committing crimes but for going back to the joint. I was starting to feel – if only vaguely – that I didn't want to live inside anymore. I was about thirty-four years old, getting older, and the game didn't seem as exciting.

John Wilson recalls walking with Tony around the exercise yard in those first days of doubt.

'It was a cool fall day – I remember a few leaves were blowing around the yard. Tony was in an unsettled mood, a mood I didn't understand at the time. Because I'd been on the street ten years and had just come back in, from a con's point of view I was an expert on the straight life.

'"John, I'm tired of this life, man, but how can I stay on the street?" Tony asked me.

'"You have to disassociate, stay away from rounders, live with square johns," I told him. "It's the only way to make it out there."

'Tony just kept looking at me and nodding in disagreement. He couldn't accept that position.

'"There's got to be a way you can be with your people and still stay out of jail," he answered me.

'I had no answer for that one. I didn't realize at the time what he was wrestling with. Whatever thoughts he was having about the straight life, though, he was far from ready to act on them. But a germ of change was turning over in his mind.'

For another three years I kept thinking that I'd had enough, but I didn't know how to break the pattern. During those three years I was just living day to day, working in the kitchen and doing leathercraft. The wheeling and dealing kept me going. Money inside is worth two for one. If you got money outside, in a bank maybe, or front money – the cash the administration confiscates when you come into the joint – you write me a cheque for one hundred dollars and I'll give you fifty cash.

Leather is real expensive and I was deep into leathercraft, even had an assembly line going with ten guys. We were making purses and belts, selling them like mad inside and outside the joint. So I had to find an inmate who needed cash. That was easy. I got him to tell the crafts officer that he wanted to start a leather hobby. Then the Man would take five hundred dollars from this guy's front money to buy leather he'd sell me for two hundred fifty cash. Then I'd have cheap leather and he'd have some cash to deal in the joint for dope or booze. Maybe he'd spend it all on chocolate bars. I didn't care.

Chocolate bars reminds me of a funny incident with baked Alaska. My pal, Jackie, told me, 'I'm gonna die if I don't taste baked Alaska, Tony.'

I didn't want him to die, so I stole the ingredients to make one. Except the staff cook caught me.

'McGilvary, looks like you're planning to make a baked Alaska. That's fine by me, but you know you can't take it out of the kitchen. You make it and you eat it in here.'

'No way. I'm makin' that thing, and it's gonna be eaten by someone who ain't in the kitchen. All the trouble I went ta ta steal the ingredients. Ya think I won't deliver?'

Now I had his dandruff up, and mine was up too. This cook was good people, but he got his shit in the air that day. A competition was on. Guess what? That baked Alaska went up – disguised as pudding. We put the baked Alaska in the bottom of a homemade double boiler we made look like a single large pot. Not only did it go up, but I sneaked out of the kitchen with it, went to the common room and served Jackie, a white towel over my arm. The guy bawled like a baby, not the behaviour you'd expect from a safe-cracker and armed robber.

In 1970 I got a temporary pass to a half-way house in Hull, Quebec. I'd served about ten years by then. You must understand that a normal guy on a pass got one main thing on his mind – getting laid. Even if he isn't normal, he's probably got the same thing on his mind. But instead of giving you some freedom to live like a regular joe, certain passes are very restrictive. They require you to work, supposedly to prepare you for the square life. In Hull they stuck me in an upholstery workshop at Les Ateliers Dominique, a 'sheltered workshop,' which is double-talk for places where they exploit handicapped and cons. They paid me a dollar an hour, then stole back two bucks for lunch. A six-dollar work day – now, that's some training for the square life! They'd give us a couple of hours after work to go out and play before curfew. So much for being on a pass! Like parole, many passes are just prison beyond the bars. And it's no wonder guys break their passes and their paroles.

On temporary parole – which is what they called my pass to Hull – you can't leave your designated area without permission from your parole officer. To visit my family in Cornwall I got a pass. But I didn't report back to St Dominique's on time. Instead I was in bed with the prettiest little thing you ever want to meet. I'd look at the clock and back at her and say, 'To hell with it.' And even though I went back to prison for another two years, it was worth it. That night was mine and nobody could take it away from me. Lots of guys break passes because of women.

Don't forget, there's only two choices in prison. You can go the homosexual way or you can use your hand, and I used my hand for twenty-two years. At least the cells are pretty private in Joyceville, one man to a cell with a wooden door that has a peep slot. The guards aren't interested in seeing you on the crapper or masturbating.

I love women, I always have. And I met them easy, at bars, usually. Real nice bars and restaurants like the Silver Rail or Honest Ed's Warehouse. I might not have been the best-looking man, but I was a natty dresser and a smooth talker. I talked myself into dates with women you'd never dream I'd get. Besides, I always found that women find criminals exciting, dangerous. They like being associated with guys who live fast. I could do all the poontanging I wanted.

After that bit of poontanging in Cornwall I was a goner for

another two years, back in the joint doing petit point till I was almost blind. And eating, of course. Every Christmas they allow you to buy goodies with your front money. That year I bought a hundred dollars' worth of salamis because you can hang them to dry. My cell looked like an Italian cantina. I slept under a ceiling full of them. Once in a while a salami would drop. I could knock off two of them little fat jobbies for lunch. That was it. Salami and petit point, very unexciting. But there was drama in store.

I had one more beef to go up on, a safe-cracking job. They transferred me to the Don Jail to await trial. One day a guard told me my mother died. Just like that. 'Tony, your mother died, and I don't know what she died of.' I felt sort of numb but I was okay, I thought. A police escort took me to her funeral in Cornwall. When the pallbearers were carrying her casket out of the church, I stepped into the aisle and took the place of the lead pallbearer. I didn't think it was right that I shouldn't carry my mother. I stayed with her to the hearse.

Then something scary started happening inside me. I didn't know what it was because it had never happened before.

'Take me back to the Don right now,' I said in panic to the escort. 'I don't know what's happenin' ta me, but I won't give ya no trouble. Just take me back.'

He drove pretty fast, I remember that. I felt panicked, out of control, out of touch with myself and with reality. I didn't realize what was happening, but I found out later that for twenty-two days I wouldn't shave, wouldn't eat. I'd just sit in the corner of my cell silent. When I snapped out of my stupor, I looked around.

'Where am I? Who are these people? Am I in a nest of rats, stool pigeons, what?' I asked myself. I guessed they were stoolies because they were sitting in a circle ratting out on each other, saying things like, 'Joe stole an extra slice of bread' and 'I saw Mary smoke a cigarette.' 'I gotta get outta here,' I thought to myself. Except I didn't know where here was. I didn't recognize the place. I didn't know the people sitting in a group with me in it. All I knew was I had to get out.

There was a sign on the wall. It read 'Don't get up without permission of the counsellor.' But I got up anyway and started walking – to where I didn't know. When they tried to stop me, I went berserk. So they maced me, gave me a needle, stripped me, and threw me in a padded cell. I was in Penetang, the psycho jail. Criminally insane.

I'll never forget the eighty-eight days I spent in that hell-hole. They play tricks on you. Experiment with people, with their minds. God knows what they put in the food. One day you can't drink the milk; next day the potatoes taste rotten but the milk's okay, and the next day the vegetables are laced with whatever drugs they're feeding you. And you're watched all the time – two-way mirrors everywhere.

After six days they transferred me out of the padded cell, after a specialist worked on my eye, which had gone completely white from the mace. They put me in B Ward, for the people who are completely nuts. I was not crazy; I was just grieving and in pain because my mother died, and they treated me like I was a lunatic rather than a man in shock. But even lunatics don't deserve to be treated like shit.

B Ward. You got your spitters and guys that eat their own shit. Everyone on heavy drugs. They gave me all kinds. Some of them made me real sick. If inmates in the regular joints got few rights, inmates in Penetang got nothing, no rights. Complain and they give you more and worse punishment, usually in the form of drugs. I was terrified I'd never get out of there. All I ever did was talk to shrinks, but they never helped me. They asked so many questions about my sex life I thought they were perverted. My sex life was not my problem – a school kid could have figured that out.

The reason I finally transferred back to Joyceville was my half-sister, Grace. I hadn't associated with my family, except my aunt and uncle occasionally, in over twenty-five years. But we met at the funeral – all us hypocrites who didn't do nothing for our mother in her lifetime. Grace, still the looker of the family even though she was in her fifties then, asked if she could visit me in the joint. She came three times to Penetang. Every visit she pushed the doctors to explain what was wrong with me. All they ever told her was shock and nerves. But her bugging was why they didn't keep me longer, I thought. If you got no one lobbying for you, they just keep you in there and use your life to do experiments.

When I was released from that black hole of torture, it was back to Joyceville via the Don and a trial on that safe-cracking beef. I got another conviction, more time. I just couldn't beat it; my life was doing crime, doing time. In some ways it didn't even matter any more. I'd give in to the inevitable, and then a little voice inside me would whisper that I'd had enough, I wanted out. Grace came in handy with getting paroled. I knew she wasn't visiting me religious every Wednesday afternoon out of love. But I also knew I could use her the way she was using me.

What good was I to her? The leathercraft. She and her husband had a store in a small town, near Picton, which I kept well stocked with leather goods. Other crafts too. I'd wheel and deal inside to get her a large supply of all types of work the guys were making. Sometimes I'd give her as many as twenty-five purses and maybe twenty-five other pieces of hobby-crafts in a week. I never asked for money, and they never offered any.

That's what I was worth to them – a little more income towards their old-age retirement. They kept inviting me to come live with them when I'd make parole. They needed someone to work their store and their house, I figured. Having family to live with outside helped me make an early parole in 1972. First thing I did when I got out was visit my wife Teresa and our son Michael. In my own sloppy way I tried to patch things up. I didn't really know how to relate to the boy, so I did what my father had done to me – I tried to buy his affection with presents. I bought him about eight hundred dollars' worth of Christmas gifts, including a bike that was way too big for him.

Within a few days at Grace's I got restless. I wasn't going to be no meal ticket. But I wasn't sure I wanted to get back into crime neither. At that time I was what cons call a 'touch case': I could go either way. I wasn't a sure bet for more crime, but I wasn't a sure bet for going straight neither. Lou Hunt, my parole officer, wanted me to make it. Lou was the kind of guy that cared about his clients. A British-looking type in tweed jackets and always smoking a pipe. He dropped by Grace's to visit me.

'Tony, you're not happy here, are you?'

'You got it,' I confessed.

'I know you're on the edge, Tony. Before you decide to do anything stupid, come see me.'

Lou was a wise man. Wiser than me. Even though I wanted to quit crime, it was the only life I knew, and all my friends were cons. It was easier to stay in the game than to give it up. From Grace's I was renewing some of my old contacts. One a them, Jerry, was eager to head south. So was I. We laid our plans.

First I needed a pass to Cornwall, because you always need permission to move when you're on parole. I got the pass. From there it was easy. We just crossed the border at Thousand Islands, sailed through like regular square johns. Between us we had a hundred dollars. By the time we got to Philadelphia we had forty bucks left. And Jerry, would you believe it, got homesick. We figured he needed thirty bucks for gas to get home. That left me ten. Ten dollars and one suitcase in beautiful downtown Philly. I knew no one. I was a fugitive. What else could I do but crime?

A Fugitive Hiding with Gypsies

10

First thing I did in Philly was go into a bar, sit on a bar stool, and nurse a Budweiser. Over in the corner I saw a guy very drunk, his wallet lying on the table. I waited. When he staggered to the toilet, I bolted for the wallet, then bolted out the door. No wonder he left it on the table; there wasn't a dime in it.

I called a buddy in Ottawa. Next morning a hundred dollars was waiting for me at the telegraph office. Plenty to get me by bus to Tampa, Florida, where I could track down Paul Miller's Carnival and Circus through the Showman's League. They were playing a shopping centre in Tampa, I learned. Even though they had a full crew, Buddy Miller, the owner's son, gave me a job. Why the favour? Because one time I chopped ferris-wheel pulleys when his hand was caught in them. He lost four fingers but saved his hand. He owed me. First he put me in the swinger, a game where you got a bowling ball on a chain. You must miss the bowling pin going but hit it when the chain's swinging back.

The money wasn't great, but I was very happy, like I'd always been on the carnival. For living quarters I teamed up with a bunch of carnies to share a motel room with extra cots. We were cramped, but we had money for food, cigarettes, and clothes, all I needed. And partying money, of course. I always spent very loose on broads, even when I didn't have the bread.

After the swinger I got into cat-racking for the winter season, playing shopping centres around Florida. The show was planning to hit Cincinnati come spring, but I was planning to be in Bay St Louis, Mississippi, with another carnival that got some old gypsy friends of mine, and a game I wanted to run called the razzle. Before leaving Paul Miller I agreed to play one big springtime gig in Cincinnati, on a coloured lot in a coloured district. Three big shows were combining there. First night I caught six coloured hookers for $1,900 in the cat-rack. They weren't too pleased about losing, so they went to find some muscle. Sure enough, they come back with their pimps, four black dudes dressed like real dandies – big fedoras, patent shoes, the whole bit.

One a them, real menacing-like, said, 'This where our broads lost all their bread?'

'This is it,' I answered. 'Why? Somethin' wrong?'

'Won't be nothing wrong when we finish with you, man. We're gonna win back that money. Just show us how to play the game.'

So I showed them. 'Hit the cat gently on the nose, knock it off the rack.'

Twenty-one hundred lost dollars later, they quit. Yes, between the hookers and their pimps, they lost four thousand dollars in the cat-rack! A gambler is a gambler; money comes easy and goes easier.

'Hey, Whitey, you must have cheat us!'

'Listen guys,' I said to them, 'I'm a rounder and you're rounders also. I'm trying to whip you for your money and you're trying to whip me for mine. That's how it goes, you know that.'

They didn't like my lecture, I could tell.

'You bet your sweet ass it ain't going down like that, Whitey,' a guy with a blade threatened me.

'Ya ain't scarin' me with that shiv. I been in worse pinches than this. Either ya put that blade away or I yell "Hey rube" an' the whole carnival comes down on ya. A lot of our guys are bigger an' meaner than you. So choose.'

They took the lecture serious. Guess they'd tangled with roughies before.

After that gig I did go to Bay St Louis to join Midway Amusements. The year was 1972; I was thirty-seven. Lots of details from the next three-year period might fade one day, but I'll always remember the racism in Mississippi. You'd see signs in restaurants like 'If Any Nigger Eats Here, His Money Goes to the KKK.' White toilets, coloured toilets. Even on the fairgrounds owned by the city government, white showers and coloured showers. Just like South Africa. What do they call that system – apartheid? Like that – separate and not equal.

I ran into some jackpots with coloured carnies, situations we had to fight our way out of. White rowdies attacking and abusing guys just because they were black. Made me sick to see the way coloured people were treated throughout the south. One time in Virginia, on a city commons, the coloured showers were on the bum. So I told my black buddy to shower in the white stalls and I'd keep watch for the rednecks. Sure enough, a gang of them came snooping around just as he was coming out. They attacked us like we were dirt, screaming all kinds of foul stuff – 'Let's get the nigger and the nigger lover.' We had a mean beef, but we got out okay.

I don't know where some of those Americans are coming from, they're so full of prejudice for blacks. What makes them think they're so shit hot? I don't see no difference. We're all people; some are good, some are bad, and it isn't colour that makes the difference. But many Americans think they're the best there is in the world; they look down on everyone.

At least my gypsy friends weren't like that. Guess they were too much the victim of prejudice to feel hatred for others. They were good people and I was very comfortable being with them. I fitted right in; they accepted me. They gave me a job as a flat-store agent, or flattie, as we called them. A flattie's a guy that runs gambling joints. Mine was called the razzle, known by Canadian law as the razzle dazzle, a game by trickery or fraud, and you can't get away playing it in Canada. But in some southern states you could because you could buy the law, which you couldn't in Canada, at least not to the same extent.

One thing about flat stores – you could not play to pregnant women or their husbands. That was the rule: do not allow pregnant women or their men to play. There was a good reason for that rule. Ever seen how hot a man that lost several thousand dollars gambling can get? Ever see how hot his wife can get at him and at the guy that took it from him? We didn't need no overexcited women having miscarriages or giving birth on the lot! And we didn't need them drawing any heat to the game either. The show owners didn't want no trouble from the law, which suited me just fine because I couldn't afford no one inquiring into my background. Sooner or later someone was bound to figure out I was a fugitive. I decided to make it a little more difficult for anyone to discover I was a runaway hood from Canada; I changed my name to Tony Maples. Not only did I become known as Tony Maples; I bought such a convincing, forged birth certificate that I was able to get a legal driver's licence.

I introduced myself as Tony Maples to two of the people at Midway that were going to be my best friends and teachers, Deltas Mitchell and Frank Spina. Del, a beautiful-looking gypsy, tall and princely, very dignified, was the lot man, among other things. He'd go ahead of us into the next town we were playing to survey the fairgrounds. By the time all our trailers and trucks rolled in, he'd have the lot marked: rides here, flat stores there, food concessions over here, private trailers over there. Deltas was one a them all-round type a guys, could do most anything. He had to be very smart to qualify as prince of the gypsy tribe. Besides being the lot man he was a booking agent and an independent ride owner, plus he owned the candy-floss concession.

Del was real good friends with Frank Spina that managed Midway. Frank was one a them small but strong-built Italians with olive skin. He was in handsome shape for a man in his early fifties. A little balding, yes, but he still had thick hair, greying at the temples. You'd always remember him from the way he dressed. Dressed to colour, everything matched. If he was wearing brown pants, you knew he'd be wearing a brown shirt, a two-tone brown sweater, and brown shoes to boot. If he had on a blue shirt, there'd be blue shoes. That was Frank. And you'd never dare say anything against his dogs. He and his wife had no children, so they treated their dogs like they were children. Even ate at the table with them.

Frank was the best patch there is. The legal adjuster, you might call him. A fixer. The guy that fixes the fuzz. Some of the American carnivals had crooked games, games more of chance than skill. Somebody had to fix the fuzz so those games could go into each town. There's no way you can play a town without the law on your side – and on your payroll. Frank saw real early what a smooth talker, hard worker, and ambitious guy I was. He saw my potential as a patch, so he appointed himself my teacher.

'Yes, I had a lot of confidence in Tony, so I took him under my wing to see what his potentials were. I had a big job, something like the mayor of a small town, and I needed an assistant to help do the bookings, get the sponsors, move the show, route the show, arbitrate grievances among the carnies, bail the odd carnie out of jail — everything.

'Tony had good potential, no question about it. He was naturally a smooth talker and he was good at reading people. I taught him to listen more and talk less, which is the best way to figure people out. Just let them do all the talking.

'And I taught him not to be too greedy. Carnivals are profitable, but you can't take it all. You just beat a guy for sixty bucks? Give him back ten in merchandise. Let him walk around with a few prizes; they only cost three or four bucks apiece. You still have fifty. "That's enough, Tony, don't forget that," I'd tell him.

'He learned. Fast. He quickly became my right arm. Soon I didn't worry whether the concessions were torn down and loaded up in the truck, then moved to the next spot and set up on time. He was good, no doubt of that. He never got in any serious trouble, though he was hot-headed and he had a nasty habit of indulging in a pill too many from time to time. I didn't allow junkies or drunks on the show. Tony was no addict and no boozer, but he was a little unpredictable. I guess the hot-headedness or the pills would get to him and he'd pick a fight with the nearest person. I admit there were times when I was tempted to kick him off the show, but finally I accepted his weaknesses because he was more good than bad, and he did more good than bad. Tony Maples was a terrific help to me.

'When he had the routine skills under his belt, I started to take him with me when I'd visit the townspeople — the mayor, the DA, the sheriff, or the police. After coming along a few times as a silent partner, I'd play the silent partner while he did all the talking. It wasn't long before I'd say "You go, Tony. Check downtown for me."'

What exactly did 'check downtown' mean?

This was how it worked. We'd move on to a new lot in a new town, planning to play there for a week. Before set-up, or during set-up if we knew the fuzz and knew we could buy them, I'd go downtown to pay the sheriff a friendly visit. I'd wear my spiffiest clothes. Let's say it was one a them iffy towns, maybe a new spot where we weren't sure about the sheriff, and I went visiting before the carnival was set up. The conversation would go roughly like this:

'Mornin', sir. Nice town ya got here. I'm Tony Maples from Midway Amusements. My show's at your lot waitin' for permission ta set up.' Usually, the guy would be experienced in pay-offs and could smell one coming, so he'd be very pleasant.

'Well, Mr Maples, we're always glad to add a little excitement to our quiet lives here. But I'll have to ask you what kind of games you have. You know the law doesn't allow any gaff games, and it's my job to uphold the law.'

'We certainly don't want to break no laws, but the people expects a certain amount of excitement from the carnival, kind of change the daily routine.' I'd know from his answer if we could buy him.

'That's true enough. But, Mr Maples, I expect that most of your games are games of skill.'

'Of course they are, sir.'

'Now, if you have just a few games with some element of chance, I suppose we can live with that.'

'I appreciate your attitude, sir. Perhaps through you we could make a donation to your favourite charity? You know, with proceeds from our more magic games.'

'As a matter of fact, we have a junior sheriff's league here.'

'Good. I wonder if that junior sheriff's league would agree ta be our sponsor also. We'd pay the usual fee: 15 per cent from our rides an' concessions. The donation, of course, would be higher, an' on top of the sponsor fees. Could you arrange it?'

See, you had to have a sponsor in every town you played. Usually one of the service or business clubs, like Lions or Rotary, did it. They'd get your licence and you'd pay them 15 per cent of your take on the legal rides and concessions. That part was legit. Then, on top of that, you'd pay off the fuzz for the gaff games. When we went into a new town, however, where we didn't know the scene, maybe we'd give the fuzz sponsor fees plus the graft.

You knew the sheriff was going to answer, 'Sure, I think I can arrange it.'

Just to make sure I'd won him, I'd add, 'While you're at it, maybe ya could arrange for two off-duty officers ta work the lot for fifty dollars a night.' That way, if we got an angry customer, the law would be on our side.

We'd shake hands, exchange knowing grins, and go to work. Last day of the fair, sure as shooting, that sheriff would show up to collect. Cash, all cash, and always cash. In an average spot, just for the gaff games, he'd take two to three thousand dollars. In a hot spot, maybe five to six grand. I must say, you could never get away with this in Canada; carnivals have to be all legal and above-board. But in some parts of the States graft is a routine part of carnival life. That's why the patch is the most important man on the show.

Del's the one that taught me how to be a good patch, how to talk to anyone high or low and make them feel comfortable. He taught me to listen. I sure didn't imagine then that I'd be using his lessons to run the HELP Program, but truth is, that's where I learned to talk to employers.

I loved being a patch. Mid-season – the main season ran April to late October or early November – I was happy as could be patching and managing the razzle. Life was going to get even better. One day while I was changing money at my concession I noticed this young girl strolling up the midway. Bare feet. Wearing one of them long, gauzy, Indian dresses. She looked like a hippie or a bohemian. She also looked about five months gone. I felt attracted to her; her being so obviously pregnant didn't discourage me one bit. People change husbands and wives all the time.

'Hey, beautiful, where ya goin?'

I could tell from her smile that she was going in my direction. She hung around the show and we got to know each other. I got to know that she wasn't married and wasn't attached to no one. She was one a them black sheep. Came from a rich, prominent family that didn't think she was proper enough for them. Her whole family was down on her and she was just kind of drifting. I aimed to fix that. Next day, I bought her a pair of shoes and put her up in my motel room. At that time I was living in motels. Even though Pat Hiltie – that was her name – was only eighteen to my thirty-seven, we seemed a good match and started out real happy together. I taught her to work the razzle in order to free me for other things. Things like more assistant-manager training and inventing and running another gaff game – the four ball. It was even crookeder than the razzle.

Frank Spina told you I was a little hot-headed. It's true, I confess.

'You bet it's true,' Frank laughs. 'Like one night in Louisiana when Tony and two gypsy friends asked me if it was all right to throw a birthday bash for one of the carnies. "Okay," I said, "but keep the noise down." I had one drink with them, then went to bed. At five a.m. I was awakened by shooting. "My God, who are they shooting?" I ran outside to see these nuts right out of a cowboy picture: one ducking behind the hood of a car, another peeking out from the end of a trailer. Shooting in the air, like it's a western. Bang! Bang! Bang! They seemed to be firing shots in the direction of a converted school bus where a carnival couple lived. First I hear all kinds of screams coming from the bus, then silence. "My God, they must have shot the woman," I thought. With brute force and help, I managed to get the guns away from the drunken idiots and to get them locked in their trailers. I was terrified of what I'd find in that bus. I knocked timidly at the door. No answer. I could only imagine the worst. Finally, the woman came to the door. She was more terrified than I was. Although she was wounded, she was just grazed, nothing serious.

'I had a serious problem on my hands. How was I going to handle this? I knew that all the parties couldn't stay together on the show. So I made a hard choice. I kept the people who were most valuable to me. I ordered the woman in the converted bus off the show, and I covered for Tony and friends when the police arrived next morning.

'"I hear there was some shooting here last night, Mr. Spina," the police chief says to me.

'"Shooting? What shooting?"

'"Don't play deaf and dumb with me."

'"Chief, you've got it all wrong. No shooting, just fireworks. That's what the person who called you must have mistook for shooting. We had a big birthday bash last night. It was a pretty rowdy party, but there were no guns."

'He probably didn't believe me, but he had no evidence, so he left the lot. I warned Tony very sternly. When I was finished, he knew he'd be finished with me if he ever pulled a stunt like that again. So he didn't. At least, that season he didn't.'

Since I'm non-violent, you might wonder why I had a gun,

especially since I never used a gun when committing crimes in Canada and almost never owned one. The States isn't like Canada; American people are much more violent. Seems like every second man got a gun, and when you're in the business of stealing their money like I was doing in the flat stores, you needed protection. They want to gamble but they don't want to lose, especially not two and three thousand dollars, like many of them did lose. On a losing streak, them Georgia crackers and southern rednecks were lunatics. One guy in Tennessee shot at me from a water tower; another guy in West Virginia also tried to shoot me. It didn't take me long in the States to realize I had to pack a small piece. My first season with Midway Amusements, though, was pretty tame. I think I only used a gun in the party Frank told you about. Otherwise, it was a real smooth stretch.

I was enjoying a little family fantasy with Pat, imagining that I'd have a normal family life like I always hungered for. I saw the strong family ties the gypsies had, and I remembered the weak family ties in my own background. I wanted to make up for time lost. The possibility of doing so seemed real strong when, on the last day of the season, Pat gave birth to Dawn Marie Maples, the kid she was carrying when we met. Perfect timing. I was prepared for a domestic winter, even bought a nineteen-foot Corsair trailer, all equipped. For the winter, the three of us moved out of the motel and into the trailer we parked on a jinxed gypsy lot in Covington, Louisiana.

Gypsies believe that if something bad happens on a lot – whether the fairgrounds or the winter trailer lot – that place is jinxed, and they won't play on it or live on it again. But since I wasn't superstitious, we lived on this lot, supposedly jinxed because a gypsy queen had been murdered there. Not only did she get done in; she also got made for untold amounts of cash. The gypsies estimated that the murderer-robber netted serious money, as much as a million dollars. The murder and robbery of that gypsy queen is a famous Louisiana crime story.

So here we were on this hexed lot playing house. For a while Pat was happy billing and cooing, but I was restless for action and money. Frank Moore, the patch for Harlam Amusements, showed up just in time to rescue me from cabin fever. Together we worked the bayous, little communities of Cajun people in the swamps of

Louisiana. When I say small settlements, I mean small. Hundreds of little villages with one church, one store, a few houses. You'd drive into them on levees, roads built up like causeways to survive the frequent floods. When we'd arrive with a miniature carnival – maybe a kiddie ferris wheel and a concession – the Cajuns would come out of nowhere to gamble.

Cajun trappers were mighty tough men. Frank was experienced in dealing with them; he knew how to buy their alligator and muskrat skins and how to rook them with the razzle. We'd tour these different bayous a day or a few days at a time. Sometimes Frank would go in alone with a punchboard and sell it for ten or twenty dollars to the store owner. An hour later I'd go in and play the punchboard as a customer, spend maybe five or six dollars trying to win. Because I knew where the winning numbers were, I could win when I wanted. First Frank Moore would take the store owner by selling him the punchboard; then I'd rob him, crooked gambling at this game he bought to make money. But the Cajuns always knew when they were being taken, and they didn't hesitate to express their anger. More than once we caught a bit of buckshot in the back of our trailer while making a quick exit from a bayou. One time, our rear end was so holey from buckshot that pigeons roosted in the pockmarks!

Meanwhile, my family fantasy fell apart. Pat and me were fighting. One time we had a big fight over my little black poodle. Pat didn't like that dog and tried to keep it outside – which I wouldn't permit. After that dog fight she said she wanted to visit her family. So I gave her my car and she drove home to Woodstock, Illinois. Would she be back? I had no idea. Del lent me $150 to buy a 1955 Olds so I wouldn't be without a car.

Deltas remembers the loan. He also remembers what Tony was like around women.

'Tony was a macho man, but he was gentle as a lamb too. He had a big weakness for girls; they could do anything with him. When Pat up and left him, big-hearted Tony broke himself. He gave her everything: the car, the trailer, all the money he had.'

Deltas leans back, turns the past over in his mind. 'Yes,' *he goes on,* 'Tony was a big-hearted man, always quick to defend carnival people from anyone *who might harm us. I remember one time in Mississippi when a young guy raped a twelve-year-old girl. A lot of things that happen in towns you play — like theft or rape — the first ones the townspeople will blame are the carnies, because people don't think of us as human beings. Anyhow, a bunch of men from town came to the cook shack where we were all sitting. One of them had a gun in his hand; he started pointing it at one of our young fellas and telling the others that he was the fella that did it.*

'*Tony jumped right in. He said to the girl with him, "Go to my camper and get my piece." Then he stopped those townspeople from accusing us, scared them away by waving his gun and sounding off in his big voice. It helped, of course, that he looked like a real bully type, a bearded big-gut man, probably 250 pounds. But truth was, he was just a marshmallow; you only had to see him around girls to know what a soft touch he was.*'

Come spring I went to San Antonio, Texas, to work for Booby Overthall. He was ninety years old at the time, still going strong but not strong enough to manage and patch for all his small carnivals touring the Texas shopping centres. I took care of one of his units, consisting of a baby ferris wheel, two kiddie rides, and two concessions. Working for Booby was just a little sideline for me; my main interest was Midway. Frank Spina called me to come back to Louisiana for the late spring action.

I went back as assistant manager — officially. I was pulling a third of the action on Frank's dozen or so concessions. But don't ever imagine I didn't work for the money. It was demanding work. Didn't matter if it was freezing cold or soaking wet, them concessions had to be torn down in one town after an eleven p.m. closing, loaded up in trucks, moved hundreds of miles overnight, and unloaded and set up by opening time in another town for eight a.m. When we were finally set up, we had to work a whole day before a night's sleep. Sure, that opening day we'd spell each other off for catnaps, but that's not enough for people that have worked so hard.

You can understand why I'd need the odd pill to pick me up or calm me down. Dexadrine to speed, tuinals to slow. The gypsies never liked my pill-popping; Del would often speak to me about it. 'Listen, Bro,' he'd say, 'we need you on the show, but you have to pull up. We don't mind a little booze, but pills are scary. We don't want our kids getting into them. I'm not saying you'd give them any, but the pushers you buy from, they're another breed.' His pressuring got to me; finally, I gave him my word I'd quit pills. I wasn't hooked, so it wasn't hard.

Don't know how I'd done it, but I had survived prisons that make many men into drunks or junkies or both. I'd survived without succumbing to either. The odd drink, the odd pill – that was all that ever tempted me. I didn't need artificial stimulation. I was always on an adrenalin high from the excitement of scoring or scheming some new scam.

Even with all my responsibility at Midway, I still needed more action to pump my adrenalin to the level I enjoyed. So I developed some sidelines. Like my magnetic-sign phase in Clinton, Illinois. Across from the fairgrounds I noticed a shop selling magnetic signs; they're made by applying heat to plastic. When the show was quiet, I'd sneak across to the shop and get friendly with the owner. Before long I had conned a sign-making machine from him – and a truck to haul the thing! I offered him 50 per cent of the business I could grab from carnies and locals. First sign I made was for John the Gypsy and his wife Rose. They were characters. John was just a little guy; Rose was twice his size. They ran a hot dog and chips stand which always had the song *Gypsy Rose* blaring.

With humour and warmth, John recalls Tony Maples. 'He was always figuring out how to make a buck – legitimate, mostly. He was an inventive guy with a good sense of humour. Even though he was after the buck, he was very generous. I told Tony my idea to sell hot dogs on sticks, and he coined the name "corn dogs." Then he went off and made me a sign that read "Corn dogs – so neat, so nice to eat," and he gave it to me, never charged me a cent. Always helping out, that was Tony Maples.'

I was best at helping myself out, sometimes at the expense of others. Couldn't help it, always the flimflam man; it was my nature. The same guy I conned for the magnetic signs I flimflammed for two concessions, got him to buy them on a shared-profit basis. Then I took those concessions on the road for a bunch of side-trips to play one-week stints at hot spots. I always wanted to be where the best action was, where the best money was. You played a lot of spots – maybe thirty – in a season, but only five or six were real money-makers. I'd take a week off here, a week off there, run back to those spots to join another carnival.

Frank and Del accepted my high jinks as long as I told them when I was leaving and when I'd be back. They accepted my coming and going because I was valuable to them; I worked hard, and I was practically family. They understood that I was a fast learner, a fast mover, and a fast liver. They accepted me like I was. It felt good being accepted and appreciated; I felt like I had a home base.

It wasn't a proper home, of course, because I had no family. I was still fantasizing about having a wife and a son. Yeah, I know, I'm a chauvinist; I wanted a son. To my surprise, Pat come back that season in 1973 – without her baby. She didn't explain much, just told me she had adopted the child out. I thought I'd have my chance then to create a family with her. Before long she was pregnant.

I was deep into my family fantasy again when an incident brought me crashing to reality. Some outside gypsy tribe was giving Del's tribe a real hard time. I didn't know what they were feuding about, but it was nasty. One day one of these outsiders pulled a gun. I ran to my trailer, grabbed my gun and came out shooting – into the ground. I frightened the guy off but drew the heat. Frank and Del talked the cops out of pressing charges, but the fuzz said I had to leave town till the episode blew over. We were in Louisiana then. I owned two cars, a house trailer, and a converted boat trailer I used to haul my concessions. Pat and me each drove a car, dragged a trailer, and headed 1,400 miles away to Appleton, Minnesota, to join Frank Moore at Harlam Amusements. I could count on Frank to give me a temporary hole to play till I could go home to Midway.

I was a rich man. I was pulling down bread in the neighbourhood of seventy thousand dollars – tax-free cash – a year. I had friends and maybe the best family I'd ever have. I thought things couldn't get better till Pat had a son – my third Michael Anthony – and made my dream of fatherhood come true at a time when I imagined I could play the part. Things were just perfect. For a couple of months, that is. Then Pat got that old suspicious urge to visit her family. Again she took off, me not knowing what to expect. Being a fugitive and not being married to the woman, I wasn't exactly in a position of authority.

Without Pat and the baby there was no point sticking around

Minnesota for the rest of the off-season. I went back to Texas, the favourite winter spot for carnies. In Houston I teamed up with a guy by the name of Pineapple. He was Hawaiian. We shared a cheap but comfortable motel room while we hired on at small carnivals in local shopping centres. It was a wild winter for girls. I teamed up with two, both daughters of concessionaires. It was a winter when I kept the old ball rolling in more ways than one.

Gigi was my first concessionaire's daughter. In her early twenties, short, blonde, and with a great build – 36-28-36, I'd say – she was a very tough lady. She had to be; she was the head roughie for her father. He just lazed around while she did all the hard work tearing down and putting up joints, as well as putting in all the stock. She worked like a man, drank like a man, fought like a man. We didn't know each other more than eighteen hours before we were in the sack together; soon after, we were bunking in together. For a while we had fun; in a couple of weeks she was gone, on to the next lot her father was playing.

Don't get the idea that all carnival people played fast and loose. Some did, some didn't. Just like people in regular society, some got high morals, some got loose morals. Some would be shacking up – like me – and some would be going to church or synagogue. That's right, the big shows like Royal American had clergymen travelling with them, including a rabbi for the Jewish carnies. As you'd guess, I wasn't spending my time in church. I was spending as much as possible of it in the sack.

Gigi had no ambitions to marry me or to marry anyone. She was very independent, just wanted to live fast and furious and told me she wanted to have a kid. I gave her one. I found that out three months later when she returned to my lot pregnant.

'Tony,' she said matter-of-factly, 'I'm pregnant. It's yours. If it's a boy, I guess you want me to name him Michael Anthony, after you, right?' I told her she was right.

Gigi moved back into my trailer and for the next few weeks we had more fun. Then she went on the road again with her father. Now, there was another concessionaire's daughter and another kid in that same period. While Gigi was on the road first time, another concessionaire from another gypsy tribe joined the show. He ran hanky-panks, fifty-cent and one-dollar games where marks can't lose much money because there's no tricker involved – you can't double up or catch up. In a hanky-pank, you bust balloons or pitch to win. Believe it or not, the concessionaire's daughter was named Rosebud.

Rosebud was also in her early twenties, with jet-black hair that went down past her bum. Inside of one day she and I were in action. The action lasted one lusty week, till she moved on to another show. Before she left, I'd already educated her to my Michael Anthony thing. Same thing happened with her as with Gigi. She came back soon after, pregnant with my kid. I lived with her for another fast week; then we parted.

I later found out that both these women had boys and both named them – you guessed it – Michael Anthony – my fourth and fifth Michael Anthony. How did I know? Because they sent messages with other carnies they knew would meet up with me on the circuit. 'You Tony Maples?' a guy asked me. 'Gigi sends her love, said to tell you she had a boy and she named him Michael Anthony.'

I never worried about those kids, and their mothers never tried to touch me for support of any kind. They were independent types, big girls that knew what they were getting into, girls that expected to raise kids on their own. By the time carnival kids are four and five years old, they're ball boys; by the time they're twelve, they're capable of running joints on their own. It's a life that produces very independent people. Walk around any midway and you'll see young girls running the joints. Many of them got boyfriends twice their age. And many of the older women take young lovers half their age.

I was glad when spring came and I could go back home, to Midway in Louisiana. The show always travelled, playing a week here, a week there in all the southern states, but Louisiana was base camp; I came to regard it as my home. Pat Hiltie knew it was my home too. She knew she could always find me there come spring. This time when she came back, I wouldn't have her. I wouldn't have her partly because she done the same thing with Michael Anthony she done with her first baby. Adopted him out. 'Why, for godsakes why?' I asked her. 'Because I couldn't take care of a child.' That was all the explanation I ever got out of her. I don't know if she knew why. If only she had told me she was going to give our son up, the gypsies would gladly have adopted him and cared real good for him. There was nothing I could do except refuse to take her back. Besides, I had another girlfriend by then, back into easy come, easy go with women.

I was also into a lifestyle I liked. I might not have been Clark Gable, but I dressed the role. I loved expensive clothes and women with expensive tastes. I loved gambling every night and buying whatever I wanted, whenever I wanted to spend. My lifestyle then was averaging a hundred dollars a day; that was high living in 1974. People in the States and Canada were getting scared of the world-wide recession that had just started, but it sure wasn't affecting my lifestyle.

By then, my third year with Midway, I had a reputation as a perfect patch. I could have stayed doing the same thing with Frank and Del, but I got lured back to Dallas by a high-line show ten times the size of Midway. This first-rate outfit picked me up because my specialty was being a quiet fixer – no grief between me and the fuzz I fixed. I had a knack for keeping everyone happy. After a week patching for that show, one of the big bosses approached me.

'Tony, this is for you.' He handed me a white cap, symbol of being a boss. 'You earned it already. One week's work and you already deserve to be one of us, to trade in your blue cap.' Blue was the symbol of being an ordinary worker on the show.

'No, thank you. I want ta wear the blue cap.' I walked away. I didn't have to prove to no one that I was a boss. It's your actions that prove who you are, not your uniform. I knew who I was. Or at least I was getting clearer about who I was. I was feeling less and less like being a fugitive, like being a crook. On impulse I called Cornwall. My cousin and friend Hector Brodeur told me that my wife, Teresa, was having a hard time raising my son, my second Michael Anthony, alone. Not that I'd had anything to do with Teresa or our son in the years since I'd left them. No contact whatsoever. But I still had this stubborn urge for having a family, for pulling it all together somehow. Hector's words pulled on my heart-strings and tugged at my guilt.

In one moment it came to me that I should go back to Canada, turn myself in. It just came to me, like that. No long think, no drawn-out process. Just like that. An impulse. Go home. Pay my dues. Get straight. Get my family together. Get my life together.

I barely bothered to say goodbye. Instead, I threw my gear in my car, hitched up my trailer, and started driving. To Cincinnati, Ohio. Drove two days on uppers without stopping. Pulled into the parking lot at the bus station, parked my 1973 Ford Galaxy, for which I still owed $2,800 to an angry friend, parked my completely paid-for, completely equipped, brand-new twenty-eight-foot Brougham trailer worth $7,000. Left the whole works – including clothes and razzle boards – on the lot, keys in the ignition. I hopped the next bus to Messina, New York, across the border from Cornwall. I called a friend to pick me up there. Just before we crossed through customs I threw my Tony Maples driver's licence into the woods and said goodbye to my false identity. We sailed across that check-point, no questions asked.

Once on the Canadian side, I said to my friend, 'Drive straight ta the parole office in Kingston. I'm gonna turn myself in.'

Freedom Is a Score: Deciding To Go Straight

11

Why was Tony McGilvary / Maples, incorrigible con, frequent fugitive, and all-round bad boy, suddenly compelled to turn himself in to the law? A number of threads were slowly tugging in the direction of a turnaround. Deltas Mitchell, Tony's carnival pal and partial mentor, feels that Tony's being part of gypsy family life for three years may partly have accounted for his rush to 'get right.'

'After we got to know each other, Tony told me he was a thief and a fugitive from Canada. Many times, in a roundabout way, he hinted that he was thinking about turning himself in. I didn't take this business about him being a crook too seriously because he was a straight man while he was with us. But I did feel that he wanted to make things right in his life.

'His feeling for making things right might have grown from being part of our tight-knit family. Tony saw that the only thing separating me and his other pal, patch Frank Spina, was the bed; otherwise, we were together all the time. Besides the close bond between us, he saw the same tightness in our family life and the life of our community.

'Many times he'd say to me, "I never met people like you before. You're real, you're good people. You do everything together, like a unit." And I know he felt like part of that unit. One of the times he was telling me how good he thought we were and how good it made him feel to be around us was one of the times he told me he wanted to turn himself in. So I guess feeling part of a family that loved him like he was may have triggered him thinking that he didn't want to be a bad guy anymore.'

Deltas got something there with how he explained my decision to go back and turn myself in. At the time it seemed to me that I was just making a spur decision. A minute after I hung up the phone from talking to my cousin in Cornwall and learning that Teresa was having such a struggle raising my boy, I decided. A spur decision, like all the major decisions I've made in my life. It just comes on me like that. I decide to make a move, there's no stopping me – I do it and that's that.

But looking back, I guess there were some things troubling me. Mostly they had to do with my troubles with women. I wanted a family so bad, yet I could just never seem to get it together. We were always getting together and breaking up. Those break-ups with Pat Hiltie really hurt me. I was tired of losing out on having a family, and I got this idea that I could make it up with Teresa and with the boy.

I dunno. Maybe things were too good for me in the States; maybe I had to shake them up. I always seemed to like tension and aggravation. Certainly, it made more sense for me to stay a fugitive. I was squeaky clean in the States. I'd even pay speeding tickets when they were due, to avoid having a record. I was a free man, really. Maybe I could have continued having the good life. But something was dragging me home.

So I just turned myself in. It was that simple. Actually, it was a little complicated because I couldn't find the parole office! The damn thing had moved. When I showed up at the old address in Kingston, I found a new regional corrections office instead of the parole office. I wanted to turn myself in to my old parole officer, Lou Hunt, because he'd cared about me.

I saw a guard delivering mail. 'Excuse me. Do you happen ta know where the parole office is? It used ta be here.'

'Yeah, I know it; in fact, I'm going there now to deliver the mail. Want a lift?'

So I drove to the new address with a guard. We just made small talk. Good thing he didn't ask me what I wanted with the parole office. I would have told him and shocked his pants off. I saw Lou Hunt right off when I entered the office. He looked exactly like I always think of him – the English tweed jacket and the same old pipe hanging out of his mouth, the professor look. I just stared. At first he didn't recognize me. Then he twigged to who I was.

'What do you know? Tony McGilvary ...' Then, a little amazed, he said, 'But we thought you were dead? We heard you had died!'

'Not dead. Very much alive. I'm here ta turn myself in.'

It was 1975. I was about to do my last three years in a penitentiary, though I figured it would be longer, probably five years. I figured I'd lose my good time, plus face the new time for breaking parole – what cons call a double-jeopardy sentence.

'I think that deserves a chat and a coffee,' Lou added, still shocked. 'Let's go to the café across the street, but first let me call the RCMP to come by for you.'

'Go right ahead.'

We drank coffee and caught up before the Mounties came to cart me away in cuffs. Lou protested. 'You don't need to cuff the man; he's turning himself in.' But they wouldn't listen. Cuffs were the rule, and you've never seen anyone like RCMP officers for following rules. Before long, I was back in my old haunt, the Kingston Pen, reception centre for inmates en route to Joyceville. Once back in Joyceville I easily got back into the familiar prison routine. It was like nothing had changed, and I even began to forget why I had come back. I just picked up where I left off in my prison life, so much so that I even went back to work in the kitchen.

Ken Waters, an easy-going man with a warm laugh, has worked in the Joyceville kitchen as a supervisor since 1959. He remembers Tony.

'I remember him all right because he was in and out and he'd always get himself a job with visibility. Tony was not an inmate to wash pots quietly in a corner. He liked to be in the forefront, including the forefront of contraband activities. I always kept an eye on him because you could be sure he'd be trying to steal something from the kitchen. You could also be sure he'd be manipulating other inmates to do much of his work while making it seem he was doing it himself. Still, he was a likeable guy, popular, circulated a lot. He always got along well with institutional staff. He knew it was to his advantage to have staff on his side.

'Not that he liked to do things the way we asked him to. Tony always liked doing things his way. His way was the only right way. I remember one time when thirty or forty cases of eggs – there's fifteen dozen to a case – were delivered. I told Tony how to handle the transfer from the delivery carts to the walk-in fridge.

'"Tony, that's too many eggs to wheel right into the fridge. Better unload the carts outside the fridge door and carry the cases in. If not, they'll spill."
'"I can wheel them in, no problem."
'"Tony, don't. I don't think it will work."
'He wouldn't listen. He gave the cart one push, and six cases crashed to the floor of the fridge. Hundreds of eggs breaking and quickly congealing from the cold. Tony was none too pleased about having to clean up that mess.'

Murray Jack is another staff veteran at Joyceville who remembers Tony. As hobby crafts officer he was the one to haggle with Tony over craft purchases and activities central to Tony's life inside.

'There was a period there when Tony was into plaster casting – matadors, bullfighters, you name it. But I had to cut him off plaster supplies because his cell was a sty. Tony is not exactly your tidiest person to begin with, with his shaggy beard and his pants always hanging down around his hips. I'm sure if you put him in a five-hundred-dollar suit, he'd still look the slob. Well, you should have seen what he and his cell looked like with plaster dust and statues all over the place! He was covered and the cell was littered. There was barely standing room. Unfortunately, it didn't get much better when he switched to leathercraft.'

I was too busy with hobby-craft to think too much about straightening out. But I did think about having a family life; that was always nagging somewhere in my mind. About a year after I turned myself in, when I started to make passes, I met a woman. By then I knew there was no future for Teresa and me. She visited me once at Joyceville, but only to talk about the divorce she wanted. It was obviously too late to make up. I agreed to the divorce; it would come through before I'd make parole again. My mind was already in another relationship anyway.

During a three-day pass to a friend's place in Kingston I'd met Julie. She was a divorced woman close to my age, and she had two kids. At the time she was on mother's allowance. We hit it off right away, and she started visiting me inside. We were a big help to each other. I'd gotten very deep into leathercraft. Fifteen to twenty purses a week plus fifty wallets a week was my average production. Julie would visit me twice a week to collect all the goods I was making. She'd sell the leather at local shops and fairs as well as private sales. We'd turn the money into supplies for more leather goods and into buying things for the life I expected to have with her when I'd get out. Earnings from the leather even went into a three-thousand-dollar deposit on a house Julie found for us. My handiwork also bought her a car.

She was a very possessive woman – I could sense that. I was hers and she didn't want nobody to fool with me. I never liked feeling tight strings on me, yet I felt her eyes always on me when I'd be on a weekend pass. But as long as I was most of the time inside prison and she was outside, and as long as she was visiting me and hawking my leathercrafts, she was a good thing for me. Her love and attention were a big support to me them last years inside.

But it wasn't enough to keep me on the straight and narrow. Guess I wasn't quite ready to give up the bandit life. Breaking the law was a reflex in me. It wasn't something I thought about doing or not doing; it was something I simply did. Give me an opportunity – when I was away from the carnivals – and I wouldn't know how not to break the law. An opportunity came. I was on a three-day pass late in 1975 when I got it into my head to rob a Becker's. Maybe it was just nostalgia for a way a life I hadn't practised for a while, or maybe I was just checking that I still had the touch. Whatever, I knew I had to do it. In the dark of night I lock-picked my way into a laundromat attached to a Becker's. Then I sledge-hammered the common cement wall to get into the store. The cops caught me dead bang. I had a case of cigarettes in my arms when the harness bulls – beat cops in uniform – put a 38 revolver to my head.

Guess I was feeling particularly stubborn that night because I decided not to tell them my name. They didn't know me; the guys on the beat don't know all the cons in the can. Because I refused to give my name, they sent me to Quinte Detention Centre in Napanee near Kingston as a John Doe. To refresh my memory they threw me in the cooler for a couple of days. Little did they suspect holes were home to me and wouldn't break my determination. Finally, they transferred me into the main corridor at Quinte, still as John Doe. One day the classification officer called me to his office. He was laughing. 'Hello, McGilvary.' I was sent to Joyceville.

The caper hadn't been as much fun as previous escapades. Maybe I was getting too old. Maybe the excitement was gone forever. All I know was that it didn't do nothing for my adrenalin. The high was gone. It seemed even less of a thrill when Judge Baker sentenced me to two more years for breaking my pass and busting Becker's.

It was no thrill at all labouring down the Joyceville corridor in leg irons and hand irons. Like I was a dangerous criminal. They were taking me to the cooler, which is routine punishment for guys coming off a broken pass. All chained up like that – that's when I first spotted Sister Marguerite Somers, the chaplain's assistant. Or I guess that's when that bothersome little broad first spotted me. I knew all about her from other institutions I'd been in. One of them busybodies with a reputation for insisting on doing good. When that little lady got a bee in her bonnet, there was no way of turning her off till she got what she wanted. I'd heard that about her, but I'd never had personal experience to confirm it. After all, she was the church and I was death on the church.

I was trying to keep my eyes from meeting hers, but I couldn't help catching a glance of her staring real sad at me. 'Tony, I'd like us to talk.' To get rid of her, I said, 'Sure Sister, we'll talk sometime.' At that moment I was glad to be going to the hole where that holy lady couldn't get to me. Except I never made it to the hole. Out of nowhere came the assistant warden, who ordered the guard to take me to my cell. Why, I didn't know; Sister might have some clues.

After that Sister Marguerite started sending me notes and messages with some of the guys and some of the guards. I ignored her requests to meet. One day she showed up in my cell. Them days, women, including nuns, were not allowed on the ranges.

'Sister, you could get in trouble for coming here.'

'All right. If you don't want me to get in trouble, come talk to me.'

'Okay, okay, I'll come.' I figured if she had enough moxie to visit the range, I had enough guts to talk to the church. Not too much happened in that first chat. She pushed a little but not too hard, asked me a bunch of questions. I withdrew a lot, gave her a bunch of evasions.

'How about coming back next week, Tony?'

'Okay.'

Come next week, I didn't go back. At the appointed hour for our meeting she came back to my cell. So back I trotted to her office.

That's when she hit me with the line that made me turn myself around.

'Aren't you tired of hurting yourself, Tony?'

Yeah, I was tired, real tired.

Sister Marguerite, known to many inmates as Sister Sunshine because of her bubbly personality and sparkling blue eyes, recognized the responsive chord she struck in Tony with that simple question, 'Aren't you tired of hurting yourself?'

'For him, that was the moment he turned it around. For me, that was the day we talked, and that's what enabled him to turn it around. I'll never forget the expression on his face. It reminded me of the quote from Isaiah, "He was a man acquainted with sorrow." I'll never forget Tony's sorrowfulness that day.

'That day, he told me his life story, and I'm sure he shared with me a Tony he'd never before talked about with anyone. Much of the discussion focused on his mother. The message that he was responsible for her being institutionalized was too much for a six-year-old child to handle. He grew up feeling guilty for his mother's incarceration, and he grew up feeling he never belonged anywhere. It was so obvious that his anxieties about his mother were central to his experience of life. I felt it would be important for him to learn more about why she had been in a mental hospital, so I decided to track down information.

'I was able to get a report from the Brockville Psychiatric Hospital records department. The most significant thing in it for Tony was a statement that his mother knew she had a loving husband and a healthy son. That was the only reference to him in the report. Yet it was enough for a wave of relief to wash over Tony, as if his mother in some way came back to visit him. The prison psychologist urged me to share only selected details of the report with Tony because the report alleged a long history of mental retardation in his mother's family. The psychologist worried that Tony might wonder about his own mental powers. I, on the other hand, felt Tony had a right to read the whole thing, so I gave him the report. All that seemed to matter to him was that one statement where his mother acknowledged his existence.

'Tony revealed himself to me that day as a man riddled with sorrow, as a deeply sensitive man who had been deeply wounded and as a man who cared deeply for others, even if he hadn't as yet found a vehicle for expressing his caring. I remember the way he talked about his son, the boy he'd had with

Teresa. Tony didn't deny that he was an absentee father, yet he shared with me the special love he carried for Michael Anthony. That's why it doesn't surprise me that he made a spur-of-the-moment decision to turn himself in when he heard that Teresa was having difficulty raising the child alone. Even if he never acted on it, his conscience would bother him a lot at that moment. Tony, as I would learn more and more later and as the HELP program would prove, resonates to the distress of others.

'He resonates to distress in others,' Sister repeats slowly, emphasizing each word as if she has just struck on the essence of Tony McGilvary, 'resonates even if he can't do anything about it. His sadness is not only for himself; it's also for others.

'Over the months of getting to know him in prison, I kept seeing that special quality. I recall his reaction to a paraplegic man Tony talked with at one of our Awareness Days in Joyceville. The man recounted his story to Tony – his motorcycle accident, his anger, his struggle to progress, his feeling of being imprisoned by his body. The bonding that took place between him and Tony was almost visible. I kept seeing him react over and over again to the pain of others. Once Tony started to open up, it was like he finally found the freedom to be who he is. It's the depth of his own suffering that enabled him to relate so profoundly to the suffering of others – and for me it's the key to his success with HELP.'

Tony credits Sister Marguerite with responsibility for his turnaround decision. Others agree that Sister Marguerite was the right person saying the right thing at the right time to a man who was making a decision to right himself.

I made that decision after her famous line, 'Aren't you tired of hurting yourself?' That line kept going around in my head. I'd sit in my cell and pound leather, turning out purse after purse. Still her words would echo in my brain. Suddenly, I threw my rubber mallet in the air. It hit the ceiling of my cell. 'Yes! I am tired of hurting myself.' I said it aloud. Over and over. 'I am tired of hurting myself.' And I understood that when I could stop hurting myself, I could stop hurting other people. 'I'll never steal again as long as I live.' I said that aloud too. I'll always remember the swing of my hammer as my moment of decision.

Shortly after that hammer hit the ceiling, Tony met John Wilson in the

Joyceville yard. John, then a con doing time, now a past co-ordinator of a Toronto HELP *office, vividly recalls his impression of Tony that day. He pulls down the peak on his Greek sailor's hat, leans forward, smiles, nods a yes.*

'You always know when a guy is finished. Lots of guys say they're finished; then they tell you about their one last get-rich-quick scheme. Tony told me that he'd had it, that he couldn't cut the con's life any more. I've never heard a guy speak of quitting with so much passion. I could see that his drive was changing, his priorities were changing, and I could see that he was doing a lot to prepare for a change. You might say he was blooming where he was planted, doing the best he could to prepare for another life, a straight life outside. He was cranking out that leather, stashing away his earnings, building a relationship with a woman outside. All the indications were strong that he'd go straight.'

Nothing was going to set me back; my mind was made up. I was feeling high, on a natural high, not drug-induced. There was one small jolt of pain still coming my way — learning about my father's death. He had died while I was in the States, but no one had told me, and since we really had nothing between us, I hadn't visited him since I had turned myself in. One day a letter arrived from one of my sisters. She mentioned my father's death like I already knew. But that was the first I'd heard. It was just a moment's jolt, not more. We never had anything between us, but I never resented him neither. He was just an old Romeo that lived a good score and died in his late eighties.

After my conversion decision I settled back into prison routine to serve out my time. The best thing that happened to me in that last stretch was working in the pilot project where they train guys in real work for the real workaday world. You worked the same hours as square johns, with fifteen-minute breaks rather than the two-hour breaks we were used to in the slammer. I was responsible for the tool crib, where all the machine tools were stored. I built that crib from an empty room and maintained a lot of expensive and complicated tools. I had to convince them to let me on the pilot project; then I had to work like blazes to build the crib. It took me about five months to get it in shape. I was very proud of myself. It made me feel I would be able to do anything I wanted on the street.

By the time I was in the tool crib, it was well into my second year after turning myself in. I still had a lot of time left to do – about three years on my original sentence when I split for the States, plus the two Judge Baker gave me for the Becker's caper. It seemed like I was fixed for about five years, but I was prepared to face it.

I wasn't going around bragging about my resolution because institutional staff would never believe a word of it, and most inmates wouldn't believe me either. But inside me I knew it was the truth. I may have been settling in for the duration, but Sister wouldn't settle for me being inside. A few months after our critical discussion she came to me with parole application papers. Now, I was an expert on filling out parole papers. I knew the form by heart, and I'd invented more than my share of lies to fill it out before. When Sister brought me the forms, I laughed right in her kisser.

'You gotta be kidding! You think the parole board will believe me just because you do. First I broke parole to the States and then I broke a pass after turning myself in. Why should they trust me?'

I couldn't convince her it wasn't even worth a try. She bugged me to death, till I finally relented and scribbled something on the form. I concocted no lies. Instead I wrote simply, 'I'm tired of it all, I've had enough.' Signed Tony McGilvary. There – that would get that annoying nun off my back. Would you believe – they granted me a parole hearing!

I remember sitting on the bench outside the hearing room. The busiest little prison nun strutted past me, her nose in the air. She spoke to the board. Forty minutes later she waltzed out, still paying me no heed. Ten minutes later I was standing before them, up on that same old carpet I'd prostrated myself on many times before. Only this time I had no cons cooked up. They asked me a bunch of questions, many about my relationship with my mother. I couldn't go through the story again like I did with Sister Marguerite. I gave a few feeble answers till I couldn't control my emotions no more. The tears just came, the first time I ever lost control like that.

I was shocked that they had granted me a hearing, but I was much more shocked that they granted parole. It was designed as a gradual-release program, but it was parole none the less. First I was to have two days of unescorted passes a month for five months, followed by release to a provincial half-way place, Portsmouth House. Then, after eight months at Portsmouth, two years of parole on the street.

I wasn't the only one who couldn't believe what was happening. My classification officer, Claude, was as stunned as I was.

'Tony was known for his grass-roots diplomacy. Yes, he was liked by both sides, by inmates and staff alike, and that would certainly count in his favour at a parole hearing. Yet you had to look at his record. I liked Tony, but I couldn't support his parole application. I didn't trust that he had really changed. Obviously, the parole board did. I could never understand why they acceded.'

But agree they did. It seemed like no time at all till, in 1977, I was living at Portsmouth. That's still a jailhouse because you got so many rules and regs to live by, but I was on my way to freedom, to going back on the street as a new man, a man that was determined to live straight. Inside me it finally struck home that maybe freedom could be a score. Maybe crime was not the only way to score. Now, what was I going to do with that freedom?

HELP: Finding Jobs for Ex-offenders

12

Here I am forty-two years old living at a half-way house in Kingston, hell-bent on getting straight and not going back to the bucket. If I was going to make it on the street, I knew I had to work, so I immediately found a job cooking on the graveyard shift at the Voyageur bus terminal. Obviously, I would have to play my parole strictly by the book. At Portsmouth House, the ancient, rambling mansion that would be home for a while, I followed the endless rules and regs governing my movement – checking out, signing in, observing curfews, kowtowing to petty requirements. I was determined to play it by the book, and I did, except for one little incident that forced a bit of deceit on me.

One morning at half past three I roll in from Voyageur dead tired. So as not to disturb my roommate, I crawl into bed quietly with the lights out. I'm just nodding off, my face to the wall, when I hear heavy breathing very close to me. Stunned, I roll over quick to peer through the darkness. The breathing is getting heavier and the sheets is definitely heaving. 'Oh my God, what am I gonna do?' Panic takes hold of me. Don't get me wrong – I'm no prude, as you might have noticed from my romantic career, but having women in the rooms was strictly forbidden. If my roommate got caught, I'd go down for it too. Back to prison for breaking parole by being an accomplice. My mind was in turmoil; I wasn't ready to go down for another man's pleasure, but I couldn't rat him out either. I decided to do nothing. When they quieted down, nothing said between us, we all went to sleep. At six a.m. my roommate shakes me awake. 'You know I got a woman in my bed, man. And you know what they'll do if they catch me. You got to help me get her out of here.'

I didn't ask no questions or make no protests. I knew what I had to do. I run downstairs, put on the coffee, distracted the commissionaire with a non-stop flood of babblespeak. Ordinarily, a little gambit like this was nothing more than a game to me; I never before worried about the stakes for cheating the Man. But this time, because I wanted so bad to stay on the street, my heart was in my mouth when I heard the front door squeak open and shut. The commissionaire didn't notice the noise; I was sweating.

Other events that made me sweat with worry while I was at Portsmouth had nothing to do with violations, except my sense of what was right and wrong getting violated. It just wasn't right the way things was developing in the relationship between me and Julie. She watched me like a hawk; I felt like I had myself a new jailer. I'd get off my shift at Voyageur at three in the morning, and she'd be waiting to chauffeur me to Portsmouth House. She should have been home in her bed because she had to go to work a few hours later at eight. But no, she couldn't let me do nothing without her. Like I was a helpless kid that needed taking care of. I was feeling smothered and I wanted out. I tried to tell her nice that it was no good between us, but she wouldn't let go. The more I pulled back, the more she lunged forward, forcing herself on me. When her begging didn't work, I guess she got desperate; she started to stage these real scary, bizarre scenes.

One afternoon my boss and friend at Voyageur, also Julie's friend, Audrey, called me. 'Tony, you must meet me right away at Julie's house. It's an emergency.' I agreed to go, but my instincts told me to take another witness. I asked the second-in-command at Portsmouth to come along. He agreed. When we all went into Julie's house, the place was in darkness, window shades drawn against the daylight. Very silent. Julie was laid out on her couch like a corpse. Serene, hands folded across her chest, holding a cross, decked out in a fancy dressing-gown. On the end-table, candles and incense were burning; flowers and my photograph were on the table too. Not surprising, there were empty pill bottles scattered around. Julie had a real fetish for expensive, fussy furniture and house fixings, so the whole picture was pretty weird, like a movie set for a spooker.

The others were scared. They hovered over her, checked her pulse, slapped her face, tried to get a response. This suicide scene didn't surprise me or scare me; by then I was accustomed to Julie's hysterics. 'Don't worry – she's not dead,' I told them. 'Let's look for the pills; they're around here someplace. Don't worry; she didn't take them.' In no time we found the pills stashed in a kitchen container. When I said, 'Okay, Julie, the game's up. You can come back from the dead now,' she started to sob uncontrollably. Audrey comforted her; we left.

But that wasn't the end of it. About a week later Julie came to pick me up at midnight from a new job I had by then, cooking at Cloverleaf Bowling Lanes. I'd left Voyageur because she was working there too and driving me nuts. I refused to get in the car, so, as I started to walk home, she followed me along the highway. She pulled up alongside me and hollered all kinds of names at me. I took off on a short cut through a big field. She ditched the car and come tearing after me. Now that must have been a sight – this big, fat guy in kitchen whites running across a field, pursued by an angry lady. Me – a con – running to the safety of a half-way house! I finally reach Portsmouth, run breathless inside. 'What's wrong?' the guy on the desk asks, a look of real concern on his face. 'You'll find out soon enough,' I tell him, as I dash upstairs to hide under my blankets.

Next thing I hear is Julie at the back door screaming to let her in, she needs to use the toilet. Normally, no women are allowed in the building after eleven, but if you gotta go you gotta go, so the guard lets her in. I'm listening at the top of the stairs, hoping she won't work an angle to get up here. She worked an angle, all right. Locked herself in the john and refused to come out. The security guard made me come downstairs to plead with her. I pleaded.

She answered, between sobs. 'If you promise to come back with me, I'll come out.'

I couldn't promise, and she wouldn't come out. For over four hours we pleaded with her – me, the guard, and some Portsmouth brass we called in. It was useless. We gave up, called the fire department. Firemen broke the door down, scraped her up off the floor – which was a lot of scraping, since she weighed about 210 pounds – and carried her on a stretcher to the cop shop. Julie refused to walk. Then the cops carried her to the cruiser and delivered her to the mental hospital.

My personal life was not exactly getting off to the most promising start on the outside, but I was developing a real friend in Audrey, and I was working steady, staying clean, and developing some new interests. Sister Marguerite got me going on one that sort of foreshadowed what I was going to do with my freedom. She introduced me to Bob Weissbach, a teacher at Gananoque high school. Bob invited me to talk to his sociology classes about crime and punishment. I didn't know what I was getting into. I didn't know how I'd feel about the kids.

Weissbach had some suspicions about what Tony was getting into. 'Tony was an instant hit with the kids, especially with sixteen young guys who already had trouble with the law and were on probation. He came from the same background as most of these kids; he had been poor and unloved like they were. He could identify with them; they felt his understanding. I saw in Tony many of the qualities that would later contribute to his success with HELP. *He was very perceptive, even picked up on my nervousness about dealing with an ex-con, and he was very forthright. I didn't confess to my uneasiness; rather, he confronted me, made me discuss it. I also saw the enormous caring he was carrying around for these kids and their troubles. Very quickly he became personally involved with them – within weeks, he was meeting them for individual counselling sessions. Soon after I was taking students who'd had run-ins with the police to visit Tony at Portsmouth House. I saw how the boys respected him. I also saw Tony's leadership qualities.*

'It didn't take him long to lead me. He started advocating for a boys' club to keep kids off the street. "What you need, Bob, is a student employment agency based in the school. The kids could make up their own brochures, go door-to-door offering their services shovelling snow, babysitting, stuff like that. They don't have to sit around waiting for Manpower to call; they can create their own jobs."

'I didn't grasp the importance of what he was proposing, so I

procrastinated. But Tony kept pushing till I finally got the thing in motion. It turned into a very successful venture, especially for the boys and girls in trouble with the law.

'Tony sees possibilities that others don't see. He has the kind of vision that makes me imagine him either as a hard-nosed Catholic bishop working in the inner city or as the head of a successful company. I saw that he had the kind of commitment and sense of purpose that could create success for his ideas. As the HELP *program developed, all those qualities I saw in embryo when he first started working with the kids and working on me, those talents just exploded.'*

I was loving my involvement with those kids, beginning to sense that I could do something worthwhile on the street, but I had no plan yet. I just kept working my cooking jobs while I served out my eight months at Portsmouth House. A buddy, another ex-con who seen I had no trouble finding jobs for myself, asked me to help him get work. I knew the man's going back to jail if he doesn't find work, so I said 'Sure, I'll help you find a job.' It was a cinch; I got him a place working with me at Voyageur. I did him a favour, that was all. I never thought more about it. But I guess he did because he put the word out on the con grapevine that McGilvary can get jobs. Suddenly, I got three ex-offenders working with me at Voyageur. Suddenly, I'm Canada Manpower!

You can only find so many jobs in one bus station; I'd exhausted the openings at Voyageur. Next time a guy asked me for help getting work, I decided to try somewhere else. Fast as I got that guy a job, another was at my door. 'Help me, Tony.' I was hearing that plea over and over. Before I knew it, I was knocking on doors at restaurants, service stations, small businesses. I found myself convincing employers to give an ex-offender a break. Some said yes, some said no. I wouldn't accept no; I'd keep going back to that employer, keep grinding away at his refusal. Eventually, my persistence would wear him down, and just to get me off his back he'd let me place one worker.

Wade Greek, owner of Kanata Manufacturing, a steel-fabricating business, wasn't resistant to the idea of hiring ex-offenders. But his first impression of Tony was to 'quickly let him speak his piece, then escort him out the door.' Why? 'Because on first approach and appearance, Tony looks like a real hard person. His heavy beard and his worn cap don't help, and he doesn't exactly look or sound like a normal businessman.

'However, when he told me what he was trying to do — help ex-inmates get a fresh start — I felt I should do whatever I could to help him along. Tony was very convincing. I liked him and quickly forgot my first impression when I saw him rushing in our door from his battered old car. He was outgoing, spoke very well — not polished like business people usually are, but he spoke honestly about himself and his criminal past, and clearly about his program. From scepticism at first glance, I ended up congratulating him for turning his own life around. I felt I could trust him, and that started our relationship with HELP.

'Between 1977 and 1983, when I closed that business, I hired about fifteen workers through HELP. The majority worked out very well. At one time eight of my fourteen staff came from HELP. They worked on the assembly line earning five to eight dollars an hour, the same rates as other employees. Tony's people were always very willing to learn.

'I had good and bad experiences with the HELP workers, as every employer has with all staff. The majority stayed with me until they got better jobs or got into training programs. The minority were difficult. I placed a lot of trust in one man, even arranged with his parole officer to send him out of the area with one of my trucks. The man ended up in jail in North Bay — with my truck. I worked with the North Bay police to bring him back to Kingston. Normally an employer would fire the man, but he'd done good work for me, and I felt if I dropped him then, he might never get another chance. So I kept him on for about another year; he's still on the street today. I guess I learned from Tony that people deserve another chance.

'My other bad experience didn't involve the law. It was another kind of tragedy. After work one day a young man locked himself in my garage in one of my trucks and asphyxiated himself. I found him next morning. He left a note apologizing and explaining he wanted me to find him rather than being found dead in the middle of nowhere by a stranger. I had no idea he was so depressed; if I had, I would have made an effort to help him some way.

'The program is a good thing, and Tony's the kind of guy to convince you that if a second chance should be given to anyone, it's through his organization that you should give it. I'm glad I did.'

Josephine Chesebrough, known as JD to friends and Mrs C to employees, was owner and manager of the restaurant at the Voyageur terminal in

Kingston. *She gave Tony his first job on his first effort to go straight, and she hired six others through him. That was before the program even had a name, in the early days when Tony was running a system of favours that would quickly become a Kingston local, then province-wide organization.*

'*My first impression of Tony was that he had a good personality, and he came across as a sympathetic and caring person. He was very open and honest with me about his background; he even gave me details to check if I wanted. I felt I could trust him, and as it turned out, I could. He was a very conscientious cook, the kind of worker who always did little extra things to please. He always seemed to be thinking about how he could help the people around him. I certainly felt appreciated as an employer.*

'*So when he mentioned that he knew another ex-offender who could fill a part-time opening I had, I trusted his judgment. I hired about six people through him over the next year or so. Four of the six worked out very well; they were better than average employees. One even married a woman I had working for me. It turned into a beautiful relationship with adopted children. The other two went back to jail for crimes they committed on the street, but they didn't do anything wrong on the job.*

'*Everyone deserves a second chance in life. Tony got his and look what he did with it; he proved that people can set amazing goals and achieve them. Someone needed to give him that chance and someone needs to give his friends that chance. That's why I hired.*'

I was one helluva fat man to be running around job hunting. My knees were paining something terrible with arthritis, but I kept going with this system of favours I was into. Meantime, in 1978 I done my eight months in the half-way house and moved out to a cozy basement apartment all my own.

I was running my no-name job-placement service from the trunk of an old car I bought. I even got business cards printed: 'If you want a job, call this number,' and I gave the number at my apartment. You'd be surprised at some of the people that called. Like probation and parole officers, even the odd prison warden. It was all unofficial, of course – it was just that I was getting a reputation as someone that could connect guys with work, which meant keeping them on the street and out of trouble. Even though the Man was calling me to help, he wasn't entirely sure what I was up to. Cons and warders alike, they figured it might be a scam. But scam or no scam, I was finding jobs, and that's what brought even the sceptics to my door.

I think I found eighty jobs before my legs gave out and the surgeons got hold of me. Convalescing at home with a cast from above my knee to mid-calf, I got to thinking. This was more than a system a favours I was running. It was a much-needed service. I realized that us ex-offenders needed a job-placement program run for us and by us. Who else could understand our dilemma? Who else could understand our problems getting jobs? Who else could understand that a job meant the difference between a chance to stay on the street and the inevitability of turning to crime?

That's when the HELP program was born. I started doodling on a brown grocery bag, drafting the concept for a logo that an artist would later translate into our emblem. I didn't get too much time to sit around playing artist, though, because there came a knock at my door. I hobbled to the door. An ex-con's standing there, looking miserable. It's a look I recognize. 'Tony, you gotta help me find a job; otherwise, I know I'm going to commit a crime. Help me, man.' What could I do? I dragged my plaster-encased leg around to employers till I found the man a job.

I couldn't help thinking about the significance of starting the program in Kingston. It's the toughest of cities, the national prison capital, with nine penal institutions in the area. Tough pens, too. A town with lots of hard feelings about inmates and with no faith that a con can become an ex-offender. In Kingston a criminal record is written in indelible ink across an ex-inmate's life. Kingston wasn't some liberal city, open to prison reform and open to any fond feelings for felons. I knew that if HELP could make it there, it could make it anywhere. I was determined that it would make it. More than anything, I understood that in creating HELP I'd found my own – and maybe only – ticket to salvation.

My body might have been on the bum, but my work was on a roll and even my personal life was looking up. Audrey and me was getting very tight. When I became more mobile, I got a job as manager and cook – it was July 1979 by then – at Aberdeen House, a provincial half-way house.

Audrey remembers even the early years of their relatively short – on and off for ten years — but mightily turbulent relationship with mixed feelings. She recalls the lovable good and the maddening bad that is Tony McGilvary.

'We were friends for a year before we started going out. When we met — I was his boss at Voyageur — Tony was in turbulence over Julie, who was also an old friend of mine. I was in turbulence too, in the middle of divorce proceedings, with four children to worry about. Tony always seemed so sympathetic. He had such a big, caring heart, and he was very sensitive. I liked that. It wasn't at all what you'd expect from the look of him. I loved it when we'd sit and talk, share our feelings and our problems. After his relationship with Julie ended, he and I became closer, but we remained just friends until after his surgery.

'Then one day I dropped by his apartment and found him hobbling around on a cast and crutches. It broke my heart to see him suffering like that with his arthritis. I felt he needed to be taken care of. It wasn't a bad instinct on my part because I eventually realized that mothering is all Tony wants from any woman. I invited him to move into a cottage I was renting near Kingston so I could help him through his convalescence. After that he never moved out. He loved my waiting on him, pampering him, treating him like a child.

'The honeymoon was over long before the marriage began. He had already started the HELP program. HELP was an obsession. I quickly got taken for granted and put in a back seat to the program. Tony had the program and he had four jobs — manager and cook at Aberdeen House plus part-time cook at three spots: the Pancake House in Gananoque, Chimo's restaurant, and Husky Buy-Rite, a truck stop. Between juggling his shifts, working seven-day weeks, and running non-stop for his sacred program, there was no time for me. Want a good laugh? I even got a weekend job at the Pancake House, on top of my full-time job at Voyageur, just so I could see Tony.'

Her lips tighten. The bitterness shows. She drags on another in the endless chain of cigarettes.

'We'd meet each other occasionally going in and out of the bathroom, or over a cup of coffee at the kitchen table when one of us was hurrying off to work. Tony shared very little with me about his program, but I knew he was always thinking about it. It was an obsession, nothing less. I supported HELP but I was also concerned with my children and their needs and problems. We could never discuss them; Tony seemed to regard them as intrusions. What little discussion we had, he wanted it to be on his concerns, *not mine. And it wasn't that the man didn't know how to care. He was always absorbed in someone's crisis, just so long as they weren't ours. My God, he could counsel a husband and wife who were practically killing each other; he'd have them hugging in twenty minutes!*

'But,' Audrey adds with tighter lip while stubbing out her fifth cigarette of the hour, 'he couldn't work through any of our differences. When we had big fights over the years, he just moved out. He left me four times over arguments about my grown kids because he was jealous of the attention I gave them. Or he left over arguments we had about his program because I was jealous of the attention he gave it. Just packed up and left while I was at work! I always felt part hurt and part relieved to be free of him. I guess I deserve someone who treats me better, but I always took him back three weeks or three months, or even a year later, when he showed up.

'When he'd return, nothing ever changed. I knew the kind of nitty-gritty problems he was involved in because our phone rang with them all hours of the night. Always a fresh supply of crisis. How many schoolgirls phoned late at night with their suicide talk? How many parents called worried about a kid out drinking or doing drugs or getting in trouble with the law? And how many times did Tony go out in the middle of the night in search of some lost kid? Meantime, my own kids were lost; they had problems, normal growing-up problems. Tony wasn't much of a help even if he was a good provider. I appreciated the material things he gave me and my kids, but it wasn't things I needed. I needed Tony to share himself with us; he didn't know how.

'The sympathetic man with the big belly-laugh and the fun-loving nature, the Tony I'd known our first year as friends – that Tony was long gone. The new Tony didn't laugh and never had time for fun. He became impossibly moody. I felt like I was sitting on a firecracker, never certain when it would explode.'

A hard memory. Audrey shudders mildly. She opens her dark eyes. With the tone of a resigned woman who has borne too much with too little protest, she tells the story of a nightmarish Christmas when Tony exploded.

'I always thought of Tony as sensitive, but I guess I didn't realize just how short his fuse could be. Maybe I didn't understand how deep his frustrations were – from all those years behind bars and all the pressures he had at HELP. *I got my first inkling of his frustrations, and his temper, our first Christmas together. Not only was it our first together; it was the first one Tony had ever had as an adult outside a prison.*

'We'd been out at one of my girlfriend's and had a few drinks. Tony holds liquor well and doesn't drink too much, so he definitely wasn't drunk. We came home and went to bed; it was Christmas Eve. I don't know what triggered him, but suddenly he went berserk. Like a wild man. He tore our place apart. Hung on the chandelier like an ape, tore it off the ceiling. He grabbed the tree and smashed all the bulbs.

'I had no idea what he was enraged about. He said what most men say to women when they lose control. You're this, you're that — I can't repeat the words he used. He even chased Judy, my twenty-year-old daughter, around the room with a knife. Judy was dating a guard's son at the time, a guard Tony didn't like. I guess that's why he picked on her, though he threatened all four kids during his rampage.'

Audrey takes a deep breath, then sighs with relief. 'It was a dangerous incident, but Tony came to his senses in time. Instead of harming any of us, he bent the blade in half.'

Tony calmed down, backed off, left the house. He called Sister Marguerite Somers. She remembers that middle-of-the-night conversation clearly. 'Tony was absolutely broken. Here it was his first Christmas on the street, and he'd behaved like a madman. He didn't know what caused it and I didn't know either, but I think it could have been guilt. He knew all the guys inside were having a hellish Christmas, and he may have been asking himself how he could deserve to be having anything better than they were.

'What Tony did was terrifying for him. To me, it spoke of two threads in his life. First, his guilt over believing himself responsible for his mother's mental illness, and second, his feeling that he had no right to a good life as long as others were suffering. To me, Tony always had that Christ-figure quality.'

'Christ figure?' Audrey laughs in disbelief. 'He can have a big heart, all right, but let's not get carried away. The guy who came home to me nights was no Christ figure. You could never count on what mood he'd arrive in. He went up and down with the small developments and setbacks in the program. Depending on how I reacted to his mood, he might blow up or stay cool. Luckily, he never repeated the Christmas blow-out. It's wasn't so much temper with Tony as frustration. He wanted to do so much, but he could never get it done fast enough to suit him.

'And yet, knowing all this, I married him on 2 May 1980. I guess I still hoped the old Tony would return to me. Like so many other misguided women, I imagined I could change my man. What happened at our wed-

ding should have convinced me that I'd lost him forever to the program.'

I can't blame Audrey for being hot at me about the wedding. I guess my timing was in bad taste. See, Judge Baker – that gave me two years for breaking one of my paroles – married us; he was a judge and a JP. Right after the ceremony, while we're still standing in front of him, I said, 'Well, Judge Baker, one time you sentenced me to two years; now you're sentencing me to life.' But that's not what got her mad. Then I added, 'Do you know about the HELP program?'

'The what? The HELP ...?'

'Yeah. The HELP program, for finding jobs for people like myself, ex-cons.'

Audrey hauled back and swung at me, hit me over the head with her purse. 'Tony, have a heart. This isn't the time to start talking HELP program.'

I couldn't help it. Nothing else really existed for me except the program. I knew I had a good woman, but I also knew that I could only make the program a success if I ate it, slept it, and breathed it. It was taking off, that was for sure. The staff at Aberdeen House was real supportive of my program. They even gave me the program's first office, a little hole in their basement. The minute I had a space to call an office, I put my old conning skills to work, bumming all the things I needed to create a proper office. I rounded up some volunteers from the John Howard Society. I put a guy on the phone calling lumberyards bumming building supplies and calling office-furniture outlets bumming a desk and chairs. I even convinced Bell to donate a telephone for our first month. Just try getting anything free from Ma Bell! Well, I did it.

Between stirring the stew and baking the bread, I'd be running up and down the stairs to answer calls in the office and follow up on contacts I'd made with ex-offenders and employers I was trying to match up. While someone else watched the pot roast, I'd go out on the street and hustle a new employer. Very fast, it became obvious I needed a secretary. I got one of them for free too, from the Workmen's Compensation Board.

Pat Walker was the assistant director of Aberdeen House at the time. 'My most vivid memories of Tony are of him wiping his hands on his apron – he was dressed in cook's whites all the time – and sitting down to a serious, involved talk with someone who drifted into the kitchen, someone who'd heard about him and his program. And I recall him running up and down the stairs between the kitchen and the basement office. The man never stopped; he was constant motion.

'Tony brought so much life to Aberdeen House. His big, booming voice and his laugh filled the place. I liked him the minute I met him when he applied for the job. The dynamic personality and the force he comes at you with – it's overwhelming. It involves you almost against your will. Besides being likeable, he was a man with a lot of experience in what it meant to be a loser, someone who always screwed up. He understood the guys who came to see him because he'd been there himself. And he observed the con code, which gave him a lot of credibility with the men he was helping. For example, if anyone was stealing at Aberdeen or bringing stolen merchandise in, Tony would never tell me what was happening, but I knew he was down in that basement retreat backing some guy up against the wall. If he couldn't persuade a guy to observe his parole, he might come to me and say, 'Are you at all worried about so-and-so?' That was my cue to start working with the man.

'What made Tony different was that he really cared. He related to the ex-offenders as "his people." Working with them wasn't just a job to him like it is to most social workers.'

Pat Walker was a real ally; she really helped me get started. I knew just how solid a foundation I'd built when one day at Aberdeen a parole officer called to say he was referring an ex-offender to me. I decided to test my reputation.

'Uh, uh. Don't send him alone. Bring him. Come with him,' I said.

He did. Here we were sitting in my office, a little threesome chatting away. A parole officer and two ex-cons – in my office! That parole officer wasn't comfortable, that's for sure, but he stuck it. That afternoon I found his guy a job. Next morning he brought over another man. That afternoon there were two parole officers, each with a new client in tow, in my office.

My little operation was starting to outgrow my basement space. Besides, the Aberdeen brass weren't thrilled to see guys from federal pens walking around their provincial turf. Here I am with a job and an office under their roof, and mostly I'm serving cons from the federal system. I knew they wanted me to move my office, and I was ready for more space too. So I wrote to seventy – yes, seventy – churches in the Kingston area. Don't forget, Kingston's a town of sinners and saints, cons and Christians. Except none of those so-called Christian churches wrote back; none of them had any interest in my proposal. One day I was discussing my office problem with this blind parole officer I knew, a guy that was working voluntary in the parole system – people with handicaps is always getting ripped off – and this guy tells me his wife, who was also blind, is a member of Alliance Church. Maybe she could get an entrée for me. 'Great,' I said.

She did open that door for me. I'll always remember the night I met those church elders. It was real windy, dark night. The church looked like it belonged in one of them haunted-house movies. I knocked at the only door inside where light was visible around the door frame. When someone opened the door an inch, I saw thirteen bowed heads. The last supper, I guess.

'We'll be right with you,' the man said.

A few minutes later they called me in. Under my arm I got a little box.

Pastor David spoke first. 'You understand all the elders here must agree to your request before we can grant it. Even one dissenting vote means we will have to say no.'

'I understand. Now I got to tell you some things. I know this is a church, but you know that my people smoke, and I'm the biggest culprit of them all. So we need an office where we can smoke. Also, you might hear the odd curse word – and that could be me also.

'Then I told them a little about my program, how I'm finding jobs for guys getting out of prison. I opened up the box. It was full of applications. I start taking the cards out and laying them down on the table – seventeen, eighteen, twenty cards. And I get emotional – that happens to me sometimes. As I'm stacking them cards up, the tears start rolling down my face. Because I'm fighting for my people, see. To me, it was my big chance to keep HELP going. I believed in it heart, body, and soul. But I was scared nobody else would give it a shot. I got through half the box and I stopped.

'That's enough. If you can't see what I'm doing and what my

people need from you, then there's nothing more I can do to convince you.'

Next morning Pastor David tells me we can have the corner room in their basement. 'You can have it, but there are certain rules you must follow: first, only your staff can use the washrooms; second, you must know where your staff and clients are in the building at all times.'

There were a few more rules; I forgot them.

'And you are on six months' probation. You can be told to leave at two months' notice.'

'Fine.' I was jubilant. First rule we broke the second day because my people had to have a washroom. The rest of the rules, we bended them a little. I guess we didn't bend them too much, though, because we got along real good with the elders and they helped us a lot. HELP really took off under their roof. In my own mind I'm finally beginning to grasp what I've created, beginning to grasp how solid it is and what its potential is. And I'm beginning to dream much bigger dreams.

A Critical Partnership: HELP Meets Frontier College

13

I started to dream about a nation-wide program of ex-cons helping other ex-cons get jobs and get straight. Stay on the street. Stay out of the slammer. Every time I'd close my eyes – which wasn't often because I was working day and night – I'd imagine a new office with new staff, all ex-cons like me, opening in a new town or city. In my dream world I was dotting the map of Canada with HELP offices. In my waking hours I knew my big dreams would need big bread, but I didn't have a legal line on that kind of money. I didn't exactly have the manners or the polish necessary to raise it, neither.

I knew something I wished wasn't true. HELP, if it was going to get big and better and famous, needed a front. Legit. Respectable. One of them do-gooder organizations with an 'unbleachable' reputation. I had no contacts in those places except maybe John Howard Society, and I wasn't about to team my program up with any group involved in probation and parole, any organization that could be part of policing ex-offenders and party to sending them back to prisons. You can't mix after-care and parole supervision – it's giving with one hand and taking back with the other.

Almost by accident two connections just fell in my lap. First, I connected with Joe, another ex-con involved in another job-placement scheme for ex-offenders. Second, through Joe I connected with Frontier College in Toronto. Frontier, a national adult-literacy organization, was running the scheme Joe was hooked into. For three years Frontier had been operating this experimental job-placement program for ex-offenders in Manitoba. They'd hired Joe to review their program. He liked what he saw in Winnipeg. He also liked the grapevine gossip about my activities in Kingston. He thought we should talk, so he tracked me down and called me up. In 1979 we met. It was love at first discussion, love of an idea; we had the same idea of what ex-cons needed.

We were destined to be partners. We had the same goals but different talents. Joe was respectable-looking and -sounding. He could wear a suit and pass for a businessman. He could talk and write the Queen's English. He could speak the language that big people with big money in big positions like to hear. He could talk to bureaucrats; he could make simple things sound complicated. And he had the patience to do their dances, to fill out forms in quadruplicate and fill in all the reports that fill the files of Ottawa. He could represent our needs in a world that couldn't accept me nearly as fast – the world of power and money.

I would be better on the beat, pounding pavement for jobs, convincing employers that my people deserved a second chance. I knew how to deal with the nitty-gritty day-to-day needs and demands, crisis and fears of habitual losers. I knew how to build them up to believe in themselves and how to build up employers to have some faith in them too. I was better in the front lines; Joe was better in the back rooms. Both roles had to be played out if we were going to pull off the biggest score of our lives.

My life had trained me not to trust no one. On the one hand I knew we needed a straight sponsor. No one – neither community nor con – was going to trust a bunch of ex-inmates with a lot of bread. Everyone would suspect we were running a scam. On the other hand I didn't trust no do-gooder agencies; I figured they'd take us over and dictate how things would get done. I figured they'd rob us of our independence. But the side of me that knew we needed a legitimate front to handle the cash agreed to meet Frontier College, Joe's contact. I walked into those first meetings in August of 79 with a head full of resentment and a heart full of suspicion.

Jack Pearpoint, Frontier's president, recalls some of his thoughts from that first encounter.

'Throughout our meeting, I was mostly conscious of a recent failure – a very expensive one – we'd had supporting another ex-offender on a scheme similar to the one Tony was proposing. I knew Tony's idea was a good one, one of those profound pieces of common sense that no one had pulled off before. But whether this obviously intense, compelled, mistrusting character could pull it off was another matter. I was open to the possibility that he could, but for all I knew he was just a con artist. What convinced me initially was Joe's confidence in Tony. He told me that if anyone could do it, Tony could. On that recommendation I was willing to give Tony some seed money and support to see what he could do. The meeting ended with me agreeing to hand over six hundred dollars. Little did I suspect that six hundred dollars would turn out to be a small down payment on a major partnership for the college.'

The HELP–Frontier College partnership that would develop over the next eight years turned out to be a meeting of organizations with plans that meshed. It has also been the pairing of personalities, with McGilvary and Pearpoint at the centre. It is a curious partnership. In some ways these men are opposites; yet in some ways they are identical. Pearpoint looks the polished president of an important organization. With his CUSO background and homey office decorated with treasures from developing countries, the tall, wholesome boy from Shaunavan, Saskatchewan, is clearly doing good in what he finds a bad society. Dressed in his soft beige llama-wool sweater from a recent hiking tour of Peru, he is, at forty, the picture of mannish good health.

Talking with him, you know you are with someone who comes from the right side of the tracks. You also learn fast that he is full of indignation with a system that denies others the breaks that he has had from birth. He seems in full control of what Frontier can do about some of the imbalances.

Tony, by contrast, couldn't be more unpolished. He looks mildly menacing and clearly comes from the wrong side of the tracks. Far from a picture of good health, he is grossly overweight and seemingly out of control. He rushes, chain-smoking, from crisis to crisis, reacting to events that seem beyond his control.

Yet these two people share a palpable bond, a driving need to be at the centre of action directed at giving losers a chance to become winners.

So much happened so fast after I met Jack and Frontier donated that seed money. Fast suited me just fine; it's the only speed I know.

First Joe and Frontier found $10,400 from a small family foundation that became a loyal ally and supporter of HELP. That first grant let me quit three of my four part-time jobs and concentrate on the program while I kept my one job at Aberdeen. Then I hired my first field worker, Bob Young.

When Bob Young first met Tony, he must have felt as though he was facing his mirror image. Bob has more hair and less girth, but the two men have a remarkably similar aura. Too much bulk on too-small frames. Relatively short men (Bob is five-foot six, weighs around two hundred pounds; Tony is five-foot ten, weighs around three hundred) who fill up large psychological spaces. Perhaps the dissimilar appearance – the curly haired, ash-blonde, blue-eyed Bob against the spare-haired, brown-eyed Tony – yet similar impact comes from their parallel experience of life. Hard backgrounds, harder lives, hardened cons. Both ready to reverse their history, make amends, help others.

'I was at a point where I wanted to help other people, wanted to save the world to save myself, I guess, but I didn't know how to go about it,' Bob admits. 'I was filled with frustration and resentment; I had a chip on my shoulder bigger than my body. I was running my own upholstering business, hiring other ex-cons like myself, trying to give them and me a new start, but I was no businessman and these guys were ripping me off. My wife and my parole officer saw how frustrated I was. Independently they were both pushing me to check Tony out because they knew about his program and they knew he needed help.

'I'd met him once at Portsmouth House. The meeting left me with a really bad impression of the guy. I'd wandered into the half-way house one day and this super-chubby guy shoved his card in my face. I didn't like his manner. He waddled off, and I went my way. When I later saw ads for HELP workers – "Ex-cons with life together needed to work with other ex-cons" – I hesitated because my first impression had been so bad. But my wife and my parole officer kept nagging. Finally, after six months' prodding, I arranged to meet Tony at the HELP office in Kingston Alliance Church.

'At this meeting, again I didn't completely trust him. After all, I'm a con and he's a con. He was spouting off so much about honesty I was suspicious. When you've done the amount of time we've done, you don't just flip over like that. I figured Tony for a do-gooder, somebody into doing good for personal gain. In prison you meet lots of do-gooders and you learn to steer clear of them.

'So I asked him outright: "Why are you doing this? What's in it for you?" He answered, "There's nothing for our kind — that's why I'm doing it." He'd given me the right answer. I was ready to talk. Tony conned me into teaming up with him by promising to set up an upholstery shop where I could train ex-cons. I was excited about that. But then Tony threw in a twist, told me I'd have to prove myself first as a field-worker who could get jobs.

'All right. I was ready to accept that for a while. "How long do I have to work as a field-worker?" I asked Tony. "A month, that's all." That sounded okay to me, so I agreed. The guy really sucked me in; to this day I haven't taught one ex-con to drive even one upholstery tack!'

Bob laughs good-humouredly. 'Tony had more ambitious plans for me. Little did I suspect I was in training to become his right-hand man. When I say training, I should say testing, because that's what he did. Tested me day and night just to see if I could hack the pace.'

What exactly was Bob in training for? What exactly was this thing called HELP? The heart of HELP was association, ex-cons associating on the street. In this concept alone Tony had launched something novel — and historically unpopular. Tom French, whose booming voice and ponderous bulk give the impression of Tony and Bob's size combined, is a recently paroled lifer who worked for the program behind bars. Now he is assistant director beyond the bars. Tom explains the significance of association.

'One of the sacred rules of parole in the penitentiary system is no association. The system has always told us that anyone released to the street who associates with other ex-cons will inevitably wind up back in jail. A reasonable assumption? Yes. But it is also an impossible demand — insisting that ex-cons don't associate on the street. Let me explain why.

'First we are confined to the system to live out our lives. There, we develop the only friends and contacts most of us will ever know. At various points we're thrown out on the street again, thrown out with nothing — in many cases no skills for making an honest living, often no money, no family or old friends who still accept us. Finally, we're forbidden, on pain of parole violation and punishment, to associate with our only friends. We don't have anyone else to associate with! That's why there was genius in Tony's idea. He understood that association is all we've got; he figured an angle to make association pay.'

Ex-con and past co-ordinator of one of two Toronto HELP offices John Wilson many times tried to make it outside without association. And he didn't do badly. But, eventually he would be drawn to the familiar haunts

HELP Meets Frontier College

frequented by familiar rounders. Finally he'd be drawn back into the underworld.

'When you're on parole and you're tossed into the square world and happen to be down on your luck, there is no one else you can turn to. The con community is your community, your only community. I tried very hard to stay clear of other rounders, but I'd always come back. I don't think a month ever went by when I didn't at least sneak a peek around the corners where my kind of people hung out. Sometimes I didn't talk with anyone because a guy on parole is always wary of stoolies, but I had to at least look around my old crime neighbourhood. Tony understood that instinct in ex-cons, and instead of denying it, he built on it.'

HELP is built on that bias precisely — that ex-cons will associate with their peers. The program regards association as a positive bond to use in building positive lives for men and women who would otherwise face negative prospects. Ex-cons understand other ex-cons. They know the stigma of trying to reshape lives already misshapen by criminal records. They know the futility of trying to do it alone. They know the pressures that suck even some of the most determined turnarounds back into the vortex of crime.

The HELP concept, based on positive association among ex-offenders, is both simple and profound. But how could it be put into practice? First, and foremost, by one ex-offender helping another to find a job. If one thing is key to making it straight and staying on the street, it is paid work. Other supports matter, but work is most often the essence of self-worth and the ticket to living legally. Yet getting work can be a nightmare for ex-offenders. Inexperience and self-doubt combine with employer prejudices to discourage even the most ardent job searcher. Add the indignities of weak literacy, weak training, and weak skills that bedevil many ex-inmates, and success in a job hunt becomes a mere pipe-dream. Throw economic recession into the picture, and the undertaking becomes even more hopeless.

The trick, Tony figured, was to make life easier for ex-offenders while serving the needs of employers. Save employers the expense and aggravation of finding suitable employees. Bring carefully matched prospective workers to hiring employers. Provide this matchmaking service free of charge. All you had to do was find the employers, look for them in sectors that hire trades inmates learn inside prisons. As well, look for entry-level, on-the-job training chances and for unskilled and semi-skilled jobs. Part-time and graveyard shifts, weekend shifts — look for the hard-to-fill openings where HELP clients, eager to get straight, might be willing to start. Be available to *employers around the clock and have workers on the ready at short notice for one-shot jobs.*

Having workers on the ready was a major challenge. Sure, lots of recently released inmates were full of resolve to turn their lives around. But they had far less experience and discipline than they had good intentions. HELP *tested them, trained them for the small but essential self-disciplines like getting up early, coming to the* HELP *office to wait for job calls. 'After they made it inta the office five mornin's in a row,' Tony says, 'I knew they was ready ta work. If they only showed up the odd mornin' – sometimes hung over or lookin' shabby – I knew I'd have ta push 'em ta shape up before I could take them for an interview.*

'Guys that have spent most of their life in prisons ain't exactly got the best work habits. They're used to workin' five minutes, then takin' a two-hour coffee break. On the street they gotta learn to work two hours and take five-minute breaks. Also, bank robbers are used to big paydays; they don't know about minimum wage. A square job to them looks like a helluva lotta work for a pittance. See, there's a whole re-education that we got to do to prepare some of these guys for success on the street.'

Once an ex-offender seemed ready for the rigours of work, Tony would try to have job prospects lined up. He began making matches through the hard business of knocking on employer doors and 'rapping' with inmates. He quickly learned that it was important to attend the job interview with the candidate, to make sure the client's nerve was up for facing it and his confidence was up for faring well. If the interview was a bust, find another, more acceptable candidate for the employer and find another, more appropriate placement for the worker. Keep at it until the best match was made.

Once the ex-inmate was on the job, offer encouragement; phone or drop by to make sure the job was working out. Check that the employee was satisfied; check that the employer was satisfied. Help either or both people resolve job-related problems involving the other. Remember that the ex-offender turned worker was a rookie to the square world and that the employer was a rookie to the business of having ex-cons as staff. Be patient, supportive, sympathetic, helpful to both parties. Be there. Help make the match work.

Through trial, error, and improvisation, coupled with sharp street sense, Tony learned what it took to make HELP *work. He confronted the complexities of his simple idea of finding jobs for ex-cons. The job might be key to keeping a person straight, he discovered, but it was not the only thing* needed for success in the square world. Newcomers to a foreign lifestyle needed to talk out their feelings and anxieties, work out strategies for coping on the job and in their personal lives. He found that his clients, struggling to live outside institutions, needed help learning how to make it. Tony developed rap sessions, weekly get-togethers at HELP offices where a scared or angry or confused ex-con could spill his guts and get a gut response from peers, from empathetic employers, and from HELP staff.

Support roles, fanning out from the job core, developed as Tony, Bob Young, and a slowly developing staff of other ex-cons realized what was needed. 'You name it, we probably did it,' Tony explains. 'We got Frontier College involved in tutorin' many of our clients. Lotsa people that come up in institutions can't read and write good enough ta meet the demands of livin' on the street. Many a them got no skills either, so we managed ta buy a chip truck and three hot-dog wagons ta train ex-offenders in short-order cookin' while we gave them a job at the same time.'

Bob Young laughs at the mention of chip and hot-dog wagons. 'Oh, them,' he muses, 'yeah, Tony was a great one for new ideas. He was planning to train ex-cons in short-order cooking. Given his background in the joints and his love of food, it made a lot of sense. Except he was always too busy generating new ideas to follow through with the ones he started. So in the end, as usual, it was me in my three-piece suit in the trucks, frying grease, cleaning up, and then delivering the workers home. I was always racing into some meeting late with mustard stains on my tie!'

Bob is laughing too hard to speak.

'What's so funny? What are you remembering?'

'The HELP restaurant. Did you know we were in the restaurant business in Kingston – very briefly? A bar owner needed someone to run the food-service part of his business. Because Tony was always eager about anything having to do with food, he got us involved. We made a deal with the owner, hired a retired fraud artist as our cook, and went into the restaurant business. For starters, our cook wasn't retired enough; she bought some supplies on bad cheques. Then, before we knew it, all the ex-cons in town were doing deals at our restaurant. They figured it was a safe spot to deal because we wouldn't rat on them.

'To aggravate what was fast becoming a disaster, we were so dumb at business that we parked our own chip truck in front of our restaurant, undercut our own business! Then there were the drinkers in the bar – not a good mix for ex-cons that might have drinking problems, and a pool table in *the middle of the restaurant that encouraged guys to just hang around. We really knew the job-finding business, but we were not businessmen. Luckily, we got out of that restaurant within months.'*

HELP *learned to concentrate its efforts in its strong areas. 'We created youth groups for the youngsters ta have somethin' more than crime ta think about in their spare time,' Tony recalls. 'And we got their families involved in them groups an' social events. Ya got a lot a healin' of rifts in families ta deal with, and these groups helped bring families closer, back together after their kid done some time.'*

That wasn't all. The program started to expand its client base, started finding jobs for family members of ex-offenders. HELP *came to the conclusion that it was in the business of working with anyone affected by the corrections system, whether or not the individual had actual conflict with the law. Efforts at crime prevention were an obvious offshoot. As the program grew, as the funding base enlarged, with Frontier and Joe working tirelessly behind the scenes to raise foundation, government, and corporate donations, as the program's name gained credibility, so too did the program's field of work and influence expand. Public education became an important sideline, especially speaking engagements before young audiences in schools and colleges.*

In Kingston HELP *reached its stride, worked out its kinks, learned its strengths and realized a formula for doing what Tony set out to do — find jobs for ex-cons as the key to keeping them out of trouble.*

In Kingston the first field-workers, themselves ex-offenders, were trained to do the leg-work Tony had fine-tuned through his own trials. He trained Bob, and then together they trained others to follow in their footsteps on door-knocking rounds. They trained field-workers to prepare other ex-offenders for the workaday world. They trained field-workers in the fine art of bumming — soliciting donations, like office supplies. As the program moved from its Aberdeen House basement location to its donated space in the basement of Alliance Church to its storefront space in a Kingston shopping centre, shrewd ex-cons put conning skills to work in a new context. They became experts in the stock and trade of small, voluntary human services — getting donations in services and in kind. 'From the wall panelling to the tiniest screws we needed ta finish the inside of our office, we bummed everything,' Tony boasts. 'Finally, we were doin' somethin' honest and worthwhile with the same talents that only got us jail before.'

The job-finding focus would remain the heart of HELP. *The rules Tony and Bob put in place in Kingston would remain the program's gospel.*

First rule: observe confidentiality. A client's background is no one's business but his / her own. If an employer wants to know about the criminal record of the person he's hiring, he has a right to ask. The prospective employee can choose to explain or to refuse explanation. 'Mostly the employers do want to know,' *Tony says,* 'and mostly our clients tell them.'

Second rule: never give up on an ex-offender. Youth, and men and women who'd lived their lives as habitual losers, were not likely to become winners overnight. Even with the program's support they had patterns of behaviour stronger than their will to break them. In short, some ex-offenders were bound to screw up; it was written in their history. Make them believe they don't need to screw up, don't need to commit crimes, don't need to go back to jail.

Treat them like winners; treat them like they'll make it on the street. But understand they might fail. When they do, be there, make them feel welcome to come back for more help. If they wreck the job, counsel them to readiness for another job a little later. Keep the employer happy by replacing the original worker with one who might fare better. Keep the employer's door open. Persevere with the employer, but most of all persevere with the ex-offender. If you don't give up on him or her, next try they might make it.

Third rule: 'We believe in troot 'n' honesty,' *as Tony puts it.* 'Everybody's waitin' for the ex-con to screw up, tell a lie, steal something – do something wrong. We couldn't afford nothin' that might be dishonest.'

Fourth rule: 'We can't break no rules. We hadta live by the book, live by the Man's rules. That was easier said than done. Over the years we went through a number of co-ordinators and field-workers that still had dark secrets, was still in the game. Soon as I'd find out, I'd fire them. Even my very first field-worker – who worked a short stint before Bob Young – I had to suspend that guy for criminal activities just the day before I faced the elders at Alliance Church. There I was begging for a chance for my program and havin' to admit my only worker been charged with a crime! Another time I had a Bible thumper used ta show up ta work with a Bible under his arm. Today he's doin' life ... It wasn't easy to make sure my staff was clean and our clients too was gettin' their lives together.'

Fifth rule: 'We don't get involved in prison politics. We gotta be respected by both sides. We need the inmates' trust and we need the administration's respect.'

Sixth rule: no intimate relationships between HELP staff and HELP clients. 'I put that rule in,' Tony says, 'so the broads wouldn't be hangin' around and so the guys still inside wouldn't be worried if their wives and daughters come ta us for jobs. Also, I thought it might help keep the relationships and marriages of my staff in better shape if everyone knew there was ta be no screwin' around.'

Last rule: HELP finds jobs for all ex-offenders, irrespective of the crimes they committed. At first that was not a rule; in fact the program initially extended the con code to the street by refusing to help sex offenders. 'Rapos,' 'diddlers,' and child killers are regarded as scum by inmates. That's why prison authorities routinely segregate sex offenders from the general population. If left unprotected, their lives are at risk. Given his background, therefore, it was natural for Tony to exclude sex offenders from his roster of potential clients. However, an accident turned his view around. Unknown to Tony, he placed a sex offender in a job.

One day this guy I knew from inside approached me. 'Hey, Tony,' he said, real unfriendly, 'why are you helping rapos get jobs?'

'I ain't helpin' no sex offenders, man. Whadya talkin' about?'

'You not only got one a job; you placed him in a school with all those kids.' Then he named the school.

I got to the man's parole officer fast as I could, but the parole officer wouldn't tell me if it was true. Them days they didn't like to tell us anything about the guys they referred to HELP, but I was very insistent. Eventually, he told me the details of a very grisly rape. I speeded over to that school in my truck. I confronted the man.

'Do me a favour. Put that broom down an' quit your job.'

'I'm not quitting, Tony.'

'Oh yes you are.' He knew I'd uncovered his crime, and he knew I meant business. Down went the broom, and we both started walking away, heading off in different directions. Suddenly, I heard him calling me.

'What happens to guys like me, Tony? How do we get another chance?'

Them words really stung me. I started thinking. If the government let them out on the street – right or wrong, and I think it's wrong for them to be released; they're part of the 5 per cent of inmates that really deserves locking up in mental institutions and throwing away the key – anyway, if the government lets them on the street, then they're ex-offenders. And I was in the business of helping ex-offenders, no questions asked. So I decided to change my strategy. Yes, we'd place sex offenders. Maybe a job would help keep even people like them from committing more crimes. However, we were going to be more careful about knowing which clients were sex offenders, and we were going to be very careful about the kind of jobs we placed them in – ones where they'd have no access to kids and adolescents. Not everyone was going to love me for this decision, I knew that, but the program already had a good reputation, and I knew we could take the chance and win. I was right.

The program was growing, getting very solid. By 1982 HELP opened three more offices across Ontario and one in Winnipeg. While Tony was driving himself and driving his staff, having maximum success with maximum noise on the street, equally dedicated but quieter activities to support HELP were doing down in the back rooms. Frontier College staff and Joe, the program's official fund raiser, were knocking on doors, placing endless calls, writing numerous briefs, holding constant meetings in a drive to raise money. There were always lots of bills. Tony never worried about where money would come from and never thought twice about spending it. Even the routine bills were growing astronomically, reflecting the astronomical growth in the scope of the program. By 1982 there were bills for five offices – Kingston, Cornwall, Brockville, Toronto, and Winnipeg. (Since then Toronto has opened a second office and the Winnipeg office has closed. In addition, two administrative offices have opened in Kingston.) There were thirty-three staff, most of them ex-offenders. And there were the costs associated with the many sideline programs HELP was running – from encouraging young hookers to quit the streets and helping them to find alternatives to working with young shoplifters being diverted into HELP rather than being charged and sent to court.

Budget needs grew from the original $600 Frontier donated in 1979 to $750,000 in 1986!

Buying the Freedom Farm in 1985 certainly contributed to expenses. Getting that farm – 208 acres in Erinsville, Ontario – had been HELP's *dream project for years. Tony and Bob had dreamed of owning a farm to open trades training shops – upholstery, auto body, furniture, skids, and even computer courses. Maybe even a small business trout farming. They envisaged the farm as a refuge for newly released people, whether on day or full parole. They talked of running the farm with trades training and job-skills and life-skills training capacities.*

'Our idea,' Bob Young explains, 'was to have ex-offenders working days at the farm as paid trainees or employees until HELP *could place them in jobs. We figured the Freedom Farm would help inmates break their links with prison life and forge new links with a new life.'*

But where does all the money for running the programs come from? From a multitude of sources: foundations, churches, private donors, federal and provincial government ministries, service and business clubs, and many fund-raising events like auctions staged by HELP. *A small family foundation that prefers anonymity has been the most consistent supporter, there with the first hand-out and still digging deep in its resources. The Donner Canadian Foundation and the Laidlaw Foundation have made substantial contributions. So has the Anglican Foundation of Canada; they helped at a critical time. In 1985 the Ontario Trillium Foundation committed a large sum to use over four years for development and expansion. Trillium is a Crown corporation built on lottery money. They use lottery profits to support causes they consider worthy.*

These and other funders – especially Correctional Service Canada – have contributed money, but HELP *has received support in other ways from other sources as well.* HELP *usually has a raft of fee-for-service contracts to find employment for ex-offenders. Correctional Service Canada, Outreach Ontario (a provincial branch of Employment and Immigration Canada), and to a small extent the Ontario Ministry of Correctional Services have all supported* HELP *on this fee-for-service basis.*

COMSOC, *Ontario's Ministry of Community and Social Services, has paid wages of welfare recipients* HELP *has hired into some positions (the bulk of program staff are ex-offenders, but not all are).* HELP *has begged, borrowed – but not stolen – money and many in-kind services and supplies from more sources than the staff can adequately thank.*

Having Frontier College as partner and dedicated ally accounts for a large part of the fund-raising success. And that is exactly what Frontier is – a dedicated ally. Officially its role is administrative trustee (read: handles the money coming in and going out) and literacy trainer for HELP *clients. In reality the college and* HELP *have become full partners with complementary roles. The college, from the board of directors to the front-line staff, is as deeply committed to the growth and success of* HELP *as is the* HELP *staff. The relationship has been a workable, although often wrenching, symbiosis. Nobody inside* HELP *or inside Frontier ever pretended that Tony was easy to work with.*

Yet in spite of the pressure and strain, or perhaps because of them, HELP *kept becoming more and more of an unrivalled success. That success can be measured by several standards, one being statistical: how many ex-offenders* HELP *helps to keep on the street. First there is the staff employed by the program. Let's take 1986 as a sample year. In 1986* HELP *employed thirty-five people, mostly ex-offenders.*

Next there are the clients. Since Tony's first favour to a friend in 1977, the program has placed over 14,000 ex-offenders in lasting jobs. Yes, 14,000! From 1981 to 1986 HELP *has found an average of 2,700 jobs a year, about half full time and the rest part time, casual, and temporary. About 25 per cent of its clients are women – ex-offenders and female relatives of ex-offenders.*

In 1986, a record-breaking year, HELP *staff knocked on 28,000 employer doors. Their efforts netted 4,545 jobs for 2,000 people – jobs from programming computers to sweeping floors.* HELP *calculates that it takes 2.3 jobs per person before a client settles into a permanent position. Someone who has just done rough time needs time to 'cool out.' Therefore,* HELP*'s job-placement pattern is to graduate a client through casual or part-time jobs to more durable jobs. The majority of the people placed are still on the street a year later; only a tiny minority have been convicted of crimes and gone back to prison. Against a national recidivism rate estimated at 50 to 70 per cent, depending on whose figures you trust, this dimension alone reveals what* HELP *means.*

Clients in HELP*'s Roamer Program have fared exceptionally well. Roamers are inmates with nothing and nobody: they don't belong anywhere. They roam. They drift in and out of prisons. Institutions consider them lost causes; they consider themselves lost causes. Ontario jailers call* HELP *when a roamer is about to be released.* HELP *field-workers visit these men and* women inside, offer them help. They offer to find individuals a place to live anywhere in Ontario that they choose; they offer to arrange housing and welfare. Most significantly, they offer to find the person a job. They also offer to stay with the individual till he or she is placed on the job. Then they keep in touch with the client for a year. Thirty-two of thirty-nine roamers helped by HELP were still on the street early in 1987.

But data are not the same as real flesh-and-blood people who have turned personally tragic and socially harmful lives into worthwhile lives. People like Charlie and Angie.

Charlie was a loser. Everyone knew it, including Charlie. After all, he was a lifer who had already done nineteen years when HELP found him. 'He was so scared of people he couldn't put two sentences together in a conversation,' Bob Young recalls. 'When he went before the parole board and they asked if he wanted to get out of prison, he told them "it don't matter"; that's how little he cared about his life. That time, they denied parole, but Tony persuaded him to try again. Tony appeared at the hearing on his behalf and we managed to get him out on day parole. Meanwhile, I'd found an employer at a real chic restaurant in Kingston who agreed to give him a job cooking, since Charlie was a cook inside.'

Not only did Charlie stick with that job three and a half years to earn his chef's papers, but he also married and had a child – his first real family. A man in his forties starting over! Once he felt secure, had proven himself on the job and to his family, he moved on to construction work, which he does today.

'The pleasure of seeing that man fit back into society after nineteen years inside, the pleasure of meeting him walking down the street with his family, is more than I can express,' Bob Young explains. 'It's a tribute to Charlie that he turned his life around, and it's a tribute to our program that an employer and society as a whole have accepted him and given him a chance to be free.'

Angie's story is also typical of the radical ruptures HELP clients can make with their past. 'When I first met her at the prison for women in Kingston,' Bob recalls, 'she was such a lost cause that even I was tempted to give up on her. She had certainly given up on herself. She had a tragic background and it looked like she'd never get beyond tragedy. Her only preoccupation was dying; she had slash marks from head to toe. Angie was nineteen then, serving four years for drugs and robbery. She wasn't open to help at that time, but three years later she was. She showed up in Winnipeg for HELP *staff interviews. "Why do you want to work for us?" I asked her. "Because nobody else will accept me." Even though she's very pretty and feminine-looking, I could understand that a woman with slash marks and tattoos would have a rugged time in the square world. We gave her a chance. She's invaluable to us now, moved up through the ranks to become a co-ordinator. To meet Angie today, a woman who would not only have turned you off but would also have ripped you off, is an eye-opener. People can change – dramatically – and HELP can help them do it.'*

Whether evaluated through impersonal statistics or appreciated through personal stories of triumph, HELP has been an unparalleled success. Several forces converged to make that success. Certainly the concept – based on association of ex-cons – held the critical seed of promise. Certainly the combination of key players and the partnership between HELP and Frontier College had everything to do with the success. But this book is about Tony McGilvary, the originator of HELP. His role as founder and first director was critical. Tony had the plan and personal power to pull it off, but he also had the limitations that would lead him to leave HELP.

A Strong Legacy: Tony Leaves HELP   14

'I regarded Tony as a career criminal,' long-time Joyceville Pen staffer Murray Jack muses. 'I wouldn't have expected him to be able to stay on the street, let alone achieve what he's achieved. Tony was an old-time con, the kind who went along with the system, did their time quietly in their cells. He was never a leadership type, always a back-seat guy.'

While Tony's tales of his bandit life may amuse, alarm, or amaze us, in convict terms he was a garden-variety crook. And a garden-variety inmate. He didn't lead riots or raise hell on inmate committees; he didn't shake up the system or shake down other inmates. He wasn't violent or volatile. Rather, he was compliant and quiet, a loner who languished long hours in a solitary cell, grinding out an endless cache of crafts. Sure, he was an itch, he ran minor scams inside — a stolen steak here, a bookie's take there — but that's garden-variety misdemeanour inside. No one who knew Tony in his outlaw life ever suspected he would achieve great things. Most didn't expect he would stay on the street. Many even had a hard time remembering him.

'Inside, Tony was one of the crowd,' Art Trono, federal deputy commissioner of Corrections in Ontario, says. 'When Tony reminds me of exchanges we had when he was an inmate and I was a warden, I don't recall them. I'm sure they happened and they were significant for Tony, but for me they were commonplace experiences I had every day with hundreds of nameless men. You remember certain inmates because their crimes are extraordinary or because they pulled off an exceptional scam. Not Tony. He never stood out as a con artist of special skill ... He may not have stood out in the prison population where he was just one of the crowd, but he's sure not one of the crowd now. On the street, he's exceptional.'

Tony Leaves HELP

Trono is what Tony calls a 'muckety muck,' a bigwig with an impressive title and matching office in the ex-mini-mansion of an ex-mayor of Kingston. Church windows rise high to the ceiling behind Tory-blue wing chairs. It's an office where guys like Tony rarely gain access. Except in this office, he is now regarded as something of a hero.

Art Trono continues. 'I'd say 90 per cent of Tony's success is the man. Others came before him to this office with proposals to do the same thing. They failed where he succeeded.

'There are a lot of reasons why he succeeded. He's driven, of course, and that helps. But he can be realistic and sensible too, and that's more important. For instance, he understood the importance of having access to correctional institutions and earning the respect of institutional staff as well as the respect of inmates. Tony and his staff, as far as we know, never abused their access to inmates, never brought contraband in or out of prison. And even though I know they had access to information about illegal goings-on inside, they never came running to us with it. Tony and his staff earned the respect of both sides – that was crucial to their success.'

Many of Tony's associates feel his ego needs account for his contribution to HELP's success. Art Trono certainly feels that way. 'He's a very needy person. He needs recognition, and he's going to get it one way or another.'

Luckily for himself and for the ex-offender community, Tony chose to get the attention he needed by creating HELP. He was a likely candidate to come up with the ingenious idea for the program because ideas come easily to him.

'Tony's vision was always huge,' Frontier president Jack Pearpoint recalls. 'He had an inexhaustible supply of ideas to fix everything wrong in the country having to do with corrections. I spent most of my time with him trying to scale down the vision, trying to rescue parts of it, single manageable ideas, so that we could actually do a few things.'

Tony's second-in-command, now HELP director, Bob Young, had the same struggle with Tony. 'He was an amazing source of ideas, all right, but he was less amazing with follow-through – not that anybody could have the ability to follow through with so many ideas. Many of Tony's ideas were workable and useful; an equal number were plain crazy.'

'Crazy' is a word one hears often in reference to Tony. Investigate its meaning and you find other qualities, like compulsive, non-conforming, and creative behind it. It is hard to get a handle on Tony; he is so many things, so many apparently contradictory things, so many wonderful things and so many maddening things. His pluses are very plus, his minuses very minus.

On the plus side he is catalyst, mobilizer, model. Educator Dr Marsha Forest, Frontier's director of SCIL (student-centred, individualized learning), points out that unorthodox, ambitious programs — the ones hardest to start — need an originator consumed by conviction, almost 'bent out of shape by single-minded determination.' Someone who will not take no for an answer, who can dismiss all the pessimists and doom-sayers. Someone who believes, without reservation, that the idea will become reality.

'Tony is that kind of person,' Marsha Forest insists, 'neurotic, driven, in love with his idea, in love with himself. Initially, he was the spark without which HELP would never have happened. He could — and did — inspire lots of people but he was also pig-headed.

'Don't for a moment imagine he got HELP started by being nice. Nice people don't change the world, or make much progress in that direction. Tony may not be someone you'd describe as nice, but he constantly reached out to "his people." He's an extremely loving — and annoying — dynamo, and that's the kind of model HELP needed in its inception.'

Tony is a force who inspired others by his own example, says Marty Silverstein, a Kingston parole supervisor. 'He'd draft you, by example and suggestion, into doing things you'd wanted to do but were never able to get yourself moving on. He got me involved driving an inmate to an outside job at half past six in the morning. By going out and doing everything himself that he demands from others and by talking about HELP with such fervour, he created a feeling of total involvement. I think Tony believes people are intrinsically good and they want to do good. On that premise he tried to mobilize everyone around him. He's a one-man whirlwind who picks you up in his wake.'

Bob Young was certainly swept up in that wake. 'For me, Tony had an aura — charisma, I guess you'd call it. Watching him work and listening to him speak, I ended up believing in what he believed in, in HELP. Tony doesn't have big words at his command, but he can certainly command attention. He can sell ideas just by being the way he is.

'I learned so much from him, just by watching him in action and then copying what he had done. Like the way he sold employers on hiring ex-cons: he'd just tell his own story, honest, straightforward, the way it was. He used himself as an example, never tried to make out he was better than or different from the workers he was representing. It worked like a charm.'

Tracy LeQuyere, a beefy, bearded, brown-eyed ex-con who turns heads with his brash manner and handsome looks, worked in Toronto as a HELP field-worker and later as a co-ordinator. Today he is one of two directors of Beat the Street, a literacy and lifestyles program for street kids in downtown Toronto. Beat the Street, started by Tracy and his partner Rick Parsons, is the Frontier-HELP model applied to a different population.

'It wouldn't be here if McGilvary hadn't happened to me,' Tracy says. 'I just wouldn't have had the conviction to carry it forward. Tony showed me that with a conviction you can do anything. I also saw that having that kind of conviction doesn't make you the nicest, most likeable guy, but I learned from his example that nice doesn't necessarily get things done. Tony, like me, was more interested in getting things done.'

To get things done, Tony needed more than mere presence; he needed skills. That's where his lifetime experience as a conniver and his twenty-two years' training in prisons came in handy. HELP was his vehicle for transferring everything he'd learned.

Better than most, lifer Tom French understands how Tony's old game shaped his new direction. 'Every time he got a job for a guy getting out of jail, that was a sting. It was Tony on the street pulling another score, being a con man. It was the same skill and the same drive that went into being a criminal. HELP, like flimflamming, was hard work, a lifestyle, something he had to be committed to twenty-four hours a day. HELP demanded that he do exactly the same as he had done to rob some poor sucker; it demanded that he con, con, con.

'But,' Tom points out, 'there was a big difference. HELP was a legal con. Tony started working the con to help people rather than to rob them.'

An unrepentant con artist? Perhaps so. But it was inevitable that Tony's life beyond bars would be indelibly shaped by his experience of life behind bars. His wife Audrey certainly sees him as the con who never quit the game, just applied it to a new purpose.

'Tony is a con man through and through,' Audrey, with mixed amusement and chagrin, says of her husband. 'He seems to be able to tie people right around his finger. He kept me in a whirlwind so I'd never know what was happening till I was in the middle of something. Always volunteered me for things I knew nothing about. When the boat people first came to our church in Kingston, Tony invited them all to our place. He told me a few people would be dropping over! Twenty-five strangers arrived, not one English speaking, no translators among them, and it was my job to feed and entertain them. I did it – with a smile on my face. Tony did that to everyone – conned them into whatever plans he had for them.'

There's no question that Tony transferred productive skills he learned as a compulsive criminal into a compulsion for good work. But he also transferred counter-productive skills into his new life. Jack Pearpoint is probably most aware of the deficiencies in Tony's training.

'There are too many examples of what Tony hadn't learned and therefore did badly in the program. I'll pick one – money. Tony never learned money management. The reason is simple; he never needed to learn. When you're in crime, money is what you have in your pocket. When your pocket is empty, you go get more money. Money is not something to be managed.

'I guess it's a kind of money management,' Pearpoint says with a less-than-affectionate smirk, 'but it's not popular or practical in square society. Tony's attitude towards money, when translated into running a program, created a nightmare for Frontier. When we'd give him the equivalent of a line of credit, he'd spend it, period. He believed it would somehow keep on coming. How was a mystery and decidedly not his problem. Like prison, I guess. Meals just came. You had a place to sleep. Your clothes got cleaned. It all just happened. Tony's incompetence around money management just about drove us crazy.'

His light-hearted attitude towards money turned up in some pretty bizarre expenditures – and attempted expenditures. 'I wasn't laughing at the time,' says Bob Young, laughing now, 'but looking back, it was pretty funny. One day after we bought the Freedom Farm – which we were running as a bare-bones operation – I got a call from some horse trader. "Where shall I deliver the horses?" he asked me. "What horses? What are you talking about?" "The two horses Mr McGilvary ordered." Needless to say, we dug ourselves out of that manure, but it was so like Tony to forget a small item like two horses! He could certainly make me laugh, but sometimes he just about drove me crazy.'

Bob Young is not alone in that claim; it's practically universal from people who worked closely with Tony. But anecdotes about Tony's pushy style invariably end on an apologetic note. Everyone seems to feel that it was the only way Tony knew to run things and, in the context of a new ex-con program, perhaps the only managerial style that could have worked. Most people excuse Tony's authoritarian style because it got results, built a strong program. Perhaps for other ex-cons it was easier to accept because it was familiar. Prison, they say, is the ultimate dictatorship.

The way Tony ran HELP was consistent with the hierarchical con culture he and his staff came from. HELP allowed ex-cons to play by rules they understood. It did not straightjacket them with typical social-service rules.

'In crime, loyal players carry out their bit parts in scams invented and controlled by a leader,' Jack Pearpoint explains. 'They respect the leader's position of authority. They don't ask questions; they obey. They are just hired guns buying in for a short stint on someone else's terms. Yes or no, in or out, those are the only questions. Individual expression and democratic process have nothing to do with a con's life inside or on the street.'

'I hadta be a tough boss,' Tony explains, 'because many of my staff didn't have their lives together. Ex-cons is used ta bein' their own bosses; they don't like nobody orderin' them around, tellin' them how ta do things. In my program I insisted that we do things my way 'cause I figured my way was the best way. HELP wasn't exactly your most democratic organization, but it was the only way I knew how ta run things.'

Bob Young, Tony's second-in-command for many years, looks like a man who'd run his own show. Although only five-foot six, he makes a much taller impression. Maybe it's the look, the rock-hard two hundred pounds or the intense blue eyes or the brusque manner. Or maybe it's the hard edge from a hard life that shows – from age seven to thirty, a life spent in institutions, from foster homes to the Big House. As a criminal Bob does not have Tony's pussycat background. Rather, Bob's story is a tale of endless violence. The impression he creates today says, 'I run my own show.'

Bob insists he didn't. 'I was just Tony's shadow, and I was happy being number-two man. It was Tony's style to always demand more; he never thanked you for what you gave. "Knock on one more door; find one more job before you quit today," was his usual chant. Day and night I'd be out hustling jobs, coming home around ten at night. The phone would ring. Before I answered, I knew it would be Tony issuing orders. "Ya gotta come back to the office right now." Or "Get in your car and drive it to Toronto. We got an emergency at the office there." I could get to Toronto to find a message from Tony saying forget it, the crisis was solved or not a crisis after all. Oftentimes he'd call at two a.m. telling me to pack for a morning flight to Winnipeg. A half-hour later he'd call back and tell me to go back to bed; he'd changed his mind. Tony thought it was normal to make those demands; he couldn't imagine that anything except HELP could matter.'

Tracy LeQuyere feels much the same. Although he seems softer than Bob, he's also no pussycat. At six-foot two, 240 pounds, with an aggressive, outspoken manner and a criminal record to scatter the faint of heart, he's a presence to rival Tony. But rivalry was not his issue any more than it was

Bob's. Trained in the con code, Tracy was too ready to be unquestioning and loyal.

'Tony's bully voice and gruff manner didn't bother me because I was used to guys with Tony's kind of joint mentality and presentation. You use your size, your look, and your voice to manipulate people. He may be the most successful manipulator I've ever met; every move was geared to a preconceived result – the goal of helping other ex-cons.

'Like Bob says, he never gave slaps on the back; he used kicks in the pants to get you going. Tony was big and bad and he drove you like mad, but I had enormous respect for him, for what he was doing. I had no beef with his methods because his way worked.'

The kind of intense environment Tony favoured inevitably created some friction. The program had its share of what you might call management-labour disputes. One time when the Toronto staff was taking an unscheduled holiday, Tracy went into the office. He found Tony sitting there alone, trying to carry on business as usual.

'What's going on, Tracy?' Tony demanded in his usual gruff manner.

'The staff has some beefs with you; you'll have to ask them what it's about,' Tracy answered.

'That don't matter. What matters is gettin' jobs. Ya ready ta go ta work?' Business as usual; that's all Tony knew.

He also knew paranoia – intimately. Given his prison background, Tony's rabid distrust of everyone was understandable. 'Bein' paranoid is a survival skill ya learn in the joint,' says Tony. Besides, Tony was wise to suspect that HELP had many enemies who didn't want him to succeed. Many professionals and bureaucrats are intimidated by so-called non-professionals who do a better job doing what professionals are paid to do. However, the scope of Tony's distrust was excessive.

Now Jack Pearpoint can laugh about it. 'I think Tony learned to trust me and Frontier, but it took a long time. After three years of shared struggles on the same team, I think he had a grudging kind of respect for us, maybe bordering on trust. Yet he was always expecting to be abandoned. I always felt I was dealing with Tony the abandoned kid all over again. He could not imagine that anyone would be any more reliable than his family had been. And no matter how loyal and giving we were – and, my God, were we loyal and giving with HELP – he couldn't trust us. But given where Tony had come from, what else could I have expected?

'I had a moment when I thought he might trust us a little. We were three years into our partnership, running a huge deficit on the program. Contract

191 Tony Leaves HELP

negotiations were under way with the Ontario Ministry of Corrections for the Kingston office. They offered us fifty thousand dollars more than we had a chance of getting from other sources. There was a hitch – we had to agree to rat on ex-offenders, to become, in effect, guards or parole officers. Tony and the HELP negotiators refused. When we walked out of the meeting together, there was probably a moment when Tony thought us worthy of trust.'

Pearpoint and others contrast Tony's way with the way HELP might have been if run by typical 'helping professionals.' They say that HELP would have been a neat, organized mini-bureaucracy with nice offices but few job placements for ex-offenders. By contrast, HELP is more chaos than order. It works out of makeshift offices with discard furniture – and places more ex-offenders in jobs than anyone else in the business.

'Just look at who Tony had working with him,' Pearpoint says, 'not exactly pristine social workers. He hired some of the roughest, toughest people with burrs on who couldn't possibly know the normal constraints of a typical social service – funding, hours, rules, decorum. They just did what had to be done, based on how they knew to do things. If you had to get up at three a.m., fine – like going out at three to commit crimes.'

With Tony's aggressive style, with staff oblivious to rules governing most helping agencies, HELP has achieved unrivalled success serving the needs of its ex-offender constituency. By the fall of 1985 business was booming. It had taken Tony to start the program, plus partnership between Frontier and HELP's team – principally Bob Young, Tom French, and fund-raiser Joe – to build it. While leadership, partnership, and teamwork had been critical, the slogging daily contributions of unsung co-ordinators, field-workers, and office staff had all converged to create the stunning success.

'Where it took one person ta start it, it took many ta build it,' agrees Tony. 'And I don't just mean our staff, though they were the most important. It took inmates and parole officers – lots of people on both sides of the fence. It took a bunch of people dedicated to one thing – givin' people help that never got it before.'

At various points over the years, when Tony felt burnt out, he had threatened to leave the program, at least to resign as its director. As early as 1983, when TV Ontario produced two half-hour programs on HELP, burn-out was in the cards for Tony. He even confessed on screen to the interviewer that he was burnt out and on his way out. But that threat to quit was a false alarm.

He'd always talk about the Freedom Farm as his eventual home base. Key *people at* HELP *and Frontier naturally assumed that Tony, when he was ready to switch to a less active role, would move to the farm. They hoped he'd become honorary lifetime director and continue doing things he was best at, like making inspirational speeches. Everyone, including Tony, knew that things had to change somehow, some day.*

Partly they were bound to change because Tony had always been unpredictable and a loner. He had never in his life stayed long at one thing in one place. He had never forged lasting ties with people, never made enduring commitments.

In November 1984 Tony collapsed, spitting blood and gasping for air. When he was hospitalized, HELP *staff pitched in for a ticket to St Lucia. Maybe a rest and a holiday would revive him.*

After ten days in the Caribbean Tony convinced the airline to change his fixed charter-flight dates and fly him back to Toronto that day. He arrived red and sun-blistered, wearing open sandals and an open-neck shirt in the icy grey bluster of winter.

Breathless with outrage against the plight of St Lucian orphans and hatching a dozen schemes to rescue them from institutions, he immediately resumed his race to the next collapse.

So it was really no surprise in the fall of 1985 when Tony announced again that he was leaving. No surprise, but nobody quite believed he'd actually leave. By this time he was so short-breathed he couldn't navigate a street-crossing without laboured huffing between puffs on his ubiquitous cigarettes.

'My health was real bad and I was just burnt out. I knew there was some good years left in me, but not for runnin' HELP,' *Tony says. The separation process was tough on everyone, toughest no doubt on Tony and on his wife Audrey, whom he left behind.*

'The last couple of weeks before he left, he couldn't sit still; I'd never seen him more restless. I didn't know what was bothering him because he didn't share his thoughts with me. I didn't know he might leave. After all, he had what he'd dreamed of – the Freedom Farm. I should have reminded myself that Tony only wants things until he gets them; then he has to create another dream.'

Audrey's dark eyes glaze. 'Every time before when Tony walked out on me, I'd felt it coming. Usually there'd been an argument; this time I had no inkling. One day, out of the blue, he turned to me and said, "Write up a resignation; I'm leaving the program." I was dumbfounded. Tony didn't mention leaving the farm – which we'd just moved to – or leaving town. Or leaving me!

'A while later he came out of his sullen silence again. He turned to me and said, "Go upstairs and pack all my clothes, I mean all of them, everything I own." "Where are you going?" I asked, stunned. "I don't know, I'm just going." He hesitated, then he said, "There hasn't been nothing between us for a long time, so I don't think it will bother you if I leave." I felt numb. Would you believe I obediently went upstairs and packed for him? He was leaving me and I packed for him! I must have been nuts. I even carried his suitcases downstairs.'

With a bitter laugh Audrey continues. 'He didn't even ask if I wanted to come.' 'And if he had, Audrey, what would you have said?' I asked her. 'No, Tony, I've had enough.'

Tony left HELP the way he had uprooted and run so many times before. Burn out. Break ties. Abandon loved ones. Flee. Start again. Always the pattern. Like the way he left his fugitive life with gypsies on the American carnival circuit. Walked out on valued friends, dumped his car and trailer on a bus-depot parking lot – keys in the ignition – and returned to Canada to turn himself in.

But there was a significant difference in his legacy this time. He left more than a memory behind. In HELP he left a bold project and an able succession who could steer HELP to yet bolder achievements.

'You know,' Marsha Forest muses, 'Tony did one extraordinary thing in his life – he created HELP, which has saved a lot of lost lives, and inspired a lot of gems' – among them Bob Young, the new leader of a revitalized HELP.

'Perhaps more important than anything,' Forest adds, 'the HELP period of Tony's life is a beacon of hope, hope for inmates and ex-offenders, hope for anyone down on his luck and struggling to believe in the possibility of change. That period of Tony's life is the promise that people can turn their lives around.

'Quite an accomplishment, wouldn't you say? No one should forget that for all his maddening craziness, it was Tony who started it all. In my books he's a real hero for doing that.'

'Forget Tony?' Bob Young chuckles. 'Not a chance. Every time my phone rings in the middle of the night, I wake up wondering whether Tony will be on the blower ordering me to race to Toronto.'

Epilogue

Tony McGilvary, now fifty-three, is living in Vancouver's kinder climate. Despite deteriorating health, he is still working with 'his people.' He is still doing the only thing that gives meaning to his life – helping ex-offenders. 'I'm very greedy,' Tony says; 'by helping other people, I keep myself on the street.'

The HELP *program, in partnership with Frontier College and under Bob Young's leadership, is flourishing.*